T0327709

Worker Voice

Employee Representation in the Workplace in Australia, Canada, Germany, the UK and the US 1914–1939

STUDIES IN LABOUR HISTORY 5

Studies in Labour History

'...a series which will undoubtedly become an important force in re-invigorating the study of Labour History.' *English Historical Review*

Studies in Labour History provides reassessments of broad themes along with more detailed studies arising from the latest research in the field of labour and working-class history, both in Britain and throughout the world. Most books are single-authored but there are also volumes of essays focussed on key themes and issues, usually emerging from major conferences organized by the British Society for the Study of Labour History. The series includes studies of labour organizations, including international ones, where there is a need for new research or modern reassessment. It is also its objective to extend the breadth of labour history's gaze beyond conventionally organized workers, sometimes to workplace experiences in general, sometimes to industrial relations, but also to working-class lives beyond the immediate realm of work in households and communities.

Worker Voice

Employee Representation in the Workplace in Australia, Canada, Germany, the UK and the US 1914–1939

Greg Patmore

LIVERPOOL UNIVERSITY PRESS

To Helen, Julieanne, Robert and James

First published 2016 by
Liverpool University Press
4 Cambridge Street
Liverpool
L69 7ZU

British Library Cataloguing-in-Publication data
A British Library CIP record is available

ISBN 978-1-78138-268-4 cased

Typeset by Carnegie Book Production, Lancaster
Printed and bound in Poland by BooksFactory.co.uk

Table of Contents

Tables

Illustrations

Acknowledgements

I wish to acknowledge the support of many people and institutions that made possible the completion of this book, the research for which began with a visit to Pueblo, Colorado in 1997. The research was funded by a variety of sources including the Faculty of Economics and Business, now the School of Business, at the University of Sydney, two grants from the Australian Research Council, and the Rockefeller Archives Center. The Department of History at Georgetown University kindly provided me with the facilities to continue my research when I was in Washington in 2011. I would also like to thank the generous assistance of the staffs of the Archives of Labor and Urban Affairs at Wayne State University, Borthwick Institute for Archives in York, Beaton Institute at Cape Breton University, the Baltimore & Ohio Museum, the Canberra office of the National Archives of Australia, the Colorado Historical Society, the Historisches Archiv Krupp, the Noel Butlin Archives Centre at the Australian National University, the Bessemer Historical Society/Steelworks Center of the West, the Modern Records Centre at Warwick University, the Friedrich Ebert Stiftung in Bonn, the Department of Labor Library in Washington, DC, the Archives of the International Labour Organisation in Geneva, the Manuscripts Division of the Library of Congress, the British Library, the Bundesarchiv in Berlin, the Siemens Archive, Provincial Archives of Nova Scotia at Halifax, the State Library of NSW, the Tasmanian Archive in Hobart, the Manuscripts Library of the State Historical Society of Wisconsin, Pennsylvania State University Libraries Labor Archives, the Labour Movement Archives and Library in Stockholm, the National Archives and Library of Canada, the Rockefeller Archives Center, the University of Colorado at Boulder Archives and the Public Records Office at Kew. I would also like to thank especially the following people for their advice, support and encouragement: Greg Kealey, Neville Kirk, Leon Fink, Joe McCartin, Jonathan Rees, Ray Markey, George Strauss, David Brody, Nikola Balnave, Jim Kitay,

John Shields, Merrilyn Bryce, Melissa Kerr, Troy Sarina and Harry Knowles. I would like to thank particularly Yasmin Rittau, who was my research assistant when I was undertaking the research with an ARC Discovery Grant in 2011 and 2012, proofed the manuscript for me before submission for publication and constructed the table of abbreviations. Thank you also to Liverpool University Press, particularly Alison Welsby, for giving me the opportunity to have the manuscript published, and Trevor Matthews for compiling the index. Finally, I would like to thank my wife, Helen Warner, my children Julieanne and Robert Patmore and son-in-law James Bunton, to all of whom this book is dedicated, for their tolerance, particularly of the travel that was involved.

Abbreviations

AACL	All Canadian Congress of Labour
AAISTW	Amalgamated Association of Iron, Steel and Tin Workers
ACTU	Australasian Council of Trade Unions
ADGB	Allgemeiner Deutscher Gewerkschaftsbund
AEU	Amalgamated Engineering Union
AF	American Federationist
AfA	Allgemeiner freier Angestelltenbund
AFL	American Federation of Labor
AFULE	Australian Federated Union of Locomotive Enginemen
AJ	*The Amalgamated Journal*
AJICIRC	Association of Joint Industrial Councils and Interim Reconstruction Committees
ALP	Australian Labor Party
ASE	Amalgamated Society of Engineers
ASLEF	Associated Society of Locomotive Engineers and Firemen
AWU	Australian Workers' Union
BB	Bundesarchiv, Berlin, Germany
BESCO	British Empire Steel Corporation
BHAS, Port Pirie	Broken Hill Associated Smelters
BHSA	Bessemer Historical Society Archives, Pueblo, Colorado
BHP	Broken Hill Proprietary Company
BI	Beaton Institute, Cape Breton University

BMWE	Brotherhood of Maintenance Way Employees
B&O	Baltimore & Ohio Railroad
BP	Beyer Papers, Library of Congress, Washington, DC
BSCP	Brotherhood of Sleeping Car Porters
CBRE	Canadian Brotherhood of Railway Employees
CCF	Co-operative Commonwealth Federation (Canada)
CCL	Canadian and Catholic Confederation of Labour
CF&I	Colorado Fuel & Iron
CFIC, CHS	Colorado Fuel and Iron Corporation Collection, Colorado Historical Society, Denver, Colorado
CIO	Committee of Industrial Organisation
CMA	Canadian Manufacturers Association
CNR	Canadian National Railroad
C&O	Chesapeake and Ohio Railway
CP	Harold T. Curtiss Papers Pennsylvania State University Libraries Labor Archives, State College
CTP	Co-operative Traffic Program
DISCO	Dominion Iron and Steel Co.
DLL	United States Department of Labor Library, Washington DC
DMV	Metalworkers' Union (Deutscher Metallarbeiter-Verband)
DOSCO	Dominion Steel and Coal Corporation
DSC	Departmental Safety Committees
DWRGWU	Dock, Wharf, Riverside and General Union
ELC, FSA	Erich Lübbe Collection, Frederich-Ebert Stiftung Archive, Bonn
EMP	Elton Mayo Papers, Baker Library, Harvard Business School, Cambridge, MA
ERO	Employees' Representation Organisation
ERP	Employee Representation Plan
EZ	Electrolytic Zinc
EZCCTAH	Electrolytic Zinc Company Collection, Tasmanian Archive, Hobart
FBI	Federation of British Industries
GB MOL	Great Britain Ministry of Labour
GM	General Motors
GMH	General Motors-Holden

GMMA	George Meany Memorial Archives, Silver Spring, Maryland
HAK	Historisches Archiv Krupp, Essen
HMSO	His Majesty's Stationery Office
IAM	International Association of Machinists
ICI	Imperial Chemical Industries
IDIA	Industrial Disputes Investigation Act
Industrial Bulletin	Colorado Fuel and Iron Industrial Bulletin
ILO	International Labour Office
ILOA	ILO Archives, Geneva, Switzerland
IOC	Imperial Oil Company
ISTC	Iron and Steel Trades Confederation
IWW	Industrial Workers of the World
JDR Jr.	John D. Rockefeller Junior
JFC SHSW	John Fitch Collection, Manuscripts Library, State Historical Society of Wisconsin, Madison, Wisconsin
JFW CHS	Jesse Floyd Welborn Collection, Colorado Historical Society, Denver, Colorado
JIC	Joint Industrial Councils
KPD	Communist Party of Germany
LDC	Local Departmental Committees
LGC	*Labour Gazette*
LII	Liberal Industrial Inquiry
LMB GGB	Lamont M. Bowers collection, Department of Special Collections, Glenn G. Bartle Library, State University of New York, Binghamton
LMS	London Midland and Scottish Railway Company
MBA	NSW Master Builders Association
MFGB	Miners' Federation of Great Britain
MRC	Modern Records Centre, University of Warwick, UK
MVKRP	Mary Van Kleeck Research Papers
NAA	National Archives of Australia
NALC	National Archives and Library of Canada, Ottawa
NAM	National Association of Manufacturers
NBAC	Noel Butlin Archives Centre, Australian National University, Canberra
NCEO	National Confederation of Employers' Organisations
NICB	National Industrial Conference Board

NIRA	New Deal National Industrial Recovery Act
NLRB	National Labor Relations Board
NS	Nova Scotia
NSS	Nova Scotia Steel
NSW	New South Wales
NSWGR	NSW Government Railways
NTWA	National Trades and Worker Association
NUC	National Union Clerks
NUER	Non-union employee representation
NUR	National Union of Railwaymen
NWLB	National War Labor Board
NYT	*New York Times*
OBU	One Big Union
PRO	Public Records Office, Kew, UK
PWA	Provincial Workmen's Association
RBIAY	Rowntrees & Co. Collection, Borthwick Institute for Archives, University of York, UK
RED KA	Railway Employees' Department. AFL-CIO Records, Kheel Archives, Cornell University, New York
RFA RAC	Rockefeller Family Archives, Rockefeller Archives Center, Sleepy Hollow, New York
RKW	Reichskuratorium für Wirtschaftlichkeit
SA	South Australia
SCC	Special Conference Committee
SMH	*Sydney Morning Herald*
SPD	German Social Democratic Party (Sozialdemokratische Partei Deutschlands)
SWOC	Steelworkers' Organising Committee
TLCC	Trades and Labour Congress of Canada
TUC	Trades Union Congress
TVA	The Tennessee Valley Authority
UAW	United Automobile Workers
UMWA	United Mine Workers of America
USPD	Independent Social Democratic Party (Unabhängige Sozialdemokratische Partei Deutschlands)
USRA	United States Railroad Administration

USWA collection, PANS   United Steelworkers of America, Sydney Lodge collection, Provincial Archives of Nova Scotia, Halifax

VDA   Vereinigung der Deutschen Arbeitgeberverbände

WAP   Sir William Ashley Papers, Add MS 42250, British Library

YMCA   Young Men's Christian Association

ZWU   Zinc Workers' Union

1

Introduction

Industrial democracy offers workers the promise of greater control over their working lives. Employers have also supported forms of industrial democracy to improve worker morale and productivity. Industrial democracy can have a variety of implications for capitalism. Workers' control of businesses through ownership by workers' cooperatives challenged the traditional notion of the capitalist firm and could ultimately supplant it. Other forms of industrial democracy are less challenging for capitalism. Representative or indirect forms of industrial democracy include works councils and joint consultation, where representatives of workers and managers sit and discuss problems. They can take the form of non-union employee representation (NUER), such as in employee representation plans (ERP) or German works councils, or involve unions, such as union-management cooperation. In the US and the UK, the term "industrial democracy" also refers to collective bargaining, in which employers recognise unions and negotiate a collective agreement that covers wages and working conditions. Direct forms of industrial democracy focus on the way work is organised at the workplace level: these can include team-focused work and semiautonomous work groups. Financial forms of industrial democracy focus on the way financial rewards are distributed through employee stock ownership and profit sharing. The terms "employee democracy," "employee involvement," and "employee consultation" are used interchangeably with "industrial democracy."[1]

This book will focus on the debates and practice relating to four versions of indirect industrial democracy in the interwar period at the workplace level – ERP, union-management cooperation, Whitley works committees and

---

[1] Greg Patmore, "Industrial Democracy", in Melvyn Dubofsky, *The Oxford Encyclopedia of American Business, Labor & Economic History, Vol. 1*, Oxford University Press, New York, 2013, pp. 363–4.

German works councils. It will examine what we can learn from the interwar period to inform contemporary debates about industrial democracy and the "representation gap" of workers without union coverage in the workplace. The book will explore the interwar experiences of these ideas in Australia, Canada, Germany, the UK and the US. ERPs and union-management cooperation emerged in the US, while the UK provided the context for the development of Whitley works committees. The German interest in works councils dates back to the mid-nineteenth century, and culminated in works council legislation in 1920. While Australia and Canada were not the source of these approaches, they are examples of economies that were looking for ideas overseas to ensure labour harmony and industrial productivity in the uncertain world that accompanied the end of the First World War. Australia and Canada also had developed economies that were dependent on larger and more powerful countries such as the US and the UK for trade and capital investment.[2]

The decline in trade union membership in many Western countries in recent years has raised concerns among scholars that workers without union representation no longer have a voice in the management of their workplaces. This "representation gap" reduces workers' potential to contribute to improving productivity and the quality of working life. Commentators and academics have looked towards the instigation of forms of NUER such as works councils or joint consultative schemes as a critical means of developing appropriate representative employee participation infrastructures at the workplace level to provide for employee voice. The advocates of these forms of representation argue that they complement the call for "high-performance workplaces" or "mutual gain enterprises" in an era of heightened global and domestic competition by encouraging decentralised decision-making, team forms of production and a climate of cooperation and trust.[3]

The problem with this debate was "organisational and public policy amnesia," which led to previous experiments in employee democracy being

---

[2] Mark Bray and Jacques Rouillard, "Union Structure and Strategy in Australia and Canada", *Labour/Le Travail*, no. 38/*Labour History*, no. 71, 1996, pp. 200–1.

[3] Paul Gollan and Glenn Patmore, "Transporting the European Social Partnership Model to Australia", *The Journal of Industrial Relations*, vol. 48, no. 2, 2006, pp. 217–57; Jean Jenkins and Paul Blyton, "Works Councils", in Paul Blyton, Nicolas Bacon, Jack Fiorito and Edmund Heery (eds.), *The Sage Handbook of Industrial Relations*, Sage, London, 2008, pp. 346–73; Bruce Kaufman and Daphne Taras, "Introduction", in Bruce Kaufman and Daphne Taras (eds.), *Non-Union Employee Representation: History, Contemporary Practice and Policy*, M.E. Sharpe, Armonk, 2000, p. 4; Shlomo Mizrahi, "Workers' Participation in Decision-Making Process and Firm Stability", *British Journal of Industrial Relations*, vol. 40, no. 4, 2002, pp. 689–708.

overlooked.[4] In Australia, for example, there have been at least three waves of interest in employee democracy. There are two major approaches to explaining this recurring interest. Firstly, Harvie Ramsay in the UK and Chris Wright in Australia have noted that employers have adopted a cyclical approach to employee participation driven by threats to managerial authority. Ramsay's approach notes that waves of interest in employee democracy are linked to management's perceptions of economic, political and industrial threats to its authority.[5] The German works councils, the Whitley Scheme and the Rockefeller Plan attracted considerable interest at the end of the First World War, when employers in all five countries examined in this book faced industrial unrest and the Bolshevik threat. Another wave of interest in the Rockefeller Plan arose among US employers during the early 1930s in response to the strengthening of organised labour during the New Deal.[6]

The alternative "favourable conjunctures" thesis put forward by Michael Poole, Russell Lansbury and Nick Wailes rejects the inevitability of cycles and is more focused on factors that help explain the rise of industrial democracy. This approach acknowledges a "broad long-term trend towards greater experimentation and richness of forms" of industrial democracy. It also recognises "a discontinuous historical pattern, in which the main forms of industrial democracy have varied substantially in their incidence and impact at distinctive points in time." The favourable conjunctures model of comparative industrial democracy developed by Poole, Lansbury and Wailes suggests four main sets of variables that influence industrial democracy within organisations: macro-conditions (external organisation); the strategic choices of actors; the power of actors; and organisational structures and processes at the level of the firm. The macro-conditions include favourable economic and technological variables, culture and the legal framework. The presence of compulsory arbitration and a relatively strong trade union movement may, for example, explain the minimal impact of the Rockefeller Plan and the Whitley Scheme in Australia. Similarly, the relative weakness of labour and lack of a legislative framework for industrial relations in Canada and the US may explain the success of the Rockefeller Plan there. Poole,

[4] Greg Patmore, "Changes in the Nature of Work and Employment Relations: A Historical Perspective", in Ron Callus and Russell Lansbury (eds.), *Working Futures: The Changing Nature of Work and Employment Relations in Australia*, The Federation Press, Sydney, 2002, p. 34.

[5] Harvie Ramsay, "Cycles of Control: Worker Participation in Sociological and Historical Perspective", *Sociology*, vol. 11, no. 3, 1977, pp. 481–506; Christopher Wright, *The Management of Labour: A History of Australian Employers*, Oxford University Press, Melbourne, 1995.

[6] Patmore, Greg, "Unionism and Non-Union Employee Representation: The Interwar Experience in Canada, Germany, the US and the UK", *Journal of Industrial Relations*, vol. 55, no. 4, 2013, pp. 527–45.

Lansbury and Wailes also try to explain why particular forms of industrial democracy persist. They note that while there maybe macro-conditions that favour industrial democracy, the adoption of employee participation at the firm level is subject to organisational choice.[7]

One criticism of the Poole, Lansbury and Wailes approach is that it is teleological, implying that there is a long-term trend towards greater richness in the forms of industrial democracy. By contemporary standards, the interwar period was a very rich period for experimentation with industrial democracy, but all these ideas failed to sustain themselves significantly for the duration of the interwar period. While the German works councils were resuscitated following the Second World War, it is arguable that they represented a richer version of the Weimar experiment with works councils, particularly from a union perspective.[8] Favourable conditions at the plant level explain why some of these experiments with employee representation persisted throughout the period in the cases of Rowntree in the UK, Electrolytic Zinc (EZ) in Australia, Baltimore & Ohio Railroad (B&O) in the US and Canadian National Railroad (CNR) in Canada. Whatever its problems, both the "favourable conjectures" and the cyclical theses highlight that there is a long history of prior experimentation with industrial democracy to draw upon in evaluating the performance of contemporary proposals.

Historical debates over whether ERPs are a solution to contemporary concerns about the "representation gap" and the need for employee involvement have to some degree challenged the problem of "organisational and public policy amnesia" in regard to schemes for employee participation in the workplace. In the US and Canada, some academics have explored their historical traditions relating to ERPs prior to the outbreak of the Second World War. David Fairris and Bruce Kaufman have provided a favourable historical re-examination of ERPs during the interwar period.[9] ERPs were joint committees of employees and management representatives funded by the employer to discuss a range of issues including wages and conditions, safety and accidents, and company housing. Workers could appeal to various levels of company management and some ERPs even made provision for

   [7] Michael Poole, Russell Lansbury and Nick Wailes, "Participation and Industrial Democracy Revisited: A Theoretical Perspective", in Ray Markey, Paul Gollan, Ann Hodgkinson, Alaine Chouraqui and Ulke Veersma (eds.), *Models of Employee Participation in a Changing Global Environment: Diversity and interaction*, Ashgate, Aldershot, 2001, pp. 24–5.
   [8] Manfred Weiss and Marlene Schmidt, *Labour Law and Industrial Relations in Germany*, Wolters Kluwer, Alphen aan den Rijn, 2008, pp. 222–3.
   [9] David Fairris, "From Exit to Voice in Shopfloor Governance: The Case of Company Unions," *Business History Review*, vol. 69, no. 4, 1995, pp. 494–529; Bruce Kaufman, "The Case for the Company Union", *Labor History*, vol. 41, no. 3, 2000, pp. 321–51.

appeal to an external court if mediation failed. The company paid for all costs associated with the plan, including reimbursement for the loss of work time by employee representatives. The promoters of ERPs viewed them as alternatives to both individual contracts and independent trade unions. They argued that the ERP was part of a progressive move in US industry to promote a greater interest in more sophisticated personnel management practices in order to improve worker commitment, morale and productivity. The founders of the personnel management movement called for a recognition of the "human factor" and a more systematic approach to labour management.[10] As Brody has argued, "For the New Era's lead industrial firms, employee representation became emblematic of best practice under the aegis of advanced personnel management."[11] One recent book focusing on the ERP at Colorado Fuel & Iron (CF&I) in the US has emphasised the benefits for workers if management is committed to ERPs as an alternative form of employee voice.[12]

There are two major issues for these more favourable interpretations of the ERPs. First, Section 8 (a) (2) of the US *National Labor Relations Act* or *Wagner Act* banned ERPs in 1935 because they were viewed as an attempt to deny workers the rights to independent representation of their own choosing. Current critics of this legislation argue that it should be amended to give employees a voice in those workplaces where unions are no longer present and allow them to draw upon the re-examination of ERPs to support their case. NUER would allow workers to raise grievances and make suggestions to increase plant productivity.[13]

This approach challenges long-standing concerns within the pluralist Anglo-American industrial relations literature about the impact of NUER on trade unionism and collective bargaining. Dunlop's classic theory of industrial relations systems established the field of study on the basis of collective bargaining and organised labour and virtually ignored non-union employment. In the UK, Hugh Clegg went further and argued against NUER, claiming that only collective bargaining by unions independent of the state and management could produce genuine industrial democracy and challenge totalitarianism. He argued that only trade unions represent the interests of workers and that NUER would weaken unions. He also

[10] Patmore, "Unionism and Non-Union Employee Representation", pp. 528, 531–2.

[11] David Brody, "Why No Shop Committees in America: A Narrative History", *Industrial Relations*, vol. 40, no. 3, 2001, p. 373.

[12] Jonathan Rees, *Representation and Rebellion: The Rockefeller Plan at the Colorado Fuel and Iron Company, 1914–1942*, University of Colorado Press, Boulder, 2010.

[13] Greg Patmore, "Employee Representation Plans in the United States, Canada, and Australia: An Employer Response to Workplace Democracy", *Labor*, vol. 3, no. 2, 2006, pp. 41–2.

questioned the claims that NUER could increase productivity and reduce industrial conflict. These concerns that NUER may weaken unionism remain an important part of the industrial relations literature, particularly in the US.[14]

Where unions have been traditionally weak or non-existent, which is increasingly the case, there has been some questioning of this emphasis on unions at the expense of forms of NUER. There has been a growing willingness to examine NUER and explore workplaces where unions have no presence. In the US, Sanford Jacoby highlighted that prominent and successful firms such as IBM have remained non-union since the 1930s and developed welfare capitalism, including a range of participatory practices. He questions claims that leading American companies accepted unions as a feature of modern management.[15] In the UK, the work of scholars such as Peter Akers and Mick Marchington on NUER[16] has led some to "reject the rather conspiratorial view" that such schemes are "mainly about defeating and marginalising unions, by pointing out that management has many other goals than labour control."[17]

Second, the revisionist ERP literature, which focuses attention on the North American experience during the interwar period, begs the question as to what was happening elsewhere. There were vigorous alternative debates over worker voice in the UK and Germany, which provided for NUER that was built on freedom of association, such as Whitley works committees (UK) and works councils (Germany). These ideas were popularised during and immediately after the First World War and represent a distinct phase of international interest in NUER. Despite the great hopes surrounding the introduction of these ideas, they had not achieved the ambitions of their proponents by the outbreak of the Second World War in 1939. The impact of the Great Depression, particularly in Germany and the US, which saw dramatic political shifts towards

---

[14] Peter Ackers, "An Industrial Relations Perspective on Employee Participation", in Adrian Wilkinson, Paul Gollan, Mick Marchington and David Lewin (eds.), *The Oxford Handbook of Participation in Organisations*, Oxford University Press, Oxford, 2010, pp. 62–4; Hugh Clegg, *A New Approach to Industrial Democracy*, Blackwell, Oxford, 1961; John Godard, "Union Formation", in Paul Blyton, Nicolas Bacon, Jack Fiorito and Edmund Heery (eds.), *The Sage Handbook of Industrial Relations*, Sage, London, 2008, pp. 382–3; Bruce Kaufman, *The Global Evolution of Industrial Relations: Events, Ideas and the IIRA*, ILO, Geneva, 2004.

[15] Sanford Jacoby, *Modern Manors: Welfare Capitalism since the New Deal*, Princeton University Press, Princeton, 1997.

[16] Peter Ackers, Mick Marchington, Adrian Wilkinson, John Goodman, "The Use of Cycles? Explaining Employee Involvement in the 1990s", *Industrial Relations Journal*, vol. 23, no. 4, 1992, pp. 268–83.

[17] Ackers, "An Industrial Relations Perspective on Employee Participation", p. 70.

National Socialism in Germany and the New Deal in the US, led to the demise of the works councils in Germany and the outlawing of ERPs in the US. With some exceptions, the enthusiasm for Whitley works committees in the UK had dissipated by the mid-1920s.[18] The next wave of interest in workplace employee representation came during the Second World War, when there was a focus on improving productivity to assist wartime production, and brought "a new upsurge in workshop democracy" in the UK, according to Hugh Clegg.[19]

Expanding the study of workplace employee representation beyond North America and incorporating a comparative historical approach gives a greater depth to the discussion of these forms of industrial democracy. Comparisons are useful primarily because they enable us to see what is not there. By isolating the factors that encouraged or inhibited industrial democracy in different countries, it is possible to develop a more sophisticated conceptual framework.[20] This book looks at five countries and covers a significant period of time, which can be compared to present circumstances. To develop an argument put forward by George Strauss, the noted US industrial relations scholar, a conceptual framework, whether in labour history or industrial relations, should develop principles that "apply everywhere, not just in a single country"[21] and be applicable over time.

The book strengthens the comparative historical method by recognising the transnational dimension of history. While national boundaries provide useful platforms for comparative research, they do not prevent the flow of ideas, people and commodities.[22] Current research that examines the transferability of forms of industrial democracy, such as works councils to Australia, can only speculate on the problems and strategies. This book examines how successful the German works councils, union-management cooperation, ERPs and the Whitley schemes were in being transferred from their countries of origin to four others. It explores the factors that explain the success or failure of the transferability of industrial democracy practices. The Rockefeller Plan was successfully transferred from the US to Canada, but the Whitley and Rockefeller schemes appear to have had little impact

[18] Patmore, "Unionism and Non-Union Employee Representation", p. 529.

[19] Hugh Clegg, *The Changing System of Industrial Relations in Great Britain*, Basil Blackwell, London, 1979, p. 152.

[20] Gregory Kealey and Greg Patmore, "Comparative Labour History: Australia and Canada", *Labour/Le Travail*, no. 38/*Labour History*, no. 71, 1996, p. 2.

[21] George Strauss, "Comparative International Industrial Relations", in Keith Whitfield and George Strauss (eds.), *Researching the World of Work: Strategies and Methods in Studying Industrial Relations*, Cornell University Press, Ithaca, 1998, p. 175.

[22] Ray Markey, "The Australian Place in Comparative Labour History", *Labour History*, no. 100, 2011, pp. 177–8.

on Australia. The findings concerning historical transferability will have important implications for contemporary debates.

Labour historians have identified a number of problems in examining the impact of ideas on the management of labour. There is a "noise effect," which arises from a gap between the rhetoric and the impact with regard to change, particularly at the workplace level. Ideas such as scientific management, industrial democracy and human resource management may be widely discussed in employers' journals, academic papers and the press, but only have minimal impact on practice. Further, the changes associated with a particular idea may already be present in the workplace.[23] Aitken, in a classic study of the impact of scientific management on the Watertown Arsenal in the US, warns of the tendency of management to exaggerate the benefits of change and belittle previous practice, which may be characterised by informal organisation and an absence of written formulas.[24]

There is also the problem of "shelf life." Management has introduced some ideas such as employee participation against the background of labour shortages and high labour turnover. New policies may be introduced as part of a package of reforms by a new team of managers in an organisation to impress shareholders and the capital market. Such innovations may soon fall into disuse once they have served their purpose. Management may mix ideas with conflicting messages (scientific management and employee participation) or only apply them to a small part of their operations for public relations purposes. They may exploit "organisational amnesia" by reintroducing failed practices packaged differently. Worker resistance, opposition from within the ranks of management and state intervention can reduce the impact of any change.[25] This is not to deny that these ideas have an ideological role with regard to management authority even if not put into practice. The sociologist Michael Burawoy argued that scientific management preserved capitalism by making efficiency a "scientific question" and removing it from popular discourse.[26] The inclusion of specific firm case studies in this book alongside an examination of the industry and national levels minimises the problems of the "noise effect" and "shelf life" by providing insights into organisational choice regarding forms of employee workplace representation.

---

[23] Patmore, "Changes in the Nature of Work and Employment Relations", p. 34.

[24] Hugh Aitken, *Taylorism at Watertown Arsenal: Scientific Management in Action 1908–1915*, Harvard University Press, Cambridge, MA, 1960, p. 120.

[25] Patmore, "Changes in the Nature of Work and Employment Relations", p. 34.

[26] Michael Burawoy, "Towards a Marxist Theory of the Labour Process: Braverman and Beyond", *Politics and Society*, vol. 8, nos. 3–4, 1978, pp. 279–81.

Another problem with looking at workplace employee representation during this period is the lack of surviving archival material. Few detailed minutes and election records survive. Generally, employers have not maintained the records of these forms of employee representation. Notable exceptions to this rule include CF&I in the US, Rowntree in the UK and EZ in Australia. Many of the German and British records were lost during the Second World War. Those records not lost by Siemens, the German electrical manufacturer, during Allied bombing raids were removed by Soviet forces and sent east. The Nazis also targeted and destroyed union archives. This lack of employer archives is to some degree offset by other records found in personal, union and government archives. Steelworkers in the US and Canada and railway unions in the UK have retained material relevant to this study. Significant government archives relating to the Ministry of Labour in Germany and the UK are found in the Public Records Office in London and the German federal archives in Berlin. The British records tend to focus on the 1920s and the German on the period from 1920 to 1933, when the Nazis dismantled the works councils. Some surviving files and correspondence provide valuable insights into the operation of Whitley workshop committees and German works councils, particularly with regard to the impact on unions. There is also an extensive collection of material relating to union-management cooperation held in the Otto Beyer collection at the Library of Congress in Washington, DC, which includes long runs of union-management cooperation committee minutes. These archival limitations mean that certain industries such as railways and steel are highlighted in this study and there is a greater focus on the 1920s.[27]

This book is organised along the following lines. Chapter 2 examines the historical context in which ideas relating to employee representation in the workplace were discussed, focusing on Australia, Canada, Germany, the UK and the US. It first examines explanations of historical patterns of employee representation. The chapter then focuses on issues arising from this discussion: economic issues, the industry scale and structure, the division of labour and technology, trade unions and politics, employers and the role of the state in the five countries. The chapter provides the background for understanding the development of ideas of employee representation and the success or failure of their implementation. Chapter 3 explores in depth the four major concepts of workplace employee representation to be examined in the book – the Rockefeller Plan or ERPs, Whitleyism, German works councils and union-management cooperation. It looks at the origins of each of these ideas, their development and variations. Chapters 4 to 8 look at the

---

[27] Patmore, "Unionism and Non-Union Employee Representation", pp. 529–30.

impact of these ideas on the US, the UK, Germany, Canada and Australia respectively between 1914 and the outbreak of the Second World War. The final chapter, the conclusion, brings together the empirical evidence and arguments raised in the book.

2

The Context

This chapter provides the broad context for understanding Australia, Canada, Germany, the UK and the US during the interwar period. It first examines explanations of historical patterns of employee representation. Building on this discussion, the chapter then focuses on economic issues, industry scale and structure, the division of labour and technology, trade unions and politics, employers and the role of the state in these five countries. The chapter provides a basis for understanding the development of ideas of employee representation and the success or failure of their implementation.

Explanations of Historical Patterns of Employee Representation

There have been a number of explanations for fluctuating patterns of interest in workplace employee representation. The complexity of these empirical trends has not always been well accounted for in theoretical explanations of the historical trajectory of representative employee participation. Harvie Ramsay's influential "cyclical theory"[1] argues that support for industrial democracy grows in periods of economic expansion, when employees' bargaining power rises and employers search for alternative means of employee voice located outside the collective bargaining relationship. Conversely, support for industrial democracy wanes when economic conditions decline and employer bargaining power is strengthened. This economic determinist theory is not a sufficient explanation as it fails to account for the continuous expansion of legislation for employee representation in occupational health and safety over the past 30 years, notwithstanding major economic

[1] Ramsay, "Cycles of Control"; Harvie Ramsay, "Evolution or Cycle? Worker Participation in the 1970s and 1980s", in Colin Crouch and Frank Heller (eds.), *International Yearbook of Organizational Democracy, Organizational Democracy and Political Processes*, Wiley, Chichester, 1983, pp. 203–26.

fluctuations. There are a variety of factors that affect interest in ideas relating to workplace employee representation and their implementation.[2]

The scale and structure of industry can impact on workplace employee representation. Larger firms are concerned about the growing communication gap between management and employees and have the resources to deal with the problem, particularly where there is limited competition in the industry. There was a general move to bureaucratise employment so as to ensure uniformity and coordination in a growing enterprise. As Jacoby has argued, while "size mattered" there is no "lockstep relation between how big a company was and how its employment system was organised."[3] Some medium-sized companies can be innovators because they are not inhibited by the rigid bureaucratic control of employment practices.

Although the size of the company is important, the form of company ownership and structure can vary and impact upon employment practices. While large-scale corporations developed in the US, the traditional British firm remained family owned and managed well into the twentieth century. If large firms emerged in the UK, they were loosely organised holding companies in which subordinates enjoyed considerable autonomy. This meant that despite the size of the holding company, autonomous subsidiary companies could follow inconsistent employment policies. Within the company there are both vertical and horizontal levels. The former represents varying levels of management ranging from shop floor supervisors to CEOs, with a whole range of middle managers. If these varying levels have significant levels of autonomy they can frustrate and even undermine the labour policies of senior management. Managers and supervisors can see employee representation schemes as a challenge to their status and an assault on management prerogative. Similar concerns can arise in the horizontal levels, where different departments, such as production, sales, finance and personnel, may have high levels of autonomy and the capacity to frustrate or ignore the company's labour policy. Foreign ownership can also be important as the local Australian, Canadian or German subsidiary may introduce employment practices in accordance with head office policy in London or New York, which may be more appropriate for conditions in the UK or the US.[4]

[2] Ray Markey and Greg Patmore, "Employee Participation in Health and Safety in the Australian Steel Industry, 1935–2006", *British Journal of Industrial Relations*, vol. 49, no. 1, 2011, p. 148.

[3] Sanford Jacoby, *Employing Bureaucracy: Managers, Unions, and the Transformation of Work in American Industry, 1900–1945*, Columbia University Press, New York, 1985, p. 3.

[4] Graham Dietz, Adrian Wilkinson and Tom Redman, "Involvement and Participation", in Adrian Wilkinson, Nicolas Bacon, Tom Redman and Scott Snell (eds.), *The Sage Handbook of Human Resource Management*, Sage, Los Angeles, 2009, pp. 254–5; Howard Gospel,

Technology, which is "not just machines and technical processes, but also how these are organised and the way workers are deployed around them,"[5] can impact on labour management practices. For example, in Australia, scientific management was more applicable to industries based on assembly line technology, such as textiles, clothing, automobiles and electrical appliance manufacture, where workers were already subdivided and undertaking simple repetitive tasks, than industries such as metal fabrication and engineering, where work was organised on a jobbing or batch production basis.[6] There are similar claims that some forms of employee representation such as ERPs were more applicable to mass-production industries where there were "semi-skilled" workers.[7]

Unions, management and the state play a crucial role in developing and extending employee workplace representation. Their ability to influence events depends upon their power. They also make strategic choices, which may not necessarily be rational or well informed, or successful in the short- and long-term. There are limited choices. Management, for example, may recognise unions alongside forms of employee representation or view an employee representation system as a substitute for organised labour. The latter may antagonise unions and lead to conflict, particularly when unions are strong. Those setting up a system of employee workplace representation may choose to have workers appointed by the unions rather than elected directly by the rank and file. They may face opposition in those workplaces that have strong pre-existing networks of shop stewards or workplace delegates.[8]

There is widespread recognition that worker resistance and collective organisation can limit and shape labour policies and practices. Workers made possible the economies of speed that assisted the rise of large-scale corporations, but also delayed productive reorganisation in order to retain control over the labour process. They helped established internal labour markets in large bureaucratic organisations, to increase job security and restrict the power of foremen and subcontractors, and also aided the extensive development of corporate paternalism.[9]

Markets, Firms and the Management of Labour in Modern Britain, Cambridge University Press, Cambridge, 1992, p. 7; James Naylor, *The New Democracy: Challenging the Social Order in Industrial Ontario*, University of Toronto Press, 1991, p. 175.

[5] Gospel, *Markets, Firms and the Management of Labour*, p. 8.

[6] Wright, *The Management of Labour*, p. 218.

[7] Naylor, *The New Democracy*, p. 175.

[8] Gospel, *Markets, Firms and the Management of Labour*, p. 8; Poole, Lansbury and Wailes, "Participation and Industrial Relations Revisited", pp. 25–6.

[9] Richard John, "Elaborations, Revisions, Dissents: Alfred D. Chandler, Jr.'s *The Visible Hand* after Twenty Years", *Business History Review*, vol. 71, no. 2, 1997, pp. 190–1.

However, the impact of unions on the management of labour has been exaggerated both in popular and academic commentary. As Howard Gospel argues, "Employers had initiatory power, while union power was largely reactive and negative."[10] Further, unions can be divided on ideological and organisational lines. They may be moderate and prefer to work within the capitalist system, or be driven by radical ideologies such as communism or anarcho-syndicalism that seek to overthrow it. They can represent the interests of more moderate groups of workers such as office workers or more militant workers such as miners. Differences can also arise between the union leadership and rank-and-file members, who may challenge union authority through wildcat strikes and rival workplace-based organisation such as shop stewards and shop committees. Even where unions gain more influence through labour or social democratic parties, they may still face divisions on ideological or organisational grounds.[11]

While management plays a major role in the implementation of labour practices, it can vary in its enthusiasm and ability to introduce them. This may relate to the issues concerning corporate scale, structure and ownership raised earlier, but it can also relate to management's attitudes, values and identity. While some managers may be hostile to trade unions and develop employee representation as a means of supplanting them, others may be willing to work with unions and develop forms of employee represen-tation that recognise freedom of association and even promote trade union membership. There is also the level of professionalism of management, which can relate to the development of managerial education and the recognition of a "management ethos" or identity. Managers may form employer organi-sations and professional organisations and can use managerial consultants, which allow them access to the latest ideas and assistance in implementing them.[12]

The state can also have an influence on the forms and incidence of employee representation. Through legislation it can promote, suppress or even outlaw forms of employee representation, as occurred with Nazi Germany and the US under President Roosevelt. The state can also promote forms of employee representation without legislation by providing advice to private industry through government agencies such as departments of

[10] Gospel, *Markets, Firms and the Management of Labour*, p. 188.

[11] Dick Geary, "The Myth of the Radical Miner", in Stefan Berger, Andy Croll and Norman LaPorte (eds.), *Towards a Comparative History of Coalfield Studies*, Ashgate, Aldershot, 2005, pp. 43–64; Wright, *The Management of Labour*, p. 9.

[12] Peter Cochrane, "Company Time: Management, Ideology and the Labour Process, 1940–60", *Labour History*, no. 48, 1985, p. 54; Gospel, *Markets, Firms and the Management of Labour*, p. 7; Wright, *The Management of Labour*, p. 212.

labour, or setting an example by introducing forms of employee representation into state enterprises.

There are limits to what the state can do. In federal states there
may be constitutional restrictions on what federal and state or provincial
governments can do with regard to labour relations. There are also
ideological restraints, particularly if the party in control of the state
supports the idea of managerial prerogative in the workplace and the
principle of voluntarism, which involves non-intervention in the employment
relationship and industrial relations. As in the case of Germany during the
interwar period, there can be political parties that are antidemocratic and
frown upon forms of employee representation built upon the free election
of worker representatives and democratic practices.[13]

The state can openly reinforce the power of capital through state
repression, which increases the costs of collective action by workers and
may provide a favourable climate for the introduction of forms of workplace
employee representation that undermine workers' freedom of association.
State repression can take a variety of forms: direct physical attack on strikers,
the protection and provision of strike-breakers, and the harassment of union
activists. The agencies involved include the military, the police, intelligence
services and the courts. While state repression may be at the margins of
traditional industrial relations, the successful targeting of union activists
by the state may seriously impact upon the ability of unions to organise
and represent members' interests.[14] The defeat of relatively militant workers
such as coal miners and waterfront workers "may radically alter employee
perceptions of general union instrumentality and thereby raise the expected
costs of collective organization and action across many sectors of the
economy far removed from the direct hand of state repression."[15]

The chapter will now look at how the state and other factors influenced
the form and incidence of workplace employee representation in Australia,
Canada, Germany, the US and the UK during the period 1914 to 1939.

---

[13] Gospel, *Markets, Firms and the Management of Labour*, p. 187; Greg Patmore, "Federal
Systems of Industrial Relations", *Journal of Industrial Relations*, vol. 51, no. 2, 2009, pp. 147–9;
Wright, *The Management of Labour*, pp. 8–9.

[14] John Kelly, *Rethinking Industrial Relations: Mobilisation, Collectivism and Long Waves*,
Routledge, London, 1998, pp. 56–9.

[15] Kelly, *Rethinking Industrial Relations*, p. 59.

The Economy

The US

When the First World War began, the US was in a recession, but this soon changed. Although it did not enter the war until 1917, European demand for US products began a boom from 1914. After the US's entry into the war, demand from the US military further fuelled production. There was a growth in industrial production and industry expanded into new regions; shipbuilding, for example, expanded rapidly. European immigration to the US almost ceased with the outbreak of the war. There were labour shortages and greater opportunities for women, Afro-Americans, Mexicans and Asian workers. While workers gained wage increases, their purchasing power was eroded by inflation. The cost of living index had a base of 100 in 1914, but the cost of living grew from 107 in 1915 to 206 in 1920. The boom continued into the post-war period, fuelled by government expenditure and pent-up consumer demand. The US economy shifted from being a net debtor on international markets to a net investor and the UK and its allies were forced by the costs of war to liquidate much of their US investments. The economic bubble finally burst in late 1920, gross national product (GNP) declining by nearly 10 per cent between 1920 and 1921 and almost 5 million Americans losing their jobs.[16]

By 1922 the US economy bounced back and to 1929 enjoyed a period of sustained prosperity. The population of the US grew from 106.5 million in 1920 to 123.2 million by 1930. In the same period, the workforce grew from 42.2 million to 48.7 million. GNP rose by 38 per cent in real terms. Despite the constant size of the manufacturing workforce, manufacturing production rose by 30 per cent. Underlying this growth was a major improvement in productivity, average output per manufacturing worker increasing by 60 per cent between 1920 and 1929, and major improvements in technology and the organisation of work, which attracted international interest. The growth of the automobile industry, which saw the number of registered motor vehicles in the US tripling to over 21 million between 1919 and 1928, stimulated growth in related industries such as steel, rubber, glass, tools and petroleum refining. One new industry that grew dramatically was radios, following the first commercial broadcasting in 1920. By the end of the 1920s almost

---

[16] Alan Brinkley, *American History: A Survey. Volume II: Since 1865*, 11th ed., McGraw-Hill, New York, 2003, pp. 631, 640–1; Gerd Hardach, *The First World War 1914–1918*, University of California Press, Berkeley, 1977, pp. 289–90; Hugh Rockoff, "Until it's Over, Over There: The U.S. Economy in World War I", in Stephen Broadberry and Mark Harrison (eds.), *The Economics of World War I*, Cambridge University Press, Cambridge, 2005, pp. 310–43; Ronald Seavoy, *An Economic History of the United States: From 1607 to the Present*, Routledge, New York, 2006, p. 224.

every US family had a set. Real wages grew as wages and salaries rose by 45 per cent, but prices, reflecting falling production costs, were either steady or falling. With profits growing dramatically, the market value of shares list on the New York Stock Exchange expanded from \$4 billion in 1923 to \$67 billion in 1929. By 1929 the US was the leading financial and manufacturing power in the world economy.[17]

The prosperity of the US economy was shattered by the onset of the Great Depression. While there is a focus on the Wall Street crash of 1929, the roots of the economic downturn in the US lay in a number of factors including overproduction, the decline in European demand for US goods, debt exposure to European economies unable to make sufficient payments and the dependence of the US economy on a few sectors such as automobiles and construction to maintain prosperity. There was also uncertainty over US trade policy due to the prolonged debate that surrounded the passage of the 1930 Smoot-Hawley Tariff Act, which began as a promise by Herbert Hoover in the 1928 presidential campaign to assist farmers. GDP fell from \$104 billion in 1929 to \$76.4 billion in 1932. By 1932 it was estimated that 25 per cent of the workforce was unemployed; unemployment averaged nearly 20 per cent for the rest of the decade, never falling below 15 per cent. While the economic stimulus provided by President Roosevelt's New Deal prevented further economic deterioration and there was a limited recovery in some areas of the economy, approximately 17 per cent of the US workforce was still unemployed in 1939.[18]

The UK

While the First World War stimulated the British economy, as in the US, its performance was poor during the 1920s. The onset of the war had initially disrupted the British economy, due to uncertainty over the length of the conflict and munitions requirements, and unemployment actually rose. However, unemployment had disappeared by January 1915 with the growth due to war production and military recruitment. There were also increases in the cost of living, particularly food prices, the index of wholesale prices for Great Britain increasing from 100 in 1914 to 242 in 1919. Rising prices led to industrial unrest and demands for price control. The war stimulated

[17] Brinkley, *American History*, pp. 650–1; James Foreman-Peck, *A History of the World Economy: International Economic Relations since 1850*, 2nd ed., Prentice Hall, Harlow, England, 1995, p. 183; Neville Kirk, *Labour and Society. Volume 2: Challenge and Accommodation, 1850–1939*, Scolar Press, Aldershot, 1994, p. 273.

[18] Brinkley, *American History*, pp. 676–80, 703; Harold James, *Europe Reborn: A History, 1914–2000*, Pearson Education, Harlow, 2003, pp. 105–6, 109; Kirk, *Labour and Society*, pp. 332–3.

growth in new industries, such as chemicals and electrical engineering, but also brought new growth in traditional staple industries such as coal, iron and steel, and shipbuilding.[19] While the UK emerged from the war with an economic boom and full employment, as Howard Gospel has noted, "Britain ceased to be the centre of the world's trading network and many of Britain's export markets contracted as countries formerly dependent on its goods either sought alternative sources of supply or began to replace imports."[20]

The post-war economic boom broke in 1920, leading to a severe depression. British industrial production fell by nearly 20 per cent and exports fell by 30 per cent, with unemployment increasing from 2 per cent in 1920 to 14 per cent in 1922. The recovery from this economic downturn was not as strong as in other countries, Britain seeing an unsteady upswing between 1922 and 1929. With the exception of 1927, unemployment remained above 10 per cent, particularly impacting upon staple industries such as shipbuilding, cotton, textiles, iron and steel, mechanical engineering and the coalfields of England, Scotland and Wales. British manufacturing was placed at a cost disadvantage in world markets when the government decided to place the pound on a gold standard at an inflated rate of exchange. For workers with regular employment, retail prices fell during the 1920s and real wages improved.[21]

With the onset of the Great Depression, the British economy went into another slump that saw unemployment reach a peak of 22 per cent in 1932. However, coming from a lower productive capacity than other countries, the 1930s depression in the UK was less severe and destabilising than the economic downturn of the early 1920s. The prospects of British manufacturing improved when the UK came off the gold standard in September 1931, paving the way for lower interest rates, and the introduction of tariff protection. There was an upswing between 1932 and 1937 as exports slowly grew, the major contribution to growth coming from domestic demand. Unemployment, however, remained above 10 per cent for the remainder of the decade and British employers were generally at an advantage in the labour market for the interwar period after 1920.[22]

---

[19] Hugh Clegg, *A History of British Trade Unions since 1889. Volume II: 1911–1933*, Clarendon Press, London, 1985, pp. 141–52; Gospel, *Markets, Firms and the Management of Labour*, p. 39; Hardach, *The First World War*, p. 172; James W. Stitt, *Joint Industrial Councils in British History: Inception, Adoption, and Utilization, 1917–1939*, Praeger, Westport, 2006, pp. 10–11.

[20] Gospel, *Markets, Firms and the Management of Labour*, pp. 39–40.

[21] Derek Aldcroft, *The Inter-War Economy: Britain, 1919–1939*, Columbia University Press, New York, 1970, pp. 146–50, 364; Derek Aldcroft, *The British Economy between the Wars*, Philip Allan, Deddington, 1983, p. 108; Gospel, *Markets, Firms and the Management of Labour*, pp. 40–1; Kirk, *Labour and Society*, pp. 278–9.

[22] Aldcroft, *The Inter-War Economy*, p. 271; Aldcroft, *The British Economy between the Wars*, pp. 95, 108; Gospel, *Markets, Firms and the Management of Labour*, pp. 40–41.

Germany

The German economy was also under strain both during the First World War and the 1920s. The Royal Navy's blockade, which continued until 1919, deprived Germany of many imports essential for its industry. Germany was not self-sufficient in agriculture, importing 25 per cent of its food. While there were no deaths caused directly by starvation during the war, undernourishment was a major issue and weakened German health, morale and productivity. Unlike the French and British, the German government was excluded from foreign financial markets and had to rely on domestic borrowing to finance the war. The German government dealt with this issue by rapidly increasing the money supply through war bonds, which it believed would be paid by a defeated enemy at the end of the war. It also set up loan bureaus to lend their own money notes to state governments, local governments and private businesses. These notes had the same status as national bank notes. With large amounts of money pursuing fewer goods, inflation became a feature of German life on the home front, the cost-of-living index rising 200 per cent between 1914 and 1918. This wartime inflation, which followed a long period of relative price stability in Germany, destroyed savings and reduced real incomes. As in the US and the UK, German unemployment fell dramatically due to recruitment and increased war production.[23]

Germany's economic woes increased in the wake of its defeat in the First World War. The November 1918 revolution, which led to the abdication of the Kaiser and the establishment of the Weimar Republic, was followed by a series of political crises which fuelled economic uncertainty, including communist revolts and the Nazis' failed Munich Putsch in November 1923. The victorious Allies demanded reparations to pay for their war costs. Germans thought these payments were unjust and their government was unable to pay because of the parliament's opposition to tax increases and the reluctance of capital markets to purchase German government bonds. Wartime inflation became hyperinflation in the summer of 1922. This trend continued as the German government again increased the money supply to cover government expenditure and wage increases. There was also a slowdown in business, a decline in exports and rapidly expanding unemployment. The French and the Belgians, convinced that the Germans were not honouring their reparation payments, occupied the Ruhr, Germany's major industrial

[23] Richard Bessel, *Germany after the First World War*, Clarendon Press, Oxford, 1993, pp. 31, 38–9; Roger Chickering, *Imperial Germany and the Great War, 1914–1918*, 2nd ed., Cambridge University Press, Cambridge, 2004, pp. 35–46, 104–7; Gerald Feldman, *The Great Disorder: Politics, Economics, and Society in the German Inflation, 1914–1924*, Oxford University Press, Oxford, 1993, pp. 37–51.

region, on 11 January 1923. The German government responded with a policy of passive resistance so that whenever Allied forces entered a factory, a mine or a government office, everyone stopped work. The shutdown of the Ruhr impacted on the rest of the German economy, reducing tax revenues while the government provided subsidies to affected German companies and unemployment benefits for workers. To finance these expenditures the German government again printed money, which led to a further wild escalation of prices and the devaluation of the Deutschmark. By November 1923 the mark was practically worthless, with an exchange rate of 4.2 trillion marks to the US dollar. Hyperinflation saw the wiping out of savings and social unrest including wild cat strikes, the plundering of market stalls and stores, and hordes of urban dwellers invading rural areas and stealing food and other items. The middle class was forced to sell off household items and social resentments came to fore, worker pitted against employer, foreign speculators, including Jews, being seen as profiting off German misery.[24]

From late 1923 the economic situation in Germany began to change with a series of initiatives to stabilise the economy. There was a shift towards more conservative governments, the Catholic Centre Party leader Wilhelm Marx becoming Chancellor in November 1923. The government halted inflation by creating a new domestic currency, the Rentenmark, which was underpinned by German industrial and agricultural assets. The German currencies were also placed on the gold standard in 1924 to encourage confidence in the German monetary system. The government then slashed public expenditure by reducing civil servants' salaries and dismissing temporary employees and married women. It made major cuts to the social welfare system and allowed concessions to private sector employers on working hours and their right to dismiss workers. Negotiations with the French led to an arrangement whereby industrial production would resume in the Ruhr in exchange for goods being sent to France and Belgium as partial payment for reparations. The Allies and Germany also accepted the Dawes Plan at a London conference in July–August 1924 that provided for a more reasonable schedule of payments and a hard currency loan to stabilise the German budget. Alongside the Dawes Plan, Belgium and France agreed to withdraw their troops from the Ruhr over the next 12 months. A subsequent further round of negotiations led to the Young Plan in 1929, which reduced Germany's overall debt and set up a schedule of payments to be concluded in 1987.[25]

[24] Helga Grebing, *History of the German Labour Movement: A Survey*, rev. ed., Berg Publishers, Leamington Spa, 1985, p. 105; Eric D. Weitz, *Weimar Germany: Promise and Tragedy*, Princeton University Press, Princeton, 2007, pp. 129–42.

[25] Feldman, *The Great Disorder*, pp. 780–835; James, *Europe Reborn*, p. 87; Weitz, *Weimar Germany*, pp. 141–6.

The stabilisation programme of 1923–24 led the Weimar Republic into a period of relative prosperity that lasted from 1926 until 1929. There was an influx of US capital into Germany and there was investment in plants, equipment and housing. German GNP increased by 24 per cent between 1925 and 1928 and total industrial production again reached 1913 levels in 1927. Real wages grew and broadly regained their 1913 level the same year. There was a splurge of consumption with many consumers, even the middle class, buying on credit. German industrialists regained export markets from the British and the French. By 1930 Germany ranked second after the US among the world's exporting countries and was the first exporter of finished goods.[26]

This prosperity came to end with the Wall Street Crash of 1929, US banks calling in their short-term loans. Consumer demand collapsed and production declined, leading to the retrenchment of workers. German unemployment increased from 13.3 per cent in 1929 to a staggering 43.8 per cent in 1932. Industries particularly badly hit were machine building with 48.9 per cent and shipbuilding with 63.5 per cent unemployment. German GNP fell by 37 per cent between 1928 and 1932. Heinrich Brüning, the Centre Party Chancellor from March 1930 to May 1932, exacerbated the misery by adopting deflationary policies, cutting government expenditure on social welfare and the Civil Service, and increasing taxes. There was a shift towards stimulating the economy as Germany departed from the gold standard in 1931, allowing the government to pump more money into the economy. The economic crisis added to the growing disillusionment with the Weimar Republic and Adolf Hitler became Chancellor in January 1933. Under the National Socialists, unemployment fell during the remainder of the 1930s due to extensive public works and rearmament programmes.[27]

Canada
The fortunes of the Canadian economy during the interwar period were closely linked to the US, Canada's major trading partner and source of investment. The Canadian economy was in recession during 1913–14 and

[26] Theo Balderston, *Economics and Politics in the Weimar Republic*, Cambridge University Press, Cambridge, 2002, p. 61; Alfred Chandler, *Scale and Scope: The Dynamics of Industrial Capitalism*, Harvard University Press, Cambridge, MA, 1990, pp. 503–6; Richard Grunberger, *A Social History of the Third Reich*, Phoenix Books, London, 2005, pp. 16–17; Weitz, *Weimar Germany*, pp. 145–9.

[27] Christoph Buchheim and Redvers Garside, "Introduction", in Christoph Buchheim and Redvers Garside (eds.), *After the Slump: Industry and Politics in 1930s Britain and Germany*, Peter Lang, Frankfurt am Main, 2000, pp. 6–7; Richard J. Evans, *The Third Reich in Power: How the Nazis Won over the Hearts and Minds of a Nation*, Penguin, London, 2006, pp. 322–42; Weitz, *Weimar Germany*, pp. 161–4.

the outbreak of the First World War initially dislocated its economic recovery as export markets were disrupted. As elsewhere, however, the war soon stimulated the Canadian economy by soaking up unemployment with enlistment and increased military production, but also created the problem of rising prices. An average weekly food basket for a Canadian family increased by 46 per cent between December 1916 and December 1918, and by 82 per cent at the peak of the inflationary spiral in July 1920. By July 1920 the average weekly food basket cost 128 per cent more than it did at the outbreak of the First World War in 1914. The bargaining position of organised labour improved and by 1917 the country's employers faced a shortage of 100,000 workers. Price rises, however, contributed to a serious erosion of real wages after 1917.[28]

With the end of the war, there was an economic recession followed by a period of economic prosperity. After the Armistice, many workers lost their jobs in the munitions industry and unemployment rose steeply in the early months of 1919. Uncertainty hung over most Canadian industries until a major economic downturn in the winter of 1920–21, when unemployment increased due to enterprises closing or curtailing production. In 1921 the value of manufacturing output fell by almost a third and prices fell by 28 per cent. As in the US, however, the remainder of the 1920s was a period of economic boom with a rise in the standard of living and increased consumer demand for radios and automobiles. US investors were attracted to Canada as a place to construct branch plants to meet the demands of the British Empire behind an imperial tariff. The percentage of foreign investment represented by American capital grew from 22 per cent in 1913 to 53 per cent in 1926. While real manufacturing output had grown at a compound rate of 4 per cent between 1919 and 1925, it grew by the exceptionally high level of 9.8 per cent between 1926 and 1929. Unemployment fell from 6.2 per cent in 1921 to 1.7 per cent in 1928.[29]

The Great Depression began in Canada as early as April 1929 with the collapse of the price of wheat, an important Canadian export commodity. Immigration in the 1920s led to the full cultivation of available prairie

[28] Craig Heron and Myer Siemiatycki, "The Great War, the State and Working Class Canada", in Craig Heron (ed.), *The Workers Revolt in Canada 1917–1925*, University of Toronto Press, 1998, pp. 20–2; Naylor, *The New Democracy*, pp. 18–19; Bryan D. Palmer, *Working Class Experience: Rethinking the History of Canadian Labour 1800–1991*, 2nd ed., McClelland & Stewart, Toronto, 1992, p. 196.

[29] Robert Bothwell, Ian Drummond and John English, *Canada, 1900–1945*, University of Toronto Press, Toronto, 1987, p. 171; Heron and Siemiatycki, "The Great War", pp. 21–3; Desmond Morton, *A Short History of Canada*, 5th ed., McClelland & Stewart, Toronto, 2001, pp. 203–8; Palmer, *Working Class Experience*, pp. 214–19; Patmore, "Unionism and Non-Union Employee Representation", p. 531.

land and a bumper crop in 1929. There was also international competition from Argentina, Australia, the US and even the Soviet Union. The onset of the Great Depression in the US exacerbated the economic downturn in Canada given the economic links between the two countries. The US also worsened Canadian economic problems with the imposition of the Smoot-Hawley tariff on all agricultural goods in 1930 and the imposition in 1932 of tariffs on products such as timber and lumber. The Canadian government responded to the protectionist measures of the US and other countries by placing high tariffs on the import of manufactured goods in 1930 and 1931. From 1929 to 1933, total Canadian export prices declined by 60 per cent and earnings from wheat and flour, the top export commodities, fell by over 70 per cent. Unemployment grew from 3 per cent in 1929 to a peak of 23.9 per cent in 1933 and national income in 1933 was half that of 1929. While the Canadian federal government took a traditional deflationary view of the Great Depression, it did provide financial assistance to provincial governments to fund unemployment relief at the municipal level. Fifteen per cent of Canadians were dependent on direct unemployment relief in April 1933. The Canadian government stopped immigration during this period and the number of immigrants dropped by 93 per cent between 1929 and 1935. There was some relief for the Canadian export industries with the 1932 Ottawa Agreement on British trade preferences and the 1935 trade agreement with the US, which gave Canada the status of most-favoured nation for trade, with some exceptions, and reduced duties on 63 items, including agricultural goods and fishery products. The Canadian recovery from the Great Depression was slow and 12.8 per cent of Canadians were still unemployed at the outbreak of the Second World War in 1939.[30]

Australia

The outbreak of the First World War in Australia initially led to economic uncertainty and dislocation. The country was very dependent on exports of mineral and agricultural products. Major German markets were lost, there was uncertainty over whether British manufacturers could continue to supply Australia with most of its imports and shipping was requisitioned for

[30] Elizabeth Bloomfield, Gerald Bloomfield, Deryck W. Holdsworth, and Murdo Macpherson, "Economic Crisis", in Donald Kerr and Deryck W. Holdsworth (eds.), *Historical Atlas of Canada. Volume III: Addressing the Twentieth Century 1891–1961*, University of Toronto Press, Toronto, 1990, plate 40; H. Carl Goldenberg, "The Canada-United States Trade Agreement, 1935", *The Canadian Journal of Economics and Political Science/Revue canadienne d'Economique et de Science politique*, vol. 2, no. 2, 936, pp. 209–12; Donald Kerr and Deryck W. Holdsworth (eds.), *Historical Atlas of Canada. Volume III: Addressing the Twentieth Century 1891–1961*, University of Toronto Press, Toronto, 1990, pp. 99–101; Morton, *A Short History of Canada*, pp. 210–15; Patmore, "Unionism and Non-Union Employee Representation", p. 531.

war purposes. Unemployment increased rapidly as the sources of public and private investment dried up. Added to this was the drought during 1914–15, which reduced the wheat harvest by 75 per cent compared to the previous financial year and forced Australia to import wheat for the first time in many years. As the war continued, increased local demand and reduced imports stimulated Australian manufacturing, but the generally situation was one of stagnation and unemployment did not fall to the levels seen in Canada, Germany, the US and the UK. Remoteness from the battlefield limited the participation of Australian industry. Inflation was one of several issues that fuelled worker discontent as the war continued. Unionists believed that producers were profiteering from the war and governments were ineffective in dealing with rising prices.[31]

After the end of the First World War, with the exception of a slump in 1921, heavy foreign investment and immigration sustained a recovery. Australia's economic prosperity remained tied to the primary sector of the economy. Unemployment, however, never dropped to the levels seen in Canada and the US during the prosperous 1920s. The first signs of a major depression appeared in 1927 as the supply of overseas capital began to dry up. Estimated unemployment, based on average unemployment as a percentage of the total workforce, rose from 6.2 per cent in 1928 to 19.7 cent by 1932. These figures are considered to be an underestimate by some authors for it has been estimated that up to 35 per cent of wage earners were unemployed and another third were on work rationing or short-time to preserve their jobs. Those workers who could continue in employment faced wage cuts. But though the 1930s depression was more severe than that of the 1890s, recovery was faster. The 1930s did not suffer the repeated droughts of the 1890s. The federal government also stimulated the recovery through tariffs and currency devaluation.[32]

Unemployment data, though varying in method of calculation, provides a useful way of comparing the economic trends of these five countries. As Table 2.1 indicates, the First World War spurred production, which

[31] Ernst Boehm, *20th Century Economic Development in Australia*, 3rd ed., Longman Cheshire, Melbourne, 1993, p. 25; Greg Patmore, "Industrial Conciliation and Arbitration in NSW before 1998", in Greg Patmore (ed.), *Laying the Foundations of Industrial Justice: The Presidents of the Industrial Relations Commission of NSW 1902–1998*, Federation Press, Sydney, 2003, pp. 15–16; Patmore, "Unionism and Non-Union Employee Representation", p. 530; Glen Withers, Anthony M. Endres and Len Perry, "Labour", in Wray Vamplew (ed.), *Australians: Historical Statistics*, Fairfax, Syme & Weldon and Associates, Sydney, 1987, p. 152.

[32] Ray Broomhill, *Unemployed Workers: A Social History of the Great Depression in Adelaide*, University of Queensland, St. Lucia, 1978, pp. 16–19; Charlie Fox, *Working Australia*, Allen & Unwin, North Sydney, 1991, pp. 126–9; Patmore, "Industrial Conciliation and Arbitration", p. 19; Withers, Endres and Perry, "Labour", p. 152.

Table 2.1 Unemployment in Australia, Canada, Germany, the UK and the US, 1914–39 (%)

Year	Australia	Canada	Germany	UK	US
1914	3.3	*	7.2	3.3	7.9
1915	5.9	*	3.2	1.1	8.5
1916	3.5	*	2.2	0.4	5.1
1917	3.3	*	1.0	0.6	4.6
1918	3.4	*	0.8	0.8	1.4
1919	3.6	*	3.7	2.1	1.4
1920	3.4	*	3.8	2.0	5.2
1921	5.8	6.2	2.8	12.9	11.7
1922	6.1	4.6	1.5	14.3	6.7
1923	5.0	3.3	10.2	11.7	2.4
1924	4.8	4.7	13.1	10.3	5.0
1925	6.3	4.6	6.8	11.3	3.2
1926	4.9	3.0	18.0	12.5	1.8
1927	4.1	1.8	8.8	9.7	3.3
1928	6.2	1.7	8.6	10.8	4.2
1929	6.7	3.0	13.3	10.4	3.2
1930	9.8	10.1	22.7	16.0	8.9
1931	16.4	13.1	34.3	21.3	16.3
1932	19.7	21.4	43.8	22.1	24.1
1933	18.9	23.9	36.2	19.9	25.2
1934	16.0	17.0	20.5	16.7	22.0
1935	14.0	16.5	16.2	15.5	20.3
1936	11.0	14.7	12.0	13.1	17.0
1937	8.8	10.0	6.9	10.8	14.3
1938	7.5	12.8	3.2	13.5	19.1
1939	8.8	12.8	0.9	11.6	17.2

Source: Patmore, "Unionism and Non-Union Employee Representation", p. 530; Withers, Endres and Perry, "Labour", p. 152 – Australian figures based on Butlin estimates.

reduced unemployment in all five countries by 1918–19 and provided a favourable climate for trade unions and wage demands. The strength of trade unions, rising strike levels and concerns about the implications of the Russian Revolution encouraged legislators, liberal employers and moderate union leaders to look for orderly ways of providing a voice for workers at the workplace level. The labour markets deteriorated following the First World War, with unemployment remaining above 10 per cent in the UK for most of the 1920s. The German economy faced particular problems during the early 1920s, with hyperinflation, the payment of reparations and political unrest. Canada and the US enjoyed economic prosperity for most of the 1920s, and Australia enjoyed relatively low levels of unemployment compared to the UK and Germany, but higher than Canada and the US. All these economies faced a rapid deterioration in their labour markets with the onset of the Great Depression, particularly Germany and the United States, which saw dramatic political shifts, towards National Socialism in Germany and the New Deal in the US. With the exception of Germany, there was a limited recovery after 1932–33. In line with Ramsay's argument about economic prosperity favouring interest in employee representation, there should be increased interest in all these countries by the end of the First World War and in Canada and the US during the 1920s.[33]

Industry Scale and Structure

The scale of industry tended to be larger and more concentrated in the US, which had a large domestic market, growing from 92 million in 1910 to 132 million in 1940. The development of new technologies and the opening of new markets through the expansion of the railways led to the economies of scale and scope necessary to allow for the establishment of large multi-unit enterprises.[34] As early as 1870 the large-scale private corporation was beginning to dominate the US economy and was increasingly viewed as "a real entity with the same rights and privileges as a natural person."[35] While anti-trust legislation and litigation highlighted public concern over the economic power of these large corporations, the courts ensured a narrow approach to anti-trust regulation that legitimated concentration of economic power if certain legalities were observed. The legal and economic dominance of large-scale corporations in the US placed limitations on any

---

[33] Patmore, "Unionism and Non-union Employee Representation", p. 530.

[34] Brinkley, *American History*, p. A-38; Chandler, *Scale and Scope*, p. 18.

[35] Christopher Tomlins, *The State and the Unions: Labor Relations, Law and the Organised Labor Movement in America, 1880–1960*, Cambridge University Press, Cambridge, 1985, p. 29.

challenge by the organised labour movement, with certain exceptions such as steel and the railroads.[36]

Large-scale corporations first appeared in the railways and then spread to industrial firms such as US Steel and Standard Oil, founded in 1901 and 1912 respectively. There was a divorce between ownership and management as growing corporations had to raise funds externally and relied upon a complex management hierarchy based on a functional division of management. By 1937 American Telephone & Telegraph was the largest company of any sector in the world with a market capitalisation of $3.1 billion. These large-scale corporations grew through mergers and acquisitions. The two major forms of growth were through vertical integration, whereby the company expanded to include both suppliers and distributors, and diversification, where the corporation expanded to produce more than one distinct line of goods. While Standard Oil had its origins in the refining of oil, it undertook both backward integration into pipelines and crude oil production and forward integration into distribution and marketing. By 1930, 59 per cent of US firms were diversified, compared with 26 per cent in Australia and 21 per cent in the UK. Diversification was pursued in many leading food and chemical firms through the establishment of research laboratories that developed new products. The chemical manufacturers Proctor & Gamble and Du Pont, for example, developed washing powders. While there was reliance upon external capitalisation, founding families could still exercise a control over senior management in some corporations through minority shareholders of as little as 15–20 per cent.[37]

Just after the First World War, US firms such as Du Pont and General Motors (GM) began to shift towards a multidivisional form of organisation as the administrative efficiency of their multilevel hierarchies of professional managers was being restricted by their highly centralised nature. Within such an organisational structure there are autonomous operating divisions, each with their own functional levels of management, and a general office that provides the focal point for corporate strategy and supervises performance through a reporting system.[38]

As in the US, large-scale business or *Riesenbetriebe* in Germany emerged with the completion of new transport and communication networks, which made possible the flow of goods and services large enough for firms to exploit economies of scale and scope. Germany had a smaller domestic market and

[36] Tomlins, *The State and the Unions*, pp. 29–30.

[37] Gordon Boyce and Simon Ville, *The Development of Modern Business*, Palgrave, Houndsmills, 2002, pp. 5–15; John F. Wilson, *British Business History 1720–1894*, Manchester University Press, Manchester, 1995, pp. 66–7.

[38] Wilson, *British Business History*, pp. 134–6.

lower GDP than the US, and had to rely more on exports to sustain growth. There was, however, a greater deal of collusion and cooperation among German firms than in the US. There was a clustering of banks, training institutions and firms and trade associations or cartels were formed, particularly in coal, chemicals and steel. An example of these powerful cartels was the Rhenish-Westphalian coal syndicate, which in 1913 comprised 87 large mining enterprises and controlled 50 per cent of Germany's total coal production. While each firm had nominal independence, it was virtually impossible for any independent coal producer to operate independently in the Rhineland and the coal cartel set the price of coal. Cartels were still being formed in the interwar period -- the cartel of the chemical industry did not officially come into existence until 1925. The willingness of German courts to enforce cartels and other agreements between German firms reduced the incentive to merge into industry-wide holding companies.[39]

Despite this greater tendency towards collusion and cooperation, there was also a tendency in Germany, as in the US, towards large-scale and vertical integration with extensive use of professional managers. As a developing economy, Germany did not possess an integrated marketing or distribution system, leading German firms very early to integrate these functions into their existing activities. German firms also diversified. German company law, introduced in 1870, provided for a supervisory or control board (*Aufsichtsrat*), which was elected by shareholders and supervised the activities of management from the shareholders' perspective. The *Aufsichtsrat* dealt with strategic decisions on investment and product range, and the executive board (*Vorstand*) dealt with functional and operational management. Banks represented shareholders on the *Aufsichtsrat* and supported as well as financed trends towards concentration, integration and diversification. While self-funding remained an important part of German corporate growth, banks participated in top-level decisions more than was the case in the UK or the US, and favoured conservative investment in industries such as food and textiles rather than the chemical, electrical or automobile industries. Once a firm had developed its infrastructure and organisational capabilities, bankers became less influential.[40] Despite this, as Chandler argues, "only in Germany did the representatives of financial institutions

[39] Chandler, *Scale and Scope*, pp. 397–8, 409–11; Koppel S. Pinson, *Modern Germany: Its History and Civilization*, 2nd ed., Macmillan, New York, 1966, pp. 234–8; Wilson, *British Business History*, p. 70.

[40] Chandler, *Scale and Scope*, p. 398; Claude Guillebaud, *The Works Council: A German Experiment in Industrial Democracy*, Cambridge University Press, Cambridge, 1928, p. 188–9; Harold James, "Economic Reasons for the Collapse of the Weimar Republic", in Ian Kershaw (ed.), *Weimar: Why Did German Democracy Fail?* Weidenfeld and Nicolson, London, 1990, p. 37; Wilson, *British Business History*, pp. 71–4.

help to shape top-level policy, particularly on resource allocation, over any extended period of time."[41]

Limitations were imposed on the development of German firms along US lines. Powerful family dynasties dominated certain corporations such as Siemens, Thyssens and Krupps, and played an important role on their supervisory boards, influencing strategic decisions while delegating the functional and operational management to salaried managers. German corporations were also highly centralised. They copied the bureaucratic procedures of public administration and limited the flexibility and autonomy of the middle management and junior management levels. There were some organisational initiatives: Siemens, the leading German electrical manufacturer, adopted the multidivisional form of organisation as early as 1910. However, while a small number of individual German firms experimented with this structure during the interwar period, it made the most progress in the US and remained a rarity in Germany until the 1960s.[42]

By contrast to the German and US experience, the British economy which, like the German, depended on export markets for growth and by 1930 had only one-third of the population of the US, was long dominated by small, single-unit, family-owned and family-managed enterprises. One response of the family firms to increasing internal and external competition from the 1870s was to cooperate and form trade associations to fix prices at a mutually profitable level and allocate market quotas to offset intensifying competition and falling prices. These trade associations were found particularly in the iron and steel, textiles, metal processing and chemical industries. By 1944 there were 2,500 trade associations in Britain, 1,300 of which were in manufacturing industries. The protection of these trade associations against market competition reduced the incentive for British firms to change their structures.[43]

Even where larger multi-unit firms emerged, during the merger waves of the 1890s and 1920s, these tended to be loosely coordinated holding companies in which family control remained strong, subsidiaries had considerable autonomy and traditional methods of administration persisted. There were a few large, more unified firms with more elaborate managerial hierarchies organised on functional lines. As in Germany, multidivisional firms did not take off in the UK until the 1960s, notable exceptions in the interwar period being ICI (Imperial Chemical Industries), Dunlop and Unilever. Yet even in ICI the rationale of the multidivisional form was undermined by the

[41] Chandler, *Scale and Scope*, p. 398.

[42] Chandler, *Scale and Scope*, pp. 74–6, 136–7.

[43] Chandler, *Scale and Scope*, pp. 249–52; Gospel, *Markets, Firms and the Management of Labour*, p. 177; Wilson, *British Business History*, pp. 98–100, 155–6.

personal power and "dictatorship" of Sir Harry McGowan, the ICI chair, who restricted organisational innovation in the company.[44]

British firms tended to be slower than US counterparts in implementing growth through vertical integration and diversification. Vertical integration within British firms typically occurred during the 1920s, later than in the US. One sector where vertical integration may have been more integrated than in the US is the food industry. Reckitts, United Dairies, Unilever, Lyons, Rowntree, Bovril and Cadbury-Fry invested heavily in marketing and distribution. Diversification was less common in the UK than in the US. ICI, which arose from a merger of four of the largest firms in the British chemical industry in 1926 and brought together a level of expertise that allowed it to diversify into a range of areas including paints, plastics and fertilisers, was a rare example of diversification. By 1930, ICI was spending more than four times the amount on research of its constituent firms before the merger.[45]

While Canada had a smaller economy than Germany, the UK and the US, it was like Germany and the UK in its dependence on exports for economic growth. It was also dependent on US and British capital to develop its industries. There had been a major merger wave from 1909 to 1913 witnessing 97 mergers involving 221 firms with combined assets of more than 200 million Canadian dollars. While firms whose total sales exceeded $1 million accounted for only 15 per cent of total manufactured output in 1901, by 1921 that proportion had surpassed 50 per cent. There was another round of mergers from 1924 to 1930, when 315 mergers took place involving assets of nearly $1 billion. In addition to mergers, economic power was centralised through the formation of holding companies such as Alcan Aluminium Limited in 1928.[46] As Bryan Palmer argues, "such concentration of economic power established monopoly as the dominant force within the economy."[47] Financial intermediaries, such as investment houses and the chartered banks with which they were closely associated in *de facto* partnerships, played a crucial role in this merger movement. They also gained considerable influence over company boards. The investment house Wood Gundy, which was allied with the Royal Bank, was represented on the boards of 50 of the largest Canadian corporations.[48]

---

[44] Chandler, *Scale and Scope*, pp. 361–3; Gospel, *Markets, Firms and the Management of Labour*, pp. 46, 177–8; William Reader, *Imperial Chemical Industries:. A History. Volume Two: The First Quarter Century 1926–1952*, Oxford University Press, London, 1975, chaps. 8, 13; Wilson, *British Business History*, pp. 149–51.

[45] Boyce and Ville, *The Development of Modern Business*, pp. 10–15; Chandler, *Scale and Scope*, pp. 264–5; Gospel, *Markets, Firms and the Management of Labour*, pp. 44–5.

[46] Naylor, *The New Democracy*, p. 17; Palmer, *Working Class Experience*, p. 215.

[47] Palmer, *Working Class Experience*, p. 215.

[48] Palmer, *Working Class Experience*, p. 215.

There were other significant dimensions to this consolidation of Canadian industry. Large American corporations such as International Harvester, Ford, GM, Swift and Goodyear established branch plants to exploit Canadian domestic sales, take advantage of Canadian patent laws and operate within the British Empire's protective tariffs. By 1934 there were 1,350 US firms operating in Canada, of which 36 per cent were established between 1920 and 1929, and a further 26 per cent between 1930 and 1934. US investment dominated British investment, American capital more than doubling between 1913 and 1926, from 22 to 53 per cent.[49]

Australia, the smallest of the five countries in terms of population, tended to have the least-developed economy in terms of firm size. In 1929 the average number of wage earners per establishment in Australia was 15.6, compared with 25.3 and 41.9 in Canada and the US respectively. While the majority of enterprises in Australia remained small, the percentage of workers in large-scale enterprises grew. In manufacturing, the average number of employees per establishment fluctuated: 23.13 in 1920–21, 20.13 in 1928–29 and 21.25 in 1938–39. The number of factories in manufacturing with more than 100 employees grew, however, from 651 in 1920–21 to 725 in 1928–29 and 946 in 1938–39 – the percentage of manufacturing employees in these factories was 42.92, 43.71 and 47.52 respectively. Continued market concentration and the emergence of heavy industry assisted the growth of large-scale employers. The Broken Hill Proprietary Company (BHP) opened its steelworks at Newcastle in New South Wales (NSW) in 1915 with a workforce of 1,450 and by 1935 had absorbed its only rival at Port Kembla. Combines arose in the glass (1922), paper (1926), chemical (1928) and drug (1930) industries. Overseas companies set up operations behind tariff barriers in the 1920s. In the automobile industry, Ford established plants in Victoria in 1925 to assemble chassis and build bodies, and within a year employed 1,000 workers. GM also established a plant in 1926 and took over the local company, Holden's Motor Body Builders Ltd., in 1931. While vertical integration was not common, there was some diversification. The number of diversified Australian firms with more than 100 employees grew from 14 per cent in 1910 to 26 per cent in 1930, more than the UK (21 per cent) but smaller than the US (59 per cent). However, where diversification did occur in Australia, it was a narrow extension of existing activities. State enterprises remained large-scale employers. By 1929 the NSW Government Railways (NSWGR) and the Post Office employed 43,972 and 40,545 staff respectively.[50]

---

[49] Kerr and Holdsworth, *Historical Atlas of Canada. Volume III*, p. 14; Naylor, *The New Democracy*, p. 18; Palmer, *Working Class Experience*, p. 216.

[50] Boyce and Ville, *The Development of Modern Business*, pp. 12–15; Greg Patmore, *Australian*

The Division of Labour and Technology

The US led the way in both the reorganisation of production and techno-logical innovation. Between the 1890s and the 1920s, US employers in large-scale industries transformed their workplaces. Economic turbulence and increased competition encouraged US employers to reduce their costs of production. They altered the factory environment, changed the flow of work, introduced new production methods, adopted new technology, experimented with wage incentive schemes, reduced the arbitrary power of supervisors and centralised labour control. The systematic management movement, which included Frederick Winslow Taylor's scientific management, encouraged these trends. Taylorism promoted a set of management practices and an ideological viewpoint which challenged the populist view that workers were the sole creative factor in production and replaced it with the idea that the worker was a passive factor of production and an appendage to a machine. It also represented the bureaucratisation of the structure of control rather than employment as it lacked a notion of a career system. It is difficult to assess the impact of scientific management on management practices as most manufac-turers found Taylor's system too rigorous and adopted only those aspects that suited their particular needs. The absolute peak of managers' desire to control the production process and eliminate worker economy reached their peak in the disassembly line of meat processing plants and the automobile assembly line of Henry Ford's Highland Park plant. There was a trend towards larger-scale plants. Highland Park grew from nearly 13,000 employees in 1914 to 42,000 in 1924. Ford's River Rouge plant, which later became the largest manufacturing plant in the US and probably the world, also employed 68,000 workers in 1924. Another large-scale plant was the Goodyear Tire & Rubber plant at Akron Ohio, which employed 33,000 workers in 1920.[51]

Labour History, Longman Cheshire, Melbourne, 1991, pp. 145–6; Wright, *The Management of Labour*, p. 16.

[51] Melvyn Dubofsky, *Hard Work: The Making of Labor History*, University of Illinois Press, Urbana, 2000, pp. 186–8; David M. Gordon, Richard Edwards and Michael Reich, *Segmented Work, Divided Workers: The Historical Transformation of Labor in the United States*, Cambridge University Press, Cambridge, 1982, pp. 140–1; Craig Littler, *The Development of the Labour Process in Capitalist Societies: A Comparative Study of the Transformation of Work Organisation in Britain, Japan and the USA*, Heinemann, London, 1982, pp. 51, 58–9; Daniel Nelson, *Managers and Workers: Origins of the New Factory System in the United States 1880–1920*, The University of Wisconsin Press, Madison, 1975, p. 9; Daniel Nelson, "Scientific Management", in Melvyn Dubofsky (ed.), *The Oxford Encyclopedia of American Business, Labor & Economic History, Vol. 2*, Oxford University Press, New York, 2013, pp. 152–3; Bryan Palmer, "Class, Conception and Conflict: The Thrust for Efficiency, Managerial Views of Labour and Working Class Rebellion, 1903–22', *The Review of Radical Political Economics*, vol. 7, no. 2, 1975, p. 44.

While there was some deskilling among traditional trades such as glass-blowers and iron moulders in the US, common labourers who had once handled materials for skilled production workers became semi-skilled machine operators or parts assemblers. New forms of skill emerged, as all the basic industries, including steel and railways, needed machine makers and maintenance staff. The US mass-production system, with its assembly line and continuous flow of production, increased the vulnerability of capital to industrial action at the point of production as occurred in the automobile industry in the 1930s where key workers could bring the workflow to a halt because of their knowledge of the machinery.[52]

The developments in the US had an impact on Canada because of its geographical proximity and the growing investment by large-scale US corporations in Canada. US corporations such as Singer, Swift, International Harvester and Goodyear brought with them not only advanced forms of technology but also means of enhancing management control over the production process. US automobile manufacturers such as Ford and GM established Canadian automobile assembly plants that had the most up-to-date production design and special machinery, including the moving assembly line. To compete with the US corporations, Canadian-owned companies were forced to modernise. As in the US, Canadian employers were pragmatic in their adoption of scientific techniques, choosing what they found to be most useful. Further, the impact of technological change and productive reorganisation was uneven, Canadian logging remaining untouched, for example, and most coal mines remaining highly labour intensive.[53]

While German industry, especially those businesses involved in war production during the First World War, introduced technological and organisational changes during the war and in the post-war transformation to a peacetime economy, there was no sustained modernisation. The post-war inflation and hyperinflation further delayed modernisation as inflation permitted full employment and profits without industrial restructuring.[54] While Siemens, for example, adopted Taylorist principles in 1919–22, it established time wages instead of piece-based wage incentive systems as rapid inflation made "adjustment of the piece-based wage calculation both labour

---

[52] Dubofsky, *Hard Work*, pp. 188–94.

[53] Jacques Ferland and Christopher Wright, "Rural and Urban Labour Processes: A Comparative Analysis of Australian and Canadian Development," *Labour/Le Travail*, no. 38/ *Labour History*, no. 71, 1996, pp. 158–61; Craig Heron, *The Canadian Labour Movement: A Short History*, James Lorimer & Co., Toronto, 1996, p. 29; Palmer, *Working Class Experience*, p. 216.

[54] Mary Nolan, *Visions of Modernity: American Business and the Modernization of Germany*, Oxford University Press, New York, 1994, p. 131.

consuming and absurd."[55] Some industries, such as the Ruhr coal mines, did make changes however. Innovations such as pneumatic jackhammers and coal-cutting machines reduced the proportion of Ruhr coal being mined using manual labour and explosives from over 97 per cent in 1913 to 52 per cent in 1925.[56]

There was intense German experimentation in industrial restructuring from 1925 to 1929, following the stabilisation of the German currency and the renegotiation of reparations in 1924, which made restructuring both politically feasible and economically essential to meet reparation payments. An influx of US capital made restructuring possible and a rationalisation movement, drawn from the state and the private sector, encouraged the introduction of scientific methods to increase productivity. While some German firms introduced innovations ranging from mechanised tools to sophisticated assembly lines, the transformations within and between industries was uneven. In the steel industry, firms built new blast furnaces and Thomas and Martin steel ovens, which had larger capacities and faster operating times and required fewer workers, and time and motion studies were popular. Management integrated the different stages of production and introduced flow production. In machine making, productive reorganisation and technological innovation were limited by the diversity and multiplicity of firms and the production of specialised quality products. German car manufacturers preferred to focus on a quality vehicle for middle- and upper-class consumers, which led to US imports dominating the small car market and US cars being assembled in Germany by Ford, which opened an assembly plant in Berlin in 1926, and GM, which purchased and modernised Opel in 1929. Overall, the Fordist assembly line in Germany did not develop on a significant scale. While wages rose, so did unemployment due to the closure of inefficient factories and mines or the restructuring of others. The Ruhr mining workforce declined 33 per cent between 1922 and 1928, while production increased significantly. The economic crisis of 1929 eventually either stalled or slowed the modernisation plans of German companies. There was a revival of interest in Fordism and Taylorism after the Nazis' accession to power in 1933 and the subsequent rearmament.[57]

In the UK, new technology and methods of organisation were introduced,

[55] Heidrun Homburg, "Scientific Management and Personnel Policy in the Modern German Enterprise 1918–1939: The Case of Siemens", in Howard Gospel and Craig Littler (eds.), *Managerial Strategies and Industrial Relations*, Gower, Aldershot, 1983, p. 149.

[56] Nolan, *Visions of Modernity*, p. 138.

[57] Homburg, "Scientific Management and Personnel Policy", pp. 148–53; Nolan, *Visions of Modernity*, pp. 131–53; J. Ronald Shearer, "The *Reichskurotorium für Wirtschaftlichkeit*: Fordism and Organised Capitalism in Germany", *Business History Review*, vol. 71, no. 4, 1997, pp. 599–600; Karsten Uhl, "Giving Scientific Management a 'Human Face': The Engine

including mass production in the munitions industry, particularly during the First World War and the 1930s. In engineering, with the introduction of automatic machine tools and greater mechanisation, and mass production in certain sectors and firms, the proportion of skilled workers fell from approximately 60 per cent in 1914 to 32 per cent in 1933. While the proportion of unskilled workers declined, as in other countries, the proportion of the semi-skilled grew from about 20 per cent to 57 per cent of the labour force. In the chemical industry there was a shift from batch production to semi-continuous and continuous processes; ICI expanded its Billingham complex, where high-pressure chemical technology was used to produce nitrogen fertilisers. However, these changes were uneven, with traditional and newer types of organisation and technology existing side by side. During the Depression and in less prosperous sectors, innovation slowed down. The mechanisation of the coal industry lagged behind Germany and the US, with only 60 per cent of British coal being cut by machines in 1939, compared with virtually 100 per cent in the other two countries. As in Germany, there was a rationalisation movement in the UK, but it was more concerned with structural and financial reorganisation than with patterns of work organisation.[58]

While there was no dramatic transformation of British industry along scientific management lines during the interwar years, the US consulting firm Charles Bedaux, which established a permanent office in Britain in 1926, worked for approximately 250 firms by 1939 and implemented the Bedaux system of time study and wage incentive systems. The Bedaux system spread rapidly because many of these firms were in the industries that were new and expanding in the 1930s, such as food processing and chemicals, which did not have a traditional craft basis and depended on unskilled or semi-skilled behaviour. Bedaux was also applied in some traditional industries such as iron and steel and textiles. Some of these firms, such as ICI, were industry leaders and set the pace for other firms in their industry.[59] The impact of the Bedaux techniques should not be exaggerated because, as Gospel argues, "they were introduced into one particular plant or department and not throughout the whole company."[60]

Factory Deutz and a 'German' Path to Efficiency, 1910–1945", *Labor History*, vol. 52, no. 4, 2011, p. 511; Weitz, *Weimar Germany*, pp. 149–53.

[58] Howard Gospel, "Employers and Managers: Organisation and Strategy, 1914–1939", in Chris Wrigley (ed.), *A History of British Industrial Relations Volume II: 1914–1939*, The Harvester Press, Brighton, 1987, p. 180; Gospel, *Markets, Firms and the Management of Labour*, pp. 54–7; Wilson, *British Business History*, p. 162.

[59] Gospel, "Employers and Managers", p. 180; Littler, *The Development of the Labour Process*, pp. 105–15.

[60] Gospel, *Markets, Firms and the Management of Labour*, p. 55.

British employers generally preferred, however, to rely on traditional methods of intensifying work, such as piecework payment systems to motivate workers, than scientific management. For example, the proportion of metal fitters on piecework grew from 24 per cent in 1906 to 62 per cent in 1938. British employers did not fully adopt scientific management principles because they were concerned about union resistance and criticised scientific management for its failure to consider the human costs of production. In the automobile industry, companies, including Ford, rejected the control aspects of scientific management and mass production, preferring cooperation. They tended to introduce new machinery in an ad hoc manner and were less thorough than their US counterparts in integrating production through the assembly line. Line managers and supervisors in the UK generally were not enthusiastic about scientific management systems, which they perceived to be a threat to their traditional status in the workplace. While overall there were improvements in productivity in the UK, it lagged behind the US and Germany. There were several reasons for this. In some sectors, as labour was relatively inexpensive compared to the US, older plants were using out-dated machinery and traditional working practices. Product markets were also smaller and firms were smaller and less centrally coordinated.[61]

Due to the smaller domestic market in Australia, manufacturing was based on batch production rather than mass production. Despite this, technological change and productive reorganisation affected most industries, but had varying consequences. In coal mining the level of mechanisation actually fell – the percentage of black coal cut by machinery in NSW declined from 30.4 per cent in 1911 to 12.6 per cent in 1929. There was a slow revival to the 1911 level by 1939. Union opposition, employer reluctance to sink capital into the older fields and technical problems explain this decline in mechanisation. In flour milling, hat-making and paint manufacture there was little mechanisation after the First World War. By contrast, the production of rubber tyres changed from a hand operation in 1920 to tyre machines that were almost automatic by 1938. In the Victorian lamb and mutton export industry, the union lost a strike in 1933 against the introduction of the chain system, which subdivided the meatworker's task.

---

[61] Robert Fitzgerald, *British Labour Management & Industrial Welfare 1846–1939*, Croom Helm, Beckenham, 1988, pp. 6–7; Gospel, "Employers and Managers", p. 180; Gospel, *Markets, Firms and the Management of Labour*, pp. 56–60; Wayne Lewchuck, "Fordism and British Car Employers, 1896–1932", in Gospel and Littler (eds.), *Managerial Strategies and Industrial Relations*, Gower, Aldershot, 1983, p. 104; Gospel, *Markets, Firms and the Management of Labour*, p. 55; Arthur McIvor and Christopher Wright, "Managing Labour: UK and Australian Employers in Comparative Perspective, 1900–1950", *Labour History*, no. 88, 2005, p. 49.

There were industries where these changes expanded some skills.[62] As in the US, contemporary Australian academic economist Frank Mauldon argued, while the arrival of mass production in the automobile industry in Australia during this period replaced highly skilled craftsmen such as coachmakers with workers possessing a narrower task range, it increased the number of highly skilled toolmakers.[63]

While there was Australian interest in Taylorism and scientific management techniques were adopted in several Australian industries, they were not widespread and faced considerable union opposition. As early as 1915, the NSWGR management began timing jobs in the railway workshops. Management also experimented with card systems, which transferred the work recording function from the individual worker to the supervisor. The card system provoked the 1917 strike which resulted in the defeat of the unions. Following the strike, management adopted the voluntary bonus system proposed by Frederick Halsey, a competitor of Taylor who rejected Taylor's view that bonus schemes should be compulsory for workers. The unions were unable to stop the spread of the bonus system in the workplace but eventually persuaded a Labor state government to abolish it in 1932. General Motors-Holden's (GMH), a subsidiary of the US automobile company with a plant at Woodville, South Australia, introduced a system of time study to clear "bottlenecks" in 1928. The company suspended the study during the economic crisis of the Great Depression and revived it again in 1934.[64]

As the Australian economy revived from the 1930s depression, there was again limited interest in scientific management. As in the UK, a Bedaux consultancy was established in Sydney in 1930. In 1933 the Federated Clothing Trades Union in NSW began a successful three-year campaign against the Bedaux system. However, the retailer David Jones, which had its own clothing factory, reintroduced the system in 1936. An independent consultant established rates for piece-work based on time study at W.D. and H.O. Wills, the tobacco manufacturer, in the 1930s. Overall, scientific management failed to have an impact on Australian management practice before 1939 because of the small size of manufacturing, the limited number of expert consultants and the absence of a significant corporate managerial elite.[65]

[62] Patmore, *Australian Labour History*, pp. 145–6.
[63] Frank Mauldon, *Mechanisation in Australian Industries*, University of Tasmania, Hobart, 1938, pp. 1–77.
[64] Patmore, *Australian Labour History*, p. 148.
[65] Patmore, *Australian Labour History*, p. 148.

Trade Unionism and Politics

Table 2.2 highlights the extent to which union organisation varied between the five countries. The level of unionisation was significantly lower in Canada and the US than in Australia and the UK during the interwar period. The British trade union movement went into decline after a peak in 1920, reflecting the stagnant economy of the 1920s and 1930s, suffering a major defeat in the 1926 general strike and did not recover until the late 1930s. The German trade union movement was particularly strong during the early 1920s, but was splintered along ideological lines, with free (socialist), Christian and Hirsh-Dunker (liberal) trade unions. There were also communist and syndicalist unions. From before the First World War, German management had funded "yellow unions," mainly at the firm or plant level, to cooperate in fighting outside unions, particularly socialist ones, and promote industrial peace. The German unions were ultimately unable to prevent the rise of the National Socialists, who came to power in 1933, and their own subsequent demise. While the British unions had a national organisation, the Trades Union Congress (TUC), since 1868, the Australian equivalent, the Australasian Council of Trade Unions (ACTU) was not formed until May 1927.[66]

In both Canada and the US, unions affiliated with the American Federation of Labor (AFL) dominated the labour movement. Most of the AFL affiliates were located in competitive small-scale industries such as building. They also had a presence in railways and coal mining. They focused on collective bargaining rather than politics as a key strategy to increase the prosperity of their members. Samuel Gompers, AFL President until 1924, and the majority of the AFL rejected ideas of industrial democracy that prioritised state ownership or worker control, believing that changing ownership would not remove autocratic management. These unions did not really begin to focus on mass-production industries such as automobiles and rubber until the 1930s: the Committee of Industrial Organisation (CIO) broke away from the AFL in 1936 and began organising these industries. In Canada, while unions affiliated with the AFL belonged to a national body called the Trades and Labour Congress of Canada (TLCC), a rival All Canadian Congress of Labour (AACL) was formed in 1926, built around the Canadian Brotherhood of Railway Employees (CBRE). Within French-speaking Quebec, there was also the Canadian and Catholic Confederation of Labour (CCL), which was dominated by Catholic social doctrine and had 50,000 members in 1937.[67]

---

[66] Guillebaud, *The Works Council*, pp. 33–5; Kirk, *Labour and Society*, pp. 317–18; Patmore, "Unionism and Non-Union Employee Representation," p. 530.

[67] Chandler, *The Invisible Hand*, pp. 493–4; Dorothy Sue Cobble, "Pure and Simple

Table 2.2 Trade Union Membership in Australia, Canada, Germany,
the UK and the US, 1914–39 (%)

Year	Australia	Canada	Germany	UK	US
1914	32.8	N/A	16.9	23.0	9.9
1915	33.3	N/A	10.0	24.1	9.4
1916	36.3	N/A	8.6	25.6	9.9
1917	38.7	N/A	9.3	30.2	10.9
1918	39.7	N/A	14.9	35.7	12.6
1919	41.5	N/A	37.9	43.1	14.3
1920	42.2	N/A	52.6	45.2	16.7
1921	41.1	18.9	50.4	35.8	15.5
1922	40.3	16.3	51.0	31.6	13.0
1923	39.3	16.3	45.8	30.2	11.3
1924	39.6	14.8	31.8	30.6	10.7
1925	42.1	15.2	29.0	30.1	10.4
1926	44.6	15.2	27.6	28.3	10.2
1927	46.8	15.8	29.6	26.4	10.1
1928	46.2	15.7	32.5	25.6	9.6
1929	45.7	16.2	33.9	25.7	9.3
1930	43.5	15.2	33.7	25.4	8.9
1931	38.7	14.6	31.5	24.0	8.6
1932	36.0	13.2	n/a	23.0	7.9
1933	34.9	13.4	n/a	22.6	7.3
1934	35.3	13.4	n/a	23.5	8.9
1935	36.1	13.3	n/a	24.9	9.1
1936	37.1	15.3	n/a	26.9	9.8
1937	38.5	18.2	n/a	29.6	13.6
1938	38.8	17.7	n/a	30.5	14.0
1939	39.2	16.8	n/a	31.6	14.9

Source: George Sayers Bain and Robert Price, *Profiles of Union Growth: A Comparative Statistical Portrait of Eight Countries*, Basil Blackwell, Oxford, 1980, pp. 37, 88, 107, 123; Patmore, "Unionism and Non-Union Employee Representation", p. 530.

Generally the unions in all five countries represented mainly the interests of male blue-collar workers, and significant groups of workers were unrepresented or had to form their own unions to defend their interests. Women were denied access to many jobs and faced occupational segregation and wage discrimination. Women constituted 20 per cent of the paid Australian workforce in 1911 and 23 per cent by 1933. In 1933, 41 per cent of women worked in occupations where 90 per cent or more of workers were female and 68 per cent worked in occupations where 50 per cent or more of workers were female. Women did not work in industries such as heavy manufacturing or building and construction and from 1919 the federal basic wage for women was 54 per cent of that for men.[68] There was also discrimination on the basis of ethnicity and race. On the US railways, white unions sought to reduce and eliminate the number of Afro-American workers through strikes, threats and violence. One of the best-known groups of Afro-American railway workers, the Pullman porters, formed the Brotherhood of Sleeping Car Porters (BSCP) in 1925 to protect their interests.[69]

In Australia, the UK and Germany, prior to 1933, there were significant labour or social democratic parties that could ensure a direct voice for trade union interests in the legislature. The Australian Labor Party (ALP) had majority government both in the states of South Australia (SA) and NSW and federally by 1910. While it subsequently only held federal office before the Second World War, from 1914 to 1916 and from 1929 to 1931, the ALP did hold office at the state level, notably in Queensland from 1915 to 1929 and from 1932 to 1957. In the UK, the Labour Party benefited from the extension of the parliamentary franchise to all adult men and most women over 30 in 1918 to overtake the Liberal Party as the official opposition to the Conservative government following the 1922 national elections. The British Labour Party formed minority governments in 1924 and from 1929 to 1931 following the first election with universal adult suffrage. The German Social Democratic Party (Sozialdemokratische Partei Deutschlands or SPD) played a crucial role in the establishment of the Weimar Republic and coalitions that formed several governments before

Radicalism: Putting the Progressive Era AFL in its Time", *Labor*, vol. 10, no. 4, 2013, p. 79; Eugene Forsey, "The History of the Canadian Labour Movement", in Walter Cherwinski and Greg Kealey (eds.), *Lectures in Canadian and Working Class History*, Committee on Canadian Labour History, St. John's, Newfoundland, 1985, pp. 13–18.

[68] Patmore, *Australian Labour History*, pp. 169–70.

[69] Eric Arnesen, "Charting an Independent Course: African-American Railroad Workers in the World War I Era", in Eric Arnesen, Julie Greene and Bruce Laurie Howard (eds.), *Labor Histories. Class, Politics, and the Working Class Experience*, University of Illinois Press, Urbana and Chicago, 1998, pp. 284–309.

1933. It had a strong influence in at least four German states, including Prussia, and at the municipal level in industrial areas and large urban centres. The SPD was committed to democracy and willing to use force against the radical left, despite a long-term commitment to socialism, but its Marxist rhetoric limited its appeal beyond its traditional base among workers in industries such as coal and steel. The SPD remained the largest party in the Reichstag, the lower house of parliament during the Weimar Republic, until 1932, when the Nazis gained more seats and eventually outlawed the Social Democrats in 1933.[70]

By contrast, there were no significant labour or social democratic parties in Canada or the US. The US saw the early rise of mass political parties. By the mid-nineteenth century, universal suffrage for free white males was the norm in the US as property and taxation qualifications were removed. There were decentralised mass political parties that emphasised neighbourhood, ethnic and religious ties and hinged on the political patronage of the spoils system. These parties, which predated the rise of an industrial working class and were not based on class, persisted.[71]

In a comparison with Australia, Robin Archer has argued that there are a number of reasons for the failure of a labour party to form in the US. They include the level of state repression of the labour movement, particularly the use of the military and the police, the impact of religion on politics and socialist sectarianism. Unlike the US, unions were formed in Australia that covered large numbers of unskilled and semi-skilled workers, particularly agricultural workers in rural areas. The AFL feared that if US unions took up partisan politics then union solidarity would be undermined through political and religious loyalties.[72] These attitudes were carried to Canada by the US international unions and are an important factor in explaining the late formation in Canada of the Co-operative Commonwealth Federation

[70] Grebing, *History of the German Labour Movement*, pp. 112–13; John Moses, *Trade Unionism in Germany from Bismarck to Hitler 1869–1933. Volume Two: 1919–1933*, George Prior Publishers, London, 1982, p. 516; Patmore, *Australian Labour History*, pp. 77–83: John Shepherd and Jonathan Davis, "Britain's Second Labour Government, 1929–31: An Introduction", in John Shepherd, Jonathan Davis and Chris Wrigley (eds.), *Britain's Second Labour Government, 1929–1931: A Reappraisal*, Manchester University Press, Manchester, 2011, pp. 1–15; Andrew Thorpe, "The 1929 General Election and the Second Labour Government", in John Shepherd, Jonathan Davis and Chris Wrigley (eds.), *Britain's Second Labour Government, 1929–31: A Reappraisal*, Manchester University Press, Manchester, 2011, p. 16; Weitz, *Weimar Germany*, pp. 84–5.

[71] Robin Archer, *Why Is There No Labor Party in the United States?* Princeton University Press, Princeton, 2007, p. 74; Theda Skocpol, *Protecting Soldiers and Mothers: The Political Origins of Social Policy in the US*, Harvard University Press, Cambridge, MA, 1995, pp. 44–6; Tomlins, *The State and the Unions*, pp. 21–3.

[72] Archer, *Why is There No Labor Party in the United States?* pp. 232–43.

(CCF), which never achieved the level of electoral success of the Australian Labor Party.[73]

In all the countries examined there were radical challenges to mainstream labour politics through groups such as the Industrial Workers of the World (IWW) and communists. The IWW originated in the US and initially concentrated upon reorganising trade unions along industrial lines and forming One Big Union (OBU). However, under the influence of the Chicago school of the IWW, the movement became anti-political, rejecting labour parliamentarianism. The IWW enjoyed particular success in US mining and textiles, leading for example a strike against CF&I in 1927–28 that involved thousands of coal miners.[74] Though the membership of the IWW remained small, it faced government persecution in Australia and the US,[75] and by the 1930s it was a "shadow of its former self" in the US.[76]

Communist parties arose in all five countries in the wake of the Russian Revolution. Though they generally struggled to gain industrial and political influence in the 1920s, the fortunes of communist parties improved with the Great Depression and disillusionment with the failure of the established labour movement to protect workers. While in the US the AFL was hostile to Bolshevism and most AFL unions banned communists from union leadership during the 1920s, the CIO recognised the value of communist activism and enrolled communists as organisers to enrol new members in mass-production industries. They played a crucial role, for example, in the Steelworkers Organising Committee (SWOC), which was affiliated to the CIO. In Germany, the Communist Party (Kommunistische Partei Deutschlands or KPD) at its peak had 400,000 members in 1920 and, despite splits, 200,000 members in 1931. In the November 1932 Reichstag elections, it won 17 per cent of the popular vote and 100 seats. KPD supporters clashed violently with the supporters of the Nazis, who outlawed the KPD and other political parties after forming their first government in 1933.[77]

---

[73] Bray and Rouillard, "Union Structure and Strategy in Australia and Canada", p. 216.

[74] Roediger, "Industrial Workers of the World", p. 386.

[75] Patmore, *Australian Labour History*, pp. 81–2; David Roediger, "Industrial Workers of the World", in Melvyn Dubofsky (ed.), *The Oxford Encyclopedia of American Business, Labor and Economic History, Vol. 1*, Oxford University Press, Oxford, 2013, pp. 385–6; Ian Turner, *Industrial Labour and Politics: The Dynamics of the Labour Movement in Eastern Australia 1900–1921*, Australian National University Press, Canberra, 1965, chap. 5.

[76] Roediger, "Industrial Workers of the World", p. 386.

[77] Evans, *The Third Reich in Power*, pp. 7–14; Grebing, *History of the German Labour Movement*, pp. 134–8; Richard Hyman, "Rank-and-File Movements and Workplace Organisation, 1914–1939", in Chris Wrigley (ed.), *A History of British Industrial Relations Volume II: 1914–1939*, The Harvester Press, Brighton, 1987, pp. 141–6; Heron, *The Canadian Labour Movement*, pp. 61–4; Jennifer Luff, "Labor and Anti-Communism", in Melvyn Dubofsky

Employers and Managing Labour

Management ethos and the degree of employer organisation varied across these economies. In the US there was a greater and growing interest in more sophisticated personnel management practices to improve worker commitment, morale and productivity. The founders of the personnel management movement called for a recognition of the "human factor" and a more systematic approach to labour management. Larger firms were concerned about the growing communication gap between management and employees and had the resources to deal with the problem. These larger companies also had a significant number of university-educated managers who were steeped in the principles of scientific and personnel management. The first national conference of personnel managers was held in 1916 and the National Association of Employment Managers (soon to be renamed the Industrial Relations Research Association of America) was formed in 1918 to promote the study of employment problems. There was a range of associations with an interest in employment relations, including the Taylor Society; the National Industrial Conference Board (NICB); the Special Conference Committee (SCC), which was linked to John D. Rockefeller Junior (hereafter JDR Jr.) and established in 1919 to coordinate the labour relations policies of ten leading US corporations; and the liberal Personnel Research Federation, one of whose charter members was the AFL. A key employers' association was the National Association of Manufacturers (NAM), which had been formed in the late nineteenth century to coordinate business opposition to unions. The NAM led the Open Shop Campaign against unions in the wake of the First World War and had a membership of more than 5,000 by the early 1920s. From the late 1920s representatives from large firms began to replace the small business owners who had led the NAM.[78]

Large US firms continued to rely on welfare strategies which were developed before the First World War to ensure worker loyalty and included housing, health, education, recreational and profit-sharing schemes for employees. According to a 1926 survey of the 1,500 largest firms in the US, 80 per cent had at least one welfare programme, and approximately half,

(ed.), *The Oxford Encyclopedia of American Business, Labor and Economic History, Vol. 1*, Oxford University Press, Oxford, 2013, pp. 425–7; Patmore, *Australian Labour History*, pp. 91–3; Robert Zeiger, *American Workers, American Unions*, 2nd ed., Johns Hopkins University Press, Baltimore, 1994, pp. 54–5.

[78] Jacoby, *Employing Bureaucracy*, pp. 139, 189–91; Kaufman, *The Global Evolution of Industrial Relations*, pp. 132–4; Patmore, "Employee Representation Plans in the United States, Canada and Australia", p. 48; Kim Phillips-Fein, *Invisible Hands: The Businessmen's Crusade against the New Deal*, W.W. Norton, New York, 2009, pp. 13–14.

including Ford and US Steel, had comprehensive programmes. While the 1930s depression saw cutbacks in personnel management departments and welfare programmes, there was a revival of welfare schemes, particularly with regard to pensions and health insurance, as the economy recovered. The US, particularly during the 1920s, became a beacon for overseas managers interested in ideas such as personnel management, scientific management and mass production, and received numerous delegations and visits from Australia, Germany and the UK.[79]

In Canada, employers adopted a similar management ethos and labour management strategies to their US counterparts. University extension courses on personnel management were developed and management groups formed, such as the Employment Managers Association in Toronto in 1919, which two years later became the Industrial Relations Association of Toronto. Industrial unrest at the end of the First World War encouraged larger Canadian employers to expand welfare programmes in order to maintain employee loyalty and weaken the unions. Branch plants of US companies, such as International Harvester, GM and Imperial Oil, Standard Oil's Canadian subsidiary, had elaborate and well-publicised corporate welfare programmes. Canadian corporations in the steel industry established district offices or departments of industrial relations for the first time, introduced new pension schemes, established company newsletters to communicate with employees, adopted safety first programmes and expanded recreational programmes. While some Canadian employers may have dismantled welfare programmes as the union threat faded in the 1920s or cut specialist labour management departments to save money during the 1930s depression, these strategies persisted in some firms, such as Westclox, a US clock manufacturer based in Peterborough Ontario, while others, such as Dafasco, a steel producer in Hamilton Ontario, introduced them to counter a union resurgence in the late 1930s. Overall, caution must be exercised in assessing the impact of welfarism on Canadian industry due to the smaller scale of industry than in the US, the continued reliance by employers on a drive system in which supervisors motivated workers with the fear of dismissal in a climate of labour oversupply to ensure worker loyalty, and employer exaggeration in their claims of innovation in the area of welfarism.[80]

---

[79] Jacoby, *Employing Bureaucracy*, pp. 234–5; Kaufman, *The Global Evolution of Industrial Relations*, pp. 156–8; Nolan, *Visions of Modernity*, pp. 17–26, 105.

[80] Ferland and Wright, "Rural and Urban Labour Processes", pp. 163–6; Craig Heron, *Working in Steel: The Early Years in Canada, 1883–1935*, McClelland and Stewart, Toronto, 1988, pp. 98–111; Margaret McCallum, "Corporate Welfarism in Canada, 1919–1939", *Canadian Historical Review*, vol. 71, no. 1, 1990, pp. 46–79; Naylor, *The New Democracy*, pp. 165–75, 205–7; Joan Sangster, "The Softball Solution: Female Workers, Male Managers and the Operation of Paternalism at Westclox, 1923–1960", *Labour/Le Travail*, no. 32, 1993, p. 171;

German industry had been seen as a leader in the implementation of welfare programmes prior to the First World War. The war and the Weimar Republic saw an expansion of personnel management in large firms such as Siemens. In 1919, Carl Friedrich von Siemens created the new position of "common board adviser in personnel policy" to supervise and coordinate the company's personnel policy. All Siemen's plant managers were asked to install a work office (*Arbeitsbüro*), which reduced the functions of supervisors and relieved them of their previous autonomy in workplace labour management. The work offices centralised the hiring of workers, the setting of rates and the assignment of jobs. Carl Friedrich von Siemens also played a crucial role in the formation in 1921 of the Reichskuratorium für Wirtschaftlichkeit (RKW), which brought together industrialists, academics and government officials to promote economic and industrial efficiency along the lines promoted by Frederick Winslow Taylor and Henry Ford. The RKW did not actively seek the participation of organised labour. During the 1920s and the 1930s, Siemens continued to rely on welfare programmes such as housing and company-sponsored social activities such as sports and stamp collecting to promote employee commitment to the company.[81]

In the UK, after the First World War a management movement developed that drew upon a range of literature and individuals such the Quaker industrialist Seebohm Rowntree, whose York chocolate factory implemented various ideas including employee representation and scientific management. New research organisations were established, such as the National Institute of Industrial Psychology (1921) and the Management Research Group (1926). There was an expansion of university courses on commerce and administration. Professional institutions such as the Institute of Industrial Administration (1920) and the Institute of Cost and Work Accountants (1919) were established to harmonise practices and develop new ideas. British managers aspired to both professionalism and independence from their employers, but despite the trends towards management professionalism, patronage and nepotism remained the foundations of management in the UK.[82]

The UK also saw a strengthening of the pre-war interest in welfarism as a result of the First World War and the intense merger activity that followed it, which increased the size of business and highlighted the need for better

---

Robert Storey, "Unionization versus Corporate Welfare: The Dofasco Way", *Labour/Le Travail*, no. 12, 1983, p. 18.

[81] Homburg, "Scientific Management and Personnel Policy", pp. 149–53; Nolan, *Visions of Modernity*, p. 106; Shearer, "The *Reichskurotorium für Wirtschaftlichkeit*".

[82] Wilson, *British Business History*, pp. 149, 153–4.

communication with employees. In January 1916, the government appointed
Rowntree to be head of the newly formed Welfare Department of the
Ministry of Munitions to encourage the employment of welfare officers and
train them. There were particular concerns about the health and welfare of
the growing numbers of women being employed in munitions factories. The
number of full-time welfare officers grew from under 100 at the beginning
of the war to over 1,000 in 1918.[83] Employers formed the Industrial Welfare
Society in 1919 to promote welfarism in order to "revive the old friendly
relations between masters and men."[84] Beside the post-war increase in
the number of welfare specialists, the status of welfare work rose, to that
of personnel management, with male managers of higher status replacing
female welfare officers. Though by 1939 there were 2,000 managers engaged
full-time in labour matters in larger enterprises,[85] as Gospel argues, "it is
important not to exaggerate the sophistication of labour management in
Britain at this time."[86]

In Australia the concept of a managerial profession was underdeveloped;
there were no specific management training programmes or professional
management institutions. There was an interest in welfarism, but this was
limited to a small number of firms, particularly larger ones. During the
First World War, the NSWGR expanded existing welfare organisations
like the Railway Institute or created new ones, such as the Safety First
Movement, to enhance worker loyalty, reduce labour radicalism and improve
productivity. A period of political and industrial upheaval between 1917
and 1921 encouraged other employers such as retailers to formalise existing
practices and provide new welfare facilities. In Sydney retailing, Farmers
and Anthony Hordens employed welfare officers. By 1931, 76 establishments
in Australia had welfare schemes. There were 17 in the clothing industry
and 11 in retailing. The welfare programmes included dining, recreation and
rest rooms (53 firms), subsidised clubs and institutes (34 firms) and sick and/
or accident funds (21 firms). Although the economic problems of the 1930s
forced some employers to cut back welfare schemes, they were revived when
economic recovery permitted.[87]

Employers in all five countries adopted a range of approaches to unions.
US employers adopted an aggressive stance towards them. The Open Shop
Campaign or the American Plan, particularly during the early 1920s, targeted
the weakened labour movement through patriotism, claiming that unionism

[83] Gospel, "Employers and Managers", p. 178; Wilson, *British Business History*, p. 160.
[84] *The Times* (London, England), 24 May 1919, p. 7.
[85] Gospel, *Markets, Firms and the Management of Labour*, pp. 49–50.
[86] Gospel, *Markets, Firms and the Management of Labour*, p. 50.
[87] Patmore, *Australian Labour History*, pp. 148–51.

was a continued threat to the American spirit underlying the Declaration of Independence. Tactics included labour espionage, as used by CF&I.[88]

In the favourable legal and political environment for organised labour following the election of Roosevelt in 1932, union organisers faced continued employer hostility. Harry Bennett, who directed Ford's labour policies towards the United Automobile Workers (UAW) union, which was trying to organise its automobile plants, "personally assembled the world's largest private army, and established the most extensive and efficient espionage system in American industry."[89] Bennett's Service Department had branches in every Ford assembly plant in the US and his "service squads," supplied with a range of "persuaders," including blackjacks and pistols, would disrupt union meetings and assault union organisers. GM and Chrysler, Ford's major competitors, preferred to contract out their anti-union activities to professional labour spying agencies, GM endorsing an armed vigilante organisation in Anderson, Indiana, which threatened strikers and ransacked union offices.[90]

Canadian employers adopted similar tactics to their US counterparts. In the steel industry, attempts to organise unions were met with instant dismissal and strikers were blacklisted in the wake of unsuccessful strikes. There were networks of spies and several steel companies employed the Thiel Detective Agency, the US industrial espionage and strikebreaking agency, at the end of the First World War. These tactics continued with the resurgence of unions in the steel industry in the late 1930s. Dafasco, the steel company in Hamilton Ontario, dismissed union organisers and members of a union executive and threatened other workers with dismissal if they joined unions.[91]

In Australia, Germany prior to 1933, and the UK, employers faced a stronger collective organisation of labour and more extensive processes of industrial relations either through formal industry-wide collective bargaining or state regulation. Employers coordinated their industrial relations activities through employer associations whose strength varied according to the coverage of trade unionism in their particular industry. British employers formed the Federation of British Industries (FBI) in 1916, which desisted from dealing with labour relations after member complaints

---

[88] Patmore, "Employee Representation Plans in the United States, Canada and Australia", p. 48; Jonathan Rees, "'X,' 'XX' and 'X-3': Labor Spy Reports from the Colorado Fuel and Iron Company Archives", *Colorado Heritage*, 2004, pp. 28–41.

[89] Stephen Norwood, "Ford's Brass Knuckles: Harry Bennett, The Cult of Muscularity, and Anti-Labor Terror – 1920–1945", *Labor History*, vol. 37, no. 3, 1996, p. 367.

[90] Norwood, "Ford's Brass Knuckles", pp. 365–8.

[91] Heron, *Working in Steel*, p. 97; Storey, "Unionization versus Corporate Welfare", pp. 16–17.

concerning its progressive report on sickness and unemployment benefits, redundancy payments and the guaranteed week. Against the background of industrial unrest following the First World War, employers formed a new National Confederation of Employers' Organisations (NCEO) to coordinate their position and constitute their side on a National Industrial Council, which never eventuated. By 1920 it claimed to cover over 7 million workers and approximately 90 per cent of organised employers. The most centralised employers' organisation for industrial relations was in Germany, where the two national employers' associations merged in 1913 to form the Vereinigung der Deutschen Arbeitgeberverbände (VDA), which by 1929 had a membership of 180 employers' associations and covered approximately 6.4 million workers. Employers' associations were formed later in sectors such as retailing/wholesale and agriculture in response to the 1918 revolution and a surge of unionism in those industries.[92]

While employers' associations engaged with unions, this did not mean that the employers in the three countries (Australia, Germany and the UK) did not engage in struggles with unions at the workplace level or develop explicit anti-union strategies. BHP, Australia's major steel producer, victimised delegates, established a short-lived company union after the 1917 general strike and used salaried staff as strike-breakers. The company used a lockout and the closure of its Newcastle steel plant in 1922 as a pretext to secure cuts in wages and working conditions. For two decades following the onset of recession in 1920, British employers went on the offensive against organised labour, particularly in depressed staple sections of the economy such as cotton textiles, heavy engineering and coal mining, victimising union activists, using strike-breakers and lockouts to discipline unions.[93]

In Weimar Germany, employers became increasingly critical of the role of unions and the state in the management of their businesses, particularly in terms of welfare legislation, notably unemployment insurance, and collective agreements. Employers' associations had links with several institutions established to provide strike and lockout compensation, with premiums generally based on payrolls. The largest of these organisations was the Deutsche Streikschutz, which was affiliated with the VDA. In October 1928, Ruhr iron and steel industrialists locked out 250,000 metalworkers for

---

[92] Gospel, "Employers and Managers", p. 161; W. Krüger, "Employers Associations in Germany", *International Labour Review*, vol. 14, no. 3, 1926, pp. 313–44; McIvor and Wright, "Managing Labour", pp. 53–6; William McPherson, "Collaboration between Management and Employees in German Factories", PhD thesis, The University of Chicago, 1935, pp. 1–3; Christopher Wright, "The Formative Years of Management Control at the Newcastle Steelworks, 1913–1924", *Labour History*, No. 55, 1988, pp. 55–70.

[93] McIvor and Wright, "Managing Labour", p. 56.

five weeks in protest against a decision by an Arbitration Court to increase hourly rates, which they claimed would eliminate profits and make them uncompetitive on world markets. Employers and unions ended the lockout by agreeing to accept a decision on the wage increase by the Minister for the Interior following a further review.[94] After the Ruhr lockout, employer disillusionment with the government continued and grew to the point that by "1933 industry wanted rid of the Weimar Republic."[95]

The Role of the State

There are strong similarities in the development of the state in Australia and Canada as both were major white settler colonies of the British Empire. Both evolved into industrial capitalist, self-governing federal states with parliamentary political systems. They shared similar imperial legacies and political systems, their federal governments having a bicameral parliament as in the UK. While there was no equivalent to the largely hereditary House of Lords in the UK, senators were appointed to the federal Canadian Senate by the Canadian Governor-General on the advice of the Canadian Prime Minister and elected to the Australian Senate on an equal basis for each of the six states. One legal link to the UK initially shared by Australia and Canada was that the Judicial Committee of the Privy Council in London was the final court of appeal for both countries. While this appeal process was expensive and unpopular, the Judicial Committee's "arm's length" approach to constitutional issues could influence developments in the distribution of power between federal and state governments. One major difference was that in French-speaking Quebec there was a distinct cultural and linguistic component of Canada that had no Australian equivalent.[96]

The Constitution Act or British North America Act 1867 provided the legal basis for federal government in Canada. It was a compromise between a desire for a strong central government and the need to recognise the differing cultures and institutions of the various provinces, particularly French-speaking Quebec. The specific powers of the federal government are outlined under Section 91, which include defence, foreign policy, trade and transportation, while Section 92 sets out specific powers for the provinces,

---

[94] Dick Geary, "Employers, Workers and the Collapse of the Weimar Republic", in Ian Kershaw (ed.), *Weimar: Why Did German Democracy Fail?*, Weidenfeld and Nicolson, London, 1990, pp. 98–105; Grunberger, *A Social History of the Third Reich*, pp. 19–20; McPherson, 'Collaboration between Management and Employees', p. 3; *New York Times* (*NYT*), 3 Dec. 1928, p. 4.

[95] Geary, "Employers, Workers and the Collapse of the Weimar Republic", p. 105.

[96] Greg Patmore, "The Origins of Federal Industrial Relations Systems: Australia, Canada and the USA", *Journal of Industrial Relations*, vol. 51, no. 2, 2009, p. 152.

such as health, property and education. There were concurrent powers for immigration and agriculture. If anything fell outside these specified powers, such as industrial relations, it became a matter for the courts to decide.[97]

The writers of the Australian Constitution drew heavily upon the US Constitution. The two new houses of federal parliament were the same as the two houses of the US Congress. Specific legislative powers were given to the federal government, including power covering trade and commerce with other countries and among the Australian states, and unspecified state legislative powers. As in the US Constitution, there was a provision for Commonwealth law to override state law if inconsistency arose.[98] One specific departure from the US Constitution was a provision for the Australian federal parliament to legislate "conciliation and arbitration for the prevention and settlement of industrial disputes extending beyond the limits of any one state."[99] This provision reflected concerns over the impact of strikes, such as the 1890 maritime strike, on interstate trade, particularly from the relatively isolated Western Australia. The states still retained power over intrastate labour issues.[100]

In the US, the state was based on a decentralised federalist constitutionalist republic. While the US Constitution established a central federal government, it created ambiguity by creating structured conflicts between key institutions such as state governments and the courts.[101] The US Constitution limited the powers of the federal legislative body to specific areas such as the power "to regulate commerce with foreign nations, and among the several states, and with the Indian tribes."[102] There was also provision for federal law to pre-empt or supersede state law if there was a conflict between the two, and the tenth amendment of 1791 provided that "powers not delegated to the United States by the Constitution, nor prohibited by it to the States, are reserved for the States respectively, or to the people."[103] As in Australia and Canada, the tension over "states rights" was an important dynamic in the development of national labour relations jurisdiction. While the three countries shared a federal system, the president and state governors in the US have significant executive powers compared to the largely ceremonial role played by the Queen's representatives in Australia and Canada. The power of the legislature was enhanced in Australia and

---

[97] Patmore, "The Origins of Federal Industrial Relations Systems", p. 159.
[98] Patmore, "The Origins of Federal Industrial Relations Systems", p. 156.
[99] Australian Constitution, Section 51 (xxxv).
[100] Patmore, *Australian Labour History*, pp. 113–14.
[101] Skopcol, *Protecting Soldiers and Mothers*, pp. 44–6; Tomlins, *The State and the Unions*, pp. 21–3.
[102] US Constitution, Article 1, Section 8.
[103] US Constitution, Article 6, Amendment 10.

Canada by their common law courts following the English tradition of parliamentary supremacy.[104]

In contrast to England, in the nineteenth century and early twentieth century there was no professional Civil Service or non-judicial state elite in the US that consisted "of high-placed policymakers."[105] The lack of a rival state elite assisted the courts. The US legal and judicial elite became a major source of state and national policy in a wide range of areas including labour relations. There was no parliamentary supremacy or countervailing tradition of statutory regulation. Federal and state judges were largely drawn from wealthy Republican backgrounds and had little sympathy for labour.[106]

Germany, which also had a federal system of government, underwent a number of changes between 1914 and 1939. At the outbreak of the First World War, Germany was a constitutional monarchy with a Kaiser and an elected parliament based on franchise for males over 25. While the Reichstag authorised the funding of the war on 4 August 1914, it also delegated its powers to the Bundesrat, the less democratic German upper house that consisted of state representatives and was dominated by the Kingdom of Prussia, for the duration of the war. The military stalemate led in August 1916 to the war effort being placed in the hands of General Paul Von Hindenburg and Erich Ludendorff who, despite their victories on the Eastern Front against Russia, were unable to achieve victory by November 1918.[107]

The German Revolution of November 1918 led to the abdication of the Kaiser and the proclamation on 11 August 1919 of a new Weimar Constitution, which provided for female suffrage, the equality of men and women, the protection of basic liberties such as free speech, proportional representation and a re-established federal system of government which gave more power to the central government than the previous constitution. The Weimar Constitution also contained a provision that recognised a revolutionary government reform which made collective bargaining legally binding. A weakness of the constitution was the President, who was elected every seven years and had the power to appoint the Chancellor and the Cabinet. The President also had wide-ranging emergency powers under Article 48 of the Constitution to rule by decree, which the first President, Social Democrat Friedrich Ebert, and his successor, the staunch monarchist

---

[104] Archer, *Why Is There no Labor Party in the United States?*, pp. 92, 97.

[105] William Forbath, *Law and the Shaping of the American Labor Movement*, Harvard University Press, Cambridge, MA, 1991, p. 31.

[106] Forbath, *Law and the Shaping of the American Labor Movement*, pp. 26, 32–6.

[107] Chickering, *Imperial Germany and the Great War*, pp. 34, 79–82; Evans, *The Third Reich in Power*, pp. 3–11.

Paul von Hindenburg, who became President following the death of Ebert in 1925, used extensively and not necessarily in the interests of upholding the principles of the Weimar Republic. As there were difficulties in getting a consensus in the Reichstag due to the large number of parties elected through proportional representation, Article 48 became a regular means of governance when the Reichstag could not agree. Hindenberg, who was not sympathetic to the Weimar Constitution, appointed Chancellors such as Brüning, Franz Von Papen and Hitler, who wanted to overthrow the republic.[108]

With the accession of the Nazis to power in January 1933, the Reichstag passed an Enabling Act on 23 March 1933, which gave Hitler's Cabinet the right to rule by decree without referring to the Reichstag or the President. The Nazis won sufficient votes by threatening civil war and winning over Catholic Centre Party deputies with the promise of a Concordat with the Vatican guaranteeing Catholic rights. By the middle of July 1933, Germany was a one-party state; all opposition parties were outlawed.[109]

The role of the state in labour relations in the five countries had similarities and differences. All countries established ministries or departments of labour at national or provincial levels to investigate labour issues and promote new ideas such as employee representation. While Australia did not establish a Department of Labour or National Service until 1940, there were labour ministries at the state level, NSW being the most significant in promoting workplace employee representation. In Germany, between the November 1918 revolution and the Nazis' accession to power in 1933, there was government regulation of collective bargaining with guarantees of freedom of association for workers, the establishment of conciliation boards and a provision from November 1923 giving both the Minister of Labour and conciliation officers the power to make a binding decision in any collective dispute. There was also extensive intervention in workplace labour relations through the 1920 works council legislation and a system of labour tribunals, which commenced operations on 1 January 1927 and replaced the ordinary courts which unions considered to have a class bias. These courts had a wide jurisdiction over individual and collective labour disputes, but not the finalisation of collective agreements. They operated at three levels: the local, the state and the national (the Reich Labour Court), which was a division of the conservative Reich (Supreme) Court. While there was a principle of voluntarism in terms of limited state intervention in industrial relations in the UK, there was a legislative provision for trade boards, which were

---

[108] Evans, *The Third Reich in Power*, pp. 3–11; James, *Europe Reborn*, p. 82; Weitz, *Weimar Germany*, pp. 32–3, 118–21, 350–8.
[109] Evans, *The Third Reich in Power*, pp. 11–14.

bargaining bodies comprising representatives from business, unions and the state in low-wage industries where there was insufficient organisation among management and labour. They set legally enforceable minimum wages and conditions, which reduced wage competition and potential industrial conflict.[110]

Australia had the most comprehensive regulation of industrial relations through compulsory arbitration and wages boards. The Australian arbitration system recognised unions and gave them a role in the determination of legally binding awards. Trade unions were an essential feature of the Australian system of compulsory arbitration and there was little incentive to seek union-management cooperation. Registered unions brought grievances to the industrial tribunals on behalf of workers. Compulsory arbitration assisted union growth and gave unions a role in the determination of legally binding awards covering wages and conditions. Unions also obtained security against rival unions, rights of union entry into the workplace and clauses in arbitration awards that gave preference to unionists in promotion and retention. The compulsory arbitration system emphasised the importance of unions in giving a voice to Australian workers.[111] As Stuart Macintyre has noted, "the system of industrial arbitration transformed unions from associations tolerated by the state into protected organizations that the Court recognized, assisted and regulated."[112]

Australian employers had initially opposed state intervention through compulsory arbitration, but they also realised that it had advantages. While industrial arbitration awards reduced employer flexibility in terms of labour costs, they minimised wage competition for large firms from smaller, lower-wage producers. Arbitration tribunals provided another source of labour discipline during industrial disputes by deregistering unions, as occurred in the 1917 general strike in NSW, fining strikers and their unions, and even jailing workers and union officials. While they were independent, they favoured employers in industrial disputes for they commonly viewed the national and industry interest as one. Arbitration tribunals could also impose restraints on wage increases, as they did during the inflation of the

[110] Clegg, *The Changing System of Industrial Relations in Great Britain*, pp. 290–2, 296; Guillebaud, *The Works Council*, pp. 31–2, 36–9; Chris Howell, *Trade Unions and the State: The Construction of Industrial Relations Institutions in Britain, 1890–2000*, Princeton University Press, Princeton, 2005, pp. 68–9; Otto Kahn-Freund, *Labour Law and Politics in the Weimar Republic*, Basil Blackwell, Oxford, 1981, pp. 34–5.

[111] Patmore, *Australian Labour History*, pp. 120–1; Patmore, "The Origins of Federal Industrial Relations Systems", pp. 155–62.

[112] Stuart Macintyre, "Arbitration in Action", in Joe Isaac and Stuart Macintyre (eds.), *The New Province for Law and Order: 100 years of Australian Industrial Conciliation and Arbitration* Cambridge University Press, Cambridge, 2004, p. 61.

First World War, and even cut wages, as the Commonwealth Arbitration Court did in 1931 during the Great Depression when it reduced the basic wage by 10 per cent. The tribunals also preserved managerial prerogative by placing limits on the "industrial matters" that could be contained in industrial agreements and awards.[113]

Canadian legislation did not go as far as the Australian, only making provisions for the conciliation and investigation of industrial disputes. The most significant Canadian legislation was the federal 1907 Industrial Disputes Investigation Act (IDIA). The IDIA was drafted by William Lyon Mackenzie King, federal Deputy Minister of Labour from 1900 and federal Minister of Labour from 1908 to 1911, who later played a key role in the development of the Rockefeller ERP. The legislation designated a mandatory "cooling off" period during which strikes and lockouts were prohibited until a tripartite board, after a compulsory investigation, completed a report on the dispute. The parties were not compelled to recognise each other or to accept the terms of the report. The IDIA applied to key "public utilities," such as coal mining, whose uninterrupted operation was essential for the Canadian economy, or industries that had certain monopoly-like characteristics. The federal government claimed that the legislation's coverage of public utilities was drawn from its residual power in the Constitution to legislate for the peace, order and good government of Canada. While the IDIA did not directly cover other significant industries, such as iron and steel, parties in these industries could invoke the Act's provisions if both parties agreed. During the First World War the Canadian federal government extended the IDIA to cover munitions workers under the Wartime Measures Act.[114]

The IDIA was to run into difficulties after the First World War. The Canadian state played a major role in the defeat of the 1919 labour revolt, which involved general strikes in Winnipeg, Toronto and Amherst and was fuelled by fears of unemployment, inflation and demands for shorter hours, and the 1922 Cape Breton coal strike, shattering the notion of state impartiality regarding industrial conflict. Canadian employers also lost interest in the legislation as the Canadian trade union movement went into decline in the early 1920s. The IDIA came under legal challenge when the British Privy Council, in the *Snider* case of 1925, declared that it was unconstitutional. The provinces had the right to make laws regarding the civil rights of employers and employees, except in areas specifically within the domain of the federal government. The only time that this power could revert to the federal government was in a time of national crisis.

---

[113] Wright, *The Management of Labour*, pp. 31–2.

[114] Naylor, *The New Democracy*, p. 26; Patmore, "The Origins of Federal Industrial Relations Systems", pp. 160–1.

The TLCC lobbied the federal government to have the constitution altered to restore federal jurisdiction and ensure uniformity of labour standards. The federal government merely amended the Act to ensure that it met the constitutional limits set out by the Court and left it open for the provinces to allow local employers and unions the option of accessing the federal system. Several provinces, including British Columbia, Manitoba, New Brunswick and Saskatchewan, legislated to allow the IDIA to apply to their jurisdictions. After setting up its own local disputes machinery in the midst of the Cape Breton miners' strike of 1925, in 1926 the newly elected Conservative Nova Scotia government scrapped the legislation and decided to apply the federal IDIA to the province. Alberta decided to develop its own local system, but soon decided to apply the federal legislation to mining and public utilities following requests from the provincial Alberta Federation of Labour. Rural Prince Edward Island ignored the legislation given the low level of trade union activity in that province, and the two largest provinces, Quebec and Ontario, refused to accept the legislation, reflecting their strong views on provincial rights and the low level of industrial disputes in the industries that would be covered. They only opted to join the federal scheme following the urging of the TLCC in 1932, when industrial unrest began to increase.[115]

No federal or state legislation in the US recognised unions or gave them a role in the determination of legally binding awards. As David Brody argues, the direct impact of the state in the US before the 1930s was on the whole "essentially negative" for trade unions, its role "serving mainly to underwrite and legitimate the unilateral rights of management."[116] Even if progressive state legislature intervened in the workplace, state and federal courts would invalidate it on the grounds of state rights, "liberty of contract" and "property rights." From the 1880s courts issued an injunction, usually a temporary restraining order, on behalf of an employer against a striking union. The employer would complain that the actual or prospective strike was an "unlawful interference with the conduct of his business." There were seldom any witnesses, there was no jury and only a limited review of courts' decisions. While the injunction was in force, the employer could undermine the union through victimisation and organising strike-breakers. The number of labour injunctions in the US grew from approximately 105 in the 1880s to 2,130 in the 1920s.[117]

---

[115] Palmer, *Working Class Experience*, pp. 259–60; Patmore, "The Origins of Federal Industrial Relations Systems", pp. 161–2.

[116] David Brody, *In Labor's Cause: Main Themes on the History of the American Worker*, Oxford University Press, New York, 1993, p. 232.

[117] Irving Bernstein, *The New Deal Collective Bargaining Policy*, University of California Press, Berkeley, 1950, p. 9; Forbath, *Law and the Shaping of the American Labor Movement*,

US labour law became more favourable towards the unions during the late 1920s and the 1930s depression. The first industry to see a change was the railways, which played a key role in the national economy, and strikes, such as the 1922 national railroad shopmen's strike, could have disastrous economic effects. To bring stability to the industry, President Calvin Coolidge called upon railroad employers and unions to devise labour legislation that would prevent industrial unrest. The railway unions and their political allies in Congress secured the passage of the Railway Labor Act in 1926. It was the first comprehensive federal legislation to recognise the right of employees to form unions and engage in collective bargaining. Employers could not designate labour representatives through "interference, influence or coercion."[118]

The severe economic depression of the 1930s greatly undermined popular faith in business in the US and provided a favourable climate for pro-labour legislation. The call for change underpinned Franklin D. Roosevelt's victory in the 1932 presidential election with a margin of almost 7 million votes over the incumbent President Herbert Hoover, only six states failing to support the Democratic Party. Earlier that year, Congress had passed the Norris-La Guardia Act, which represented a fundamental turning point in US federal labour law. The legislation prohibited federal courts from issuing injunctions in any labour dispute regardless of the strike's purpose. The law prevented judges from enjoining a strike because the judge did not approve of its goal or methods. President Roosevelt's New Deal National Industrial Recovery Act (NIRA) of June 1933, which provided an economic stimulus, encouraged labour organisation in terms of both employer sponsored ERPs and trade unions. Section 7(a) of the Act "primed the pump" by recognising workers' rights to bargain and organise collectively through their own representatives without employer interference. The Supreme Court declared NIRA unconstitutional in 1935.[119]

The same year, however, Congress passed the National Labor Relations Act, referred to as the Wagner Act. An alliance of progressive liberals and the labour movement underpinned the legislation. The AFL lobbied

---

pp. 37–40, 192; William Leuchtenberg, "The Tenth Amendment over Two Centuries: More than a Trueism", in Mark Killenbeck (ed.), *The Tenth Amendment and State Sovereignty: Constitutional History and Contemporary Issues*, Berkeley Public Policy Press, Berkeley, 2002, pp. 44–5.

[118] Colin Davis, *Power at Odds: The 1922 National Railroad Shopmen's Strike*, University of Illinois Press, Urbana, 1997, p. 164; Patmore, "The Origins of Federal Industrial Relations Systems", p. 163; Robert Wechsler, "Railway Labor Act", in Melvyn Dubofsky (ed.), *The Oxford Encyclopedia of American Business, Labor and Economic History, Vol. 2*, Oxford University Press, Oxford, 2013, pp. 115–16.

[119] Patmore, "The Origins of Federal Industrial Relations Systems," pp. 163–4.

hard for the legislation. The economic problems of the Great Depression challenged its long tradition of voluntarism in industrial relations. Workers applied pressure through strikes, including sit-downs. The forces opposing the legislation, primarily business interests, including the NAM, and the Republican Party, were considerably weakened by the political and economic climate of the mid-1930s.[120]

Carefully drafted to meet Supreme Court constitutional objections, the Wagner Act established employees' right to join unions and engage in collective bargaining. It established unfair labour practices, making it unlawful for an employer to interfere with an employee's right to join a union and engage in union activities. Employers were required to bargain in good faith with unions and prohibited from discharging or otherwise discriminating against employees for engaging in union activities. The legislation outlawed the ERPs, which it condemned as "sham organizations" that impeded economic recovery. The legislation established procedures by which employees could elect their own bargaining agent and not be forced to accept ERPs. It created the three-member National Labor Relations Board (NLRB) to interpret and apply the Act. The NLRB had power to enforce its rulings and developed a body of binding case law. While the Wagner Act was concerned with whether workers preferred union representation, the Australian legislation assumed that workers preferred union representation. The majority of the Supreme Court upheld the legislation as constitutional in May 1937.[121]

While the state played a role in repressing labour unrest through the police and the military in all five countries, this was particularly notable in the US and Canada, where it played a crucial role in the extension of ERPs in several instances by weakening and even destroying trade unionism in particular workplaces. As Badger has argued, "before the New Deal the coercive power of the state had been largely arrayed against labour."[122] Public officials at all levels of government showed a willingness to use force against union activists and strikers. Local government officials tended to act as an "arm of employers" and state governors reinforced this bias by calling out the National Guard, "ostensibly to maintain law and order, in practice

[120] Patmore, "The Origins of Federal Industrial Relations Systems", pp. 164–5; Phillips-Fein, *Invisible Hands*, pp. 14–15.

[121] James Gross, "National Labor Relations Board", in Melvyn Dubofsky (ed.), *The Oxford Encyclopedia of American Business, Labor & Economic History, Vol. 2*, Oxford University Press, New York, 2013, p. 9; Patmore, "The Origins of Federal Industrial Relations Systems", pp. 164–5.

[122] Anthony Badger, *The New Deal: The Depression Years, 1933–1940*, Ivan R. Dee, Chicago, 1989, p. 119.

to protect scabs, keep plants open, and break strikes."[123] One notable US example is the Ludlow massacre, which occurred on 20 April 1914 during a violent coal miners' strike in Colorado led by the United Mine Workers of America (UMWA) against CF&I and other coal firms. A gun battle between Colorado National Guard and the miners at the Ludlow strikers' camp that left ten men and one child dead. A tent fire asphyxiated 11 children and two women after the National Guard overran the camp and put the tents to the torch. There was public outrage against CF&I and the Rockefeller family, which had the largest shareholding in CF&I, and the massacre opened the way for the introduction of the ERP at CF&I. In Canada, state repression played a major role in the suppression of labour unrest in 1919 and continued with the intervention of almost 1,000 troops and another 1,000 special police in the 1922 Cape Breton coal strike. In the wake of a defeated strike at the Sydney Nova Scotia plant of the British Empire Steel Corporation (BESCO) in 1923, which saw the deployment of machine guns and mounted police and helmeted soldiers charging picket lines with fixed bayonets, the company introduced an ERP without a vote, despite previous worker opposition.[124]

Conclusion

This chapter has examined a number of factors that have been indicated as important in promoting or retarding schemes of workplace representation. While economic prosperity can encourage schemes of workplace employee representation as a way of reducing labour turnover and increased labour unrest, the period 1914–39 saw mixed economic fortunes in Australian, Canada, Germany, the UK and the US. The US economy represents the strongest case for the economic prosperity argument with its favourable economic conditions from the outbreak of the First World War until 1929, with the exception of 1920–21. The Canadian economy, which was closely linked to the US economy, followed a similar pattern. While the UK economy was also stimulated by the war, its economic performance was poor in the 1920s, and Germany faced major strains both during the war and the

---

[123] Badger, *The New Deal*, p. 119.

[124] David Frank, *J.B. McLachlan: A Biography*, James Lorimer & Co., Toronto, 1999, pp. 300–15; Canada, Department of Labour, *Report of Royal Commission to Inquire into Industrial Unrest among the Steel Workers at Sydney, N.S.*, Supplement to *Labour Gazette* (hereafter *LGC*), Feb. 1924, pp. 12–17; Heron and Siemiatycki, "The Great War, the State and Working Class Canada", pp. 34–6; Don Macgillivray, "Military Aid to the Civil Power: The Cape Breton Experience in the 1920s", *Acadiensis*, vol. 3, no. 2, 1974, pp. 45–64; George McGovern and Leonard Guttridge, *The Great Coalfield War*, University of Colorado Press, Boulder, 1996, pp. 210–35; *The Sydney Record*, 18 Dec. 1922, p. 1, 15 Aug. 1923, p. 1.

1920s, though it enjoyed a brief period of relative prosperity from 1926 to 1929. While the Australian economy did not boom to the same extent as the other during the First World War, it recovered during the 1920s following a slump in 1921, but unemployment never dropped to the low levels of Canada or the US. After 1929, all five economies were hit by the Great Depression to varying degrees and had to wait until the outbreak of the Second World War to fully recover.

If the scale and structure of industry and the division of labour, particularly in terms of mass production, were important in encouraging employee representation, then the US would again provide the most favourable environment for the development of employee representation in the workplace. Germany and the UK also had large-scale firms, but multidivisional forms of organisation did not take off in these countries until after the Second World War, and they had a tendency to deal with internal and external competition by forming trade associations or cartels. Canadian firms had a tendency toward mergers and large US corporations formed Canadian branch plants. Australia had the least-developed economy in terms of firm size and the organisation of work.

The prospects for the adoption and success of schemes for workplace employee representation were dependent on unions, management and the state. Schemes, particularly those that saw workplace employee representation as a substitute for trade unionism, were less likely to succeed in Australia, Germany (particularly before 1933) and the UK, where there were substantial trade union movements with favourable political parties and established systems of industrial regulation either through collective bargaining or state tribunals. Where unions were weak and faced a more hostile state, as in the US and Canada, employers had a greater chance of introducing these schemes, particularly if they were part of an anti-union strategy. In the US, which had the most developed management ethos and where managers had greater access to ideas such as welfarism and personnel management, the notion of workplace employee representation had a great appeal as a means of obtaining worker loyalty and improving productivity.

The next chapter focuses on four concepts of workplace employee representation that developed between 1914 and 1939: the ERP, Whitley works committees, German works councils and union-management cooperation. The chapter looks at their origins and the essential underlying elements in terms of structure, power, legal status, relationship to management and impact on trade unionism.

3

The Concepts

Against the context for the period 1914–39 provided by the previous chapter, this chapter explores in depth the four major concepts of workplace employee representation examined in the book. They are ERPs, Whitley works committees in the UK, German works councils and union-management cooperation committees. Both ERPs and union-management cooperation were developed in the US. Whitleyism was an influence on union-management cooperation, while union-management cooperation can also be seen as an AFL response to ERPs. This chapter analyses the origins of each of these ideas and the principles underlying them in terms of their structure, power, legal status, relationship to management and their impact on trade unionism. The chapter examines some of the reactions to these ideas, both critical and supportive. It will conclude by comparing the ideas according to a number of dimensions including the relationship to unions. Later chapters focus on the impact of these ideas in the US, the UK, Germany, Canada and Australia.

Employee Representation Plans

There had been interest in the idea of ERPs in the US from at least the 1870s. Stratton & Storm, the largest manufacturer of cigars in the US by 1883, had established a board of arbitration in 1879, which comprised four elected delegates of workers, four management representatives appointed by management and a neutral selected from another branch of the company, to adjudicate matters relating to wages or working conditions that were disputed. While founder George Storm did not oppose his workers belonging to unions, he believed that unions were irrelevant to the company.[1] The Storm

---

[1] Raymond Hogler and Guillermo Greiner, *Employee Participation and Labor Law in the American Workplace*, Quorum Books, New York, 1992, pp. 13–15; Bruce Kaufman,

scheme was predicated on "political equality as a justification for enfran-chisement in the workplace; it assumed a common interest between workers and employers, and it was designed to reduce the level of adversarialism within the firm."[2]

Another notable early example of an ERP can be found in Filene's Sons, a retail clothing business in Boston. William Filene organised the Filene Cooperative Association in 1898, which had a delegated authority over certain welfare programmes such as the lunchroom and entertainment funds. The Filenes were motivated by business, humanitarian and paternalistic concerns, and were particularly aware of public perceptions of their employment of young women in sales positions. They had one of the most extensive welfare programmes in the US and were among the earliest to appoint a welfare manager. Eventually the Filenes established a representative structure known as the Cooperative Association Council, with the welfare manager as executive secretary and accountable to the Council, and an Arbitration Board resolved to settle disputes between employees and management. The Council could initiate new store rules or amend existing ones relating to discipline and working conditions, with the exception of the "policies of business." It did not need an outright majority, but two-thirds of the vote of its entire membership or a five-sixths vote of the Council itself. Management also held right of veto over any Council decision, but this could be overturned by a series of mass meetings of Association members followed by a two-thirds vote of all Association members. The company did not oppose employees being union members and they could also be members of the Association, but during the early 1920s union members were briefly discriminated against in areas such as bonuses and holidays.[3]

While the Filene example highlights the link between more enlightened approaches to labour management and an ERP, C.W. Post's National Trades and Worker Association (NTWA), formed in 1910, highlights the possibility of an ERP as an alternative to AFL trade unionism. Post was a cereal manufacturer based in Battle Creek, Michigan, a leading figure in the NAM and an outspoken national supporter of the anti-union open shop.

"Accomplishments and Shortcomings of Nonunion Employee Representation in the Pre-Wagner Act Years: A Reassessment", in Bruce Kaufman and Daphne Taras (eds.), *Non-Union Employee Representation: History, Contemporary Practice and Policy*, M.E. Sharpe, Armonk, 2000, p. 22; Daniel Nelson, "Employee Representation in Historical Perspective", in Bruce Kaufman and Morris Kleiner (eds.), *Employee Representation: Alternatives and Future Directions*, Industrial Relations Research Association, Madison, 1993, pp. 372–3.

[2] Hogler and Greiner, *Employee Participation*, p. 15.

[3] Hogler and Greiner, *Employee Participation*, pp. 15–16; Mary La Dame, *The Filene Store: A Study of Employees' Relation to Management in a Retail Store*, Russell Sage Foundation, New York, 1930, pp. 98–9, 122–3, 134–8; Nelson, "Employee Representation", pp. 372–3.

The NTWA was a "good union" with potential to become a national labour organisation that rejected strikes and picketing and relied on mediation and appeals to public opinion. Post burdened the union, however, with the management of an expensive and derelict health resort and it soon become moribund.[4] As Nelson notes, "Unlike the Filene executives, Post and his allies viewed the company union narrowly, as a representation and bargaining entity of modest scope and a bulwark against outside organizers."[5]

The firm that attracted most attention for developing an ERP, because of its size and association with the Rockefeller family, was CF&I. The company was formed in 1892 following a merger between the Colorado Fuel Company and the Colorado Coal and Iron Company. Its interests included coal mines and the steelworks at Pueblo, Colorado. Generally, management did not recognise unions or engage in collective bargaining at the Pueblo steelworks. Unions found it difficult to organise the Pueblo plant because CF&I discharged or blacklisted union activists. Some workers were union members and the International Moulder's Union, which claimed a majority of members in the steelworks foundry, was able to gain increases in wages in 1910 following discussions with the general manager. CF&I had extensive welfare programmes well before the adoption of its ERP in 1915. There was a hospital for the Colorado Coal and Iron Company's employees in Pueblo from 1881. CF&I formed a Sociological Department in July 1901, which provided educational facilities, recreational halls and reading rooms for workers and their families. From 1901 to 1904 the Sociological Department published *Camp and Plant* to encourage an *esprit de corps* among employees by providing information about the company and encouraging contributions from readers. By July 1915, the average number of employees working every day at the steelworks was 2,793 and 3,999 in the coal mines.[6] The Pueblo

---

[4] Doris McLaughlin, "The Second Battle of Battle Creek: The Open Shop Movement in the Early Twentieth Century", *Labor History*, vol. 14, no. 3, 1973, pp. 323–39; Nelson, "Employee Representation", p. 373.

[5] Nelson, "Employee Representation", p. 373.

[6] CF&I, Memorandum, J.F. Welborn, 23 Oct. 1915. Box 12, FF 293, MSS 1057, Colorado Fuel and Iron Corporation Collection, Colorado Historical Society, Denver, Colorado (CFIC, CHS); John Fitch, "Steel and Steel Workers in America. V. The Steel Industry and the People in Colorado," typescript, 1911, pp. 2–3, 23. Box 4, Folder 11, MSS937, John Fitch Collection, Manuscripts Library, State Historical Society of Wisconsin, Madison, Wisconsin (JFC SHSW); Letters J.H. Means to J.B. McKennan, 6 Jul. 1906, W.S. Hutton to J.B. McKennan, 5 Nov. 1912, Box 7 1-6, File 17. Bessemer Historical Society Archives, Pueblo, Colorado (BHSA); Nelson, "Employee Representation", p. 373; Howard Lee Scamehorn, *Pioneer Steelmaker in the West: The Colorado Fuel and Iron Company 1872–1903*, Pruett Publishing, Boulder, Co., 1976, pp. 139–55; "Report on Industrial Relations in the Colorado Fuel and Iron Company. Prepared by Industrial Relations Staff, Curtis, Fosdick & Belknap", unpublished typescript, Table IX, n.d., Box 7-1.5, File 2. BHSA.

steelworks was virtually the only steel plant in the Western US until the Second World War and workers had "no chance of finding another job in steelmaking anywhere near Pueblo."[7]

The Rockefeller family's involvement in CF&I began in November 1902, when John D. Rockefeller Sr. paid $6 million for 40 per cent of its shares and 43 per cent of its bonds at the urging of George Jay Gould. Gould hoped that his railways might receive lucrative coal-carrying contracts from CF&I. Rockefeller had become one of the richest men in the world through Standard Oil and the Rockefeller family was flush with funds from the recent sale of its Mensabi iron ore mines in Minnesota to US Steel. Rockefeller's only son, JDR Jr., who was guided by the "Christian tenets of duty, industry, honesty and humility," became a director of the company as part of the takeover. Since his graduation from Brown University in 1897, JDR Jr. had assisted Frederick T. Gates, his father's advisor on business and philanthropic matters. JDR Jr. served as a director of CF&I until 1905 and again from 1909 to 1920. He gradually took over his father's duties and Rockefeller Sr. withdrew from participation in all business activities in 1911. The Rockefeller family gained control of CF&I in 1907, when Gould was forced to sell his securities as a result of a panic in the financial market. When the firm was reorganised as the Colorado Fuel and Iron Corporation in 1936, Rockefeller interests controlled 50.4 per cent of the common stock. Despite this, JDR Jr. had "largely lost touch" with CF&I by 1933 as he had few personal ties with the company's officers. He was based in New York, and the CF&I management was located in Denver. CF&I was also on an "economic rollercoaster" with slow growth and disappointing profits. JDR Jr. had considered selling his interests as early as 1933. The Rockefeller family eventually sold their controlling interests in the company in December 1944.[8]

CF&I established the "Rockefeller Plan" in the wake of the Ludlow massacre. There was public outrage against CF&I and the Rockefeller family, which had the largest shareholdings in the company. There were protests outside the Rockefeller family home and New York offices. The United States Commission on Industrial Relations, which had been appointed by President Wilson to look at industrial unrest and improve labour-management relations, placed JDR Jr. and CF&I management under public scrutiny following the massacre. Senator Thomas P. Walsh, chair of the Commission, challenged Rockefeller Jr.'s claims that as a CF&I director he did not influence its

---

[7] Rees, *Representation and Rebellion*, p. 137.

[8] Ron Chernow, *Titan: The Life of John D. Rockefeller, Sr.*, Vintage Books, New York, 1999, p. 570; CF&I Company Minutes, 4 Oct. 1903, 26 Oct. 1905, 18 Oct. 1909, 15 Mar. 1920. BHSA; Howard Lee Scamehorn, *Mill & Mine: The CF&I in the Twentieth Century*, University of Nebraska Press, Lincoln, 1992, pp. 4, 18–24, 29, 139, 143.

policies. It was possible that the Wilson federal administration would intervene and establish grievance procedures to settle disputes. If the local committees chosen by miners could not settle grievances, then they would be referred to an arbitration board selected by the President. JDR Jr. recruited Mackenzie King, the former Canadian Minister for Labour and drafter of the IDIA, to help him frame the plan, and Ivy Lee, a founder of modern public relations, to assist with publicity. While JDR Jr. and Mackenzie King did not publicly condemn trade unions, the Rockefeller Plan was a substitution for collective bargaining with the UMWA. The idea had also been previously considered within CF&I. In 1911, F.E. Parks, the assistant manager at the Pueblo steelworks, had proposed a system of joint committees at the plant to instil in workers a "feeling of loyalty" to management. When the UMWA was defeated in the strike, the miners gave their support to the plan in a secret ballot, where 84 per cent of the 2,846 votes endorsed the scheme. JDR Jr. successfully moved the adoption of the plan at a meeting of the board of CF&I directors on 4 October 1915.[9]

One significant management casualty of the Rockefeller Plan was Lamont M. Bowers, the chair of the CF&I board of directors. Gates had originally brought Bowers, his uncle by marriage, to CF&I in 1907 to be "the man on the inside" and undermine the position of CF&I President Jesse Floyd Welborn, who had joined the Colorado Fuel Company as a clerk in 1890. While a popular appointment within CF&I, Gates saw Welborn as a George Jay Gould appointment and had little confidence in him. Bowers became the chair of the board in less than a year and made it clear that he alone represented the Rockefeller interests and his power was absolute. Welborn, technically Bowers's superior, accepted this with misgivings. While Bowers brought about improvements in CF&I's financial position,[10] he opposed

[9] CF&I Company Minutes, 4 Oct. 1915. BHSA; Letter, F.E. Parks to J.A. Fitch, 2 Jun. 1911. MSS937, Box 4, Folder 11. JFC SHSW; Letters, JDR Jr. to J.F. Welborn, 9 Dec. 1915, J.F. Welborn to JDR Jr., 15 Dec. 1915. Box 15. Folder 127. Record Group III2C. Rockefeller Family Archives, Rockefeller Archives Center, Sleepy Hollow, NY (hereafter RFA RAC); Letter, JDR Jr. to J.F. Welborn, 8 June 1914. Box 1. FF2. Letter, JDR Jr. to J.F. Welborn, 20 Oct. 1915. Box 1. FF28. MSS 1218. Jesse Floyd Welborn Collection, Colorado Historical Society, Denver, Colorado (hereafter JFW CHS); Howard Gitelman, *Legacy of the Ludlow Massacre: A Chapter in American Industrial Relations*, University of Pennsylvania Press, Philadelphia, 1988, chaps. 1–4; John Hogle, "The Rockefeller Plan: Workers, Managers and the Struggle over Unionism in Colorado Fuel and Iron, 1915–1942", PhD thesis, University of Colorado at Boulder, 1992, chaps. 3–4; Kaufman, "Accomplishments and Shortcomings", p. 22; Scamehorn, *Mill & Mine*, 53–4; Ben Selekman and Mary Van Kleeck, *Employees' Representation in Coal Mines: A Study of the Industrial Representation Plan of the Colorado Fuel and Iron Company*, Russell Sage Foundation, New York, 1924, chap. 2; *Colorado Fuel and Iron Industrial Bulletin* (hereafter *Industrial Bulletin*), 31 July 1917, p. 3.

[10] Letters, F.T. Gates to M. Bowers, 12 Nov. 1907. Box 27. File 81. Lamont M. Bowers

the ERP on the grounds that accepting it would be an admission that his previous policies had failed. Bowers also claimed during the strike that the UMWA would hail any plan as a victory for union recognition and the "open shop would be shut."[11] McKenzie King saw Bowers as the "reactionary of reactionaries," who exercised a "harmful" influence in CF&I.[12] JDR Jnr. removed Bowers. Welborn, who had only expressed moderate concerns about the plan, reasserted his authority and remained President of CF&I until January 1929.[13]

CF&I reorganised its welfare activities and extended its ERP from its coal mines to its Pueblo steelworks. CF&I abolished the Sociological Department in 1915 with the introduction of the Rockefeller Plan and handed over its activities to the industrial department of the Young Men's Christian Association (YMCA). Following the introduction of the Rockefeller Plan, CF&I management published or sponsored several publications that highlighted the extensive welfare plans and the ERP. JDR Jr. encouraged CF&I management to implement the ERP at the steelworks. He persuaded CF&I management to adopt his ideas, including the internal appointment of a CF&I President's Industrial Representative to oversee the ERP and mediate grievances. Labour unions were not seeking recognition at Pueblo and the steelworks employees made no demands for the adoption of the ERP, but voted for it by 2,321 to 863 in May 1916.[14] Warren Densmore, a leading activist in the ERP at Pueblo, later noted that the employees accepted the ERP "because they felt conditions were so bad that any alternative was worth a trial."[15]

The Rockefeller Plan for the coal miners involved workers from a particular camp being organised into four districts. The workers elected representatives to their district conference, where they met with senior representatives of the company at least three times a year. The district conferences elected

---

collection, Department of Special Collections, Glenn G. Bartle Library, State University of New York, Binghamton (hereafter LMB GGB); Scamehorn, *Mill & Mine*, pp. 29–32.

[11] Letter, L.M. Bowers to JDR Jnr., 16 Aug. 1914. Box 28. File 101 (LMB GGB).

[12] William Lyon Mackenzie King diaries, 31 Dec. 1914, 1 Feb. 1919, National Archives and Library of Canada, Ottawa (hereafter NALC).

[13] L.M. Bowers to JDR Jnr., 17 Feb. 1915. Box 21. Folder 190. Record Group III2C. RFA RAC; Scamehorn, *Mill & Mine*, pp. 54–5, 133.

[14] Greg Patmore, "Employee Representation Plans at the Minnequa Steelworks, Pueblo, Colorado, 1915–1942", *Business History*, vol. 49, no. 6, 2007, pp. 848–50; Greg Patmore and Jonathan Rees, "Employee Publications and Employee Representation Plans: The Case of Colorado Fuel and Iron", *Management and Organisational History*, vol. 3, no. 3–4, 2008, pp. 257–72.

[15] Letter, Elton Mayo to Arthur Woods, 20 Nov. 1928. Box 3B, Folder 19 Elton Mayo Papers, Baker Library, Harvard Business School, Cambridge, MA (hereafter EMP).

joint committees on employment issues, which consisted of three representatives of the employees and three of the company. The joint committee
on industrial cooperation and conciliation dealt with issues such as wages
and conditions. There were also joint committees on safety and accidents,
sanitation, health and housing. Workers could appeal to various levels of
company management and there was even provision for appeal to an external
court, the Colorado State Industrial Commission, which was established by
the Colorado Legislature in 1915 for the purpose of adjudicating industrial
disputes and administering workers' compensation if mediation failed. The
company paid for all costs associated with the plan, including reimbursement
for employee representatives' loss of work time. While there was no place for
unions in it, the original Rockefeller Plan prohibited discrimination against
employees on the grounds of union membership.[16]

Under the original ERP, the Pueblo steel plant was divided into nine
divisions and a number of subdivisions based on occupation or geographical
location in the plant. Each division was allowed one representative for every
150 employees, or a minimum of two. Employees needed three months' service
at CF&I before they could vote. The election was by secret ballot and the
company provided the ballot boxes and papers. There was no specific place for
the holding of the elections and the tellers, one appointed by management,
the other by the representatives, carried the ballot boxes round to workers on
the job. The representatives held office for one year and could call meetings
of employees in their division to discuss grievances, provided it did not
interfere with the work. Employees could raise grievances either individually
or through their representative to their supervisor or the superintendent in
the first instance and then to the CF&I President's Industrial Representative.
All the representatives held joint conferences with management representatives, three weeks after the annual election of representatives and thereafter
at intervals of not more than four months, and served on four specialist joint
committees as in the case of the ERP for CF&I coal mines, but with six
employee representatives and six management representatives.[17]

Despite the prohibition of discrimination on the grounds of union

[16] John D. Rockefeller, Jr., *The Colorado Industrial Plan*, no publisher, 1916, pp. 22–6;
Scamehorn, *Mill & Mine*, pp. 60–5.

[17] CF&I, *Industrial Representation Plan and Memorandum of Agreement Respecting
Employment and Living and Working Conditions Applicable to the Minnequa Steel Works of the
Colorado Fuel and Iron Company*, Denver, 1916. Mary Van Kleeck Research Papers, Series II
Subseries, Box 19, File 19, Folder 7. Wayne State University. Archives of Labor and Urban
Affairs and University Archives, Detroit (hereafter MVKRP): Ben Selekman, *Employees'
Representation in Steel Works: A Study of the Industrial Representation Plan of the Minnequa
Steel Works of the Colorado Fuel and Iron Company*, Russell Sage Foundation, New York, 1924,
pp. 53–60.

membership, the Rockefellers reinforced the long-standing hostility of CF&I management towards trade unions. Rockefeller Sr. saw unions as "frauds" and believed they stood for doing as little work as possible for the maximum pay.[18] While Rees emphasises that the introduction of the ERP in the steelworks was motivated by JDR Jr.'s interest in "promoting labor peace" rather than posing an immediate threat of union organisation, the ERP was an extension of CF&I's policy of anti-unionism in the Pueblo steelworks.[19] While JDR Jnr. was careful not to condemn unions outright, he expressed concern that some "organisations of Labor are conducted without just regard for the rights of employer or of the public" and "cannot be too strongly condemned or too vigorously dealt with."[20] An ERP like his was a "good" form of labour organisation that recognised the common interests of capital and labour. Kaufman and Chernow argue that the experience of the Ludlow massacre and its aftermath led JDR Jr. to recognise the right of workers to unionise. However, as will be seen in the next chapter, his actions during the 1919 steel strike at Pueblo steelworks contradicted his public approval of unions.[21]

The supporters of ERPs claimed that they were more effective than trade unions in raising employee grievances and contributing to firm productivity. The plans countered the growing gap between senior management and workers in large-scale enterprises. They provided a communication link through which workers could bring minor grievances to management's attention and management could make workers realise that improved working standards depended upon reducing overheads and increasing efficiency. Trade unions, unlike employers and employees, were "outside organizations" that were antagonistic to the firm and whose primary interest was not the good of the company.[22] Since the membership of an ERP or company union was limited to a specific firm, one contemporary commentator noted that employees "develop an interest in and a loyalty to that organization which tend to increased efficiency."[23]

---

[18] Chernow, *Titan*, p. 574.

[19] Rees, *Representation and Rebellion*, p. 106.

[20] John D. Rockefeller, Jr., *Representation in Industry*, no publisher, New York (?), 1918, p. 14.

[21] Chernow, *Titan*, p. 574; Bruce Kaufman, "Industrial Relations Counsellors, Inc.: Its History and Significance", in Bruce Kaufman, Richard Beaumont and Roy Helfgott (eds.), *Industrial Relations to Human Resources and Beyond: The Evolving Process of Employee Relations Management*, M.E. Sharpe, Armonk, 2003, pp. 52–5.

[22] Clarence Hicks, *My Life in Industrial Relations: Fifty Years in the Growth of a Profession*, Harper & Brothers, New York, 1941, pp. 87–8; Rockefeller, *The Colorado Industrial Plan*, pp. 13–14.

[23] Henry Seager, "Company Unions vs. Trade Unions", *The American Economic Review*, vol. 13, no. 1, 1923, p. 5.

Critics of ERPs argued that they did not provide an independent voice for workers as employers established and managed them. Samuel Gompers, the AFL President, criticised the Rockefeller Plan in June 1916 for being "an industrial subterfuge" that provided "a substitute for trade unions," which prevented "the formation of bona fine unions that develop democracy and a spirit of liberty among men."[24] The company generally had the right of veto over shop floor initiatives in ERPs. Workers and their representatives were unwilling to raise grievances as they could lose their jobs. The ERPs also generally dealt with minor matters and did not negotiate the general wage scale for the company or the plant. Without trade unions, workers were deprived of expert outside advice in putting their case and conducting their negotiations. Management funding compromised the integrity of these schemes and threatened union representation. Workers could not call upon outside help if employers decided to reduce wages and change working conditions. As the ERP only covered a particular plant or company, workers' knowledge of outside wages and conditions were limited.[25] While Kaufman has recently claimed that critics of ERPs such as William Leiserson reassessed in the 1920s, in May 1928 Leiserson still saw trade unions as superior to ERPs and recognised that the latter were "under the dominance" of management.[26]

Whitley Works Committees

While US employers initiated ERPs, the British government played a crucial role in initiating Whitley works committees, which were developed during the First World War against a background of industrial unrest. Union officials cooperated with the government in pursuing the war effort, which extended the collective bargaining rights of unions. But there were growing tensions between union officials and rank-and-file members, particularly in the munitions industries, over issues such as dilution or deskilling, which allowed workers to bypass the usual requirements for training to undertake war work and minimised skill shortages. Dilution played an important role in allowing the employment of women in the munitions industry. Workplace shop stewards became prominent in leading resistance to dilution and

---

[24] *American Federationist* (hereafter *AF*), Jun. 1916, p. 438.

[25] AFL, *Report of the Proceedings of the Thirty-Ninth Annual Convention*, Washington, 1919, pp. 302–3; Seager, "Company Unions vs. Trade Unions", p. 5.

[26] Letters, W. Leiserson to M.L. Cooke, 23 May 1928, 13 Nov. 1928, File – "Cooke, Morris L., 1928–1947", Box 9, MAD 4 /32/I1-J4. William Leiserson collection, Manuscripts Library, State Historical Society of Wisconsin, Madison; Kaufman, "The Case for the Company Union", pp. 333–5.

began cooperating across trades and unions in shop committees to represent rank-and-file workers. City-wide committees were formed to represent workers' interests, most notably the Clyde Workers' Committee in Glasgow, which led strikes for wage increases and against dilution agreements approved by union officials and the government. The government responded to the Clyde Workers' Committee's resistance to dilution by appointing dilution commissioners to work with moderate local union officials and form joint committees to oversee workshop changes, while repressing left-wing newspapers and arresting and deporting radical leaders from Glasgow. Employers had concerns about radical workers gaining representation on joint committees relating to munitions production. They opposed suggestions to put employee representatives on the boards of the national shell factories and were successful in having joint Local Armaments Committees abolished. Outside munitions production, there were Miners' Reform Committees on the Scottish and South Wales coalfields and unofficial vigilance committees on the railways. There was also growing demand among unions, in particular the National Union of Railwaymen (NUR), for the nationalisation of key industries such as railways and coal mining under workers control.[27]

Employers were already showing some interest in setting up joint committees at the factory level to discuss issues of mutual interest and minimise industrial conflict in a period of labour shortages. Hans Renold Limited, an engineering firm in Burnage, Manchester, decided in 1916 that, what with the growth of the firm and the uncertainty of wartime conditions, it needed better communication with staff to avoid a general breakdown in morale. Against the background of the Ministry for Munitions encouraging joint employee/employer Accident Prevention Committees, management moved to form a joint welfare committee from their nominees to consider questions relating to workplace conditions and make suggestions for improvements. But the initiative was challenged when Amalgamated Society of Engineers (ASE) shop stewards announced that they had formed a shop committee. Management decided to recognise the shop stewards' committee, which was drawn from a key group of skilled workers and had the support of other workers in the factory, but persisted with the welfare

---

[27] Rodger Charles, *The Development of Industrial Relations in Britain 1911–1939*, Hutchinson, London, 1973, pp. 83, 92–3; Clegg, *A History of British Trade Unions since 1889*, pp. 134–8; Ralph Darlington, "Strike Waves, Union Growth and the Rank-and-File/Bureaucracy Interplay: Britain 1889–1890, 1910–1913 and 1919–1920", *Labor History*, vol. 55, no. 1, 2014, pp. 13–14; Jeffrey Haydu, *Making American Industry Safe for Democracy: Comparative Perspectives on the State and Employee Representation in the Era of World War I*, University of Illinois Press, Urbana and Chicago, 1997, pp. 36–41; Ian Sharp, *Industrial Conciliation and Arbitration in Great Britain*, George Allen & Unwin, London, 1950, pp. 321–2; Stitt, *Joint Industrial Councils*, chap. 2.

committee as a means of joint consultation on matters of common concern to workers and management. The shop stewards' committee, a committee of workers only, became the negotiating committee for trade unions and held a joint meeting with management every four weeks.[28]

In the context of these developments, a general view was developing that the war offered a chance for the reconstruction of post-War British society built on wartime cooperation and the "comradeship of the trenches." In March 1916 Prime Minister Herbert Asquith established a small Cabinet subcommittee on reconstruction problems. His successor Lloyd George replaced the subcommittee in March 1917 with a Reconstruction Committee of Cabinet Ministers, which Lloyd George himself chaired. This in turn became a fully-fledged Ministry of Reconstruction in August 1917. Issues of concern for reconstruction included trade, the demobilisation of the armed forces and the removal of government regulation from industry. Those calling for a reconstruction policy also considered the future of industrial relations as one of its objects.[29]

The Whitley Committee on Relations between Employers and the Employed, appointed in October 1916, was a subcommittee of Asquith's subcommittee on reconstruction. John Henry Whitley, a prominent Liberal MP and Chair of the Ways and Means Committee, presided over the Committee. He had managed the family firm of cotton spinners S. Whitley & Co. in Halifax, Yorkshire. He was a fervent Congregationalist and widely respected for his impartiality and high principles. While he was not a social reformer, he was an advocate of co-partnership as a way of sharing responsibility with employees. Although neither the TUC nor the FBI had direct representation, there was a balance on the Committee between employers or their representatives and union members or their spokespersons. Its members included Allan Smith, Chair of the Engineering Employers' Federation; Robert Smillie, President of the Miners' Federation of Great Britain (MFGB); Susan Lawrence, Fabian and social reformer; and Sydney Chapman, Professor of Political Economy at the University of Manchester. The Committee did not call witnesses and did not keep records of its meetings.[30]

---

[28] Charles Renold, *Joint Consultation over Thirty Years: A Case Study*, George Allen & Unwin, London, 1950, pp. 18–21; Chris Wrigley, "The First World War and State Intervention in Industrial Relations, 1914–1918", in Chris Wrigley (ed.), *A History of British Industrial Relations Volume II: 1914–1939*, The Harvester Press, Brighton, 1987, pp. 57–8.

[29] Charles, *The Development of Industrial Relations*, p. 82; Stitt, *Joint Industrial Councils*, pp. 47–8.

[30] Charles, *The Development of Industrial Relations*, pp. 96–8; Allan Fox, *History and Heritage: The Social Origins of the British Industrial Relations System*, Allen & Unwin, London, 1985, pp. 293–5; Stitt, *Joint Industrial Councils*, pp. 66–8.

The Committee issued five reports during 1917 and 1918, of which the first, which is usually thought of as the Whitley Report, and the third, which looked at workplace joint committees, are the most significant for the purposes of this book. In its first report, which was signed off in March 1917 and published in June 1917, the Committee discussed industries where labour was well organised and proposed Joint Industrial Councils (JIC) composed of employer and employee representatives. Similar committees at local and workshop level would supplement JIC activities. The JIC could deal with or allocate to ancillary committees questions such as methods of fixing and adjusting earnings, technical education and training, and proposed legislation affecting industry. The Councils would also go beyond collective bargaining in that by "the better utilisation of the practical knowledge and experience of the workpeople" they would bring about the improvement in productivity necessary for Britain to trade in the post-war world. The report's recommendations were within the voluntarist traditions of British industrial relations, as employers and unions were under no obligation to do anything if they saw no need for JIC. The government would act in an advisory role in the setting up of JIC if the parties desired and provide relevant information on industrial issues. The only exception to this was the railways, which will be examined in Chapter 5. Where there was no adequate organisation of employers and employees, trade boards would continue or be established to provide statutory regulation and develop industrial organisation to the point where a JIC would be able to replace the boards.[31] In contrast to ERPs, Fox argues, Whitleyism "rested on the full recognition of the unions at all levels."[32]

The report on works committees was a supplementary report signed off by the committee in October 1917. It emphasised that the works committees were an essential element of Whitleyism and that better relations between employers and employees could only be obtained if workers had a greater say in the matters with which they were concerned. While the works committees could not alter matters in the collective agreement, they could bring grievances before local management and make suggestions concerning improvements in working conditions and production methods that would improve workplace efficiency. The Committee did not set out any particular form of constitution for these works committees, beyond recommending

[31] Charles, *The Development of Industrial Relations*, pp. 94–110; Clegg, *A History of British Trade Unions since 1889*, pp. 204–5; Fox, *History and Heritage*, pp. 294–5; Great Britain. Reconstruction Committee. Subcommittee of Relations between Employers and Employed, *Interim Report on Joint Standing Industrial Councils*, His Majesty's Stationery Office (hereafter HMSO), London, 1917, p. 6.

[32] Fox, *History and Heritage*, p. 294.

that they meet on a regular basis, not less frequently than once a fortnight, and emphasising "constructive cooperation." Given the potential benefits of the works committee for "commercial and scientific efficiency," it was recommended that a management representative in the workplace should devote a "substantial" amount of "time and thought" to the working and success of the committee. There was concern that the success of works committees would be undermined if there was any perception among workers that employers might use them as a substitute for trade unions. Trade unions and employers' associations had to cooperate in the setting up of works committees. The report recommended against setting up works committees in industries in which workers were not organised or only partially organised into trade unions, as there was a danger that employers might use works committees as an anti-union strategy.[33] As the report noted, "these committees should not, in constitution or methods of working, discourage Trade organisations."[34] While the works committees were not designed to undermine trade unions, they were a challenge to the shop committee movement and a "strategy to bypass shop steward authority."[35]

The War Cabinet gave support in principle to the Whitley Report on 9 October 1917 after obtaining responses from 103 trade unions and employers' organisations, including the FBI, which indicated that none opposed the report's principles. Some employers did have doubts, however, about the advisability of the works committees on the grounds of interference with managerial prerogative, believing that this would hamper efforts to improve workplace efficiency. Employers in staple industries such as cotton argued that Whitleyism was not applicable to them as they had developed their own industrial relations processes, but did not oppose the creation of JIC elsewhere.[36] The recognition of trade unionism was not an issue as "the war had already made this a foregone conclusion in most British industries."[37]

While the TUC did not provide a response to the Cabinet request for an opinion, the TUC Parliamentary Committee gave qualified approval to the report in April 1918, recognising the need to avoid "serious industrial strife" in the post-war reconstruction period. The Committee was concerned that

[33] Great Britain. Ministry of Reconstruction. Committee on Relations between Employers and Employed, *Supplementary Report on Works Committees*, HMSO, London, 1918.

[34] Great Britain, *Supplementary Report on Works Committees*, p. 3.

[35] Hyman, "Rank and File Movements", p. 136.

[36] Fox, *History and Heritage*, p. 296; Gospel, "Employers and Managers", pp. 162–3; Great Britain. Cabinet Office papers. Cabinet Minutes, 9 Oct. 1917. CAB/23/4. Cabinet Memorandum, "Report by the Ministry of Labour of the Attitude of Employers and Employed to Whitley Report", 26 Sept. 1917. CAB/24/27. Public Records Office, Kew, UK (hereafter PRO); *The Times*, 1 Nov. 1918, p. 3.

[37] Gospel, "Employers and Managers", p. 162.

the works committees would have "too much power," calling upon them not to interfere with general wages and conditions, which were the concern of "responsible and experienced" union officials, and rejected any form of joint negotiations that could develop into a substitute for trade unions, particularly in industries that were only partially organised. The TUC Congress of September 1918 passed a resolution by 2,374,000 votes to 758,000 calling upon the government to apply the principles of the Whitley reports to all departments of "State Service."[38]

There were divisions within the TUC that muted full endorsement by the union movement. While unions covering skilled trades with a strong shop steward organisation and collective bargaining processes, such as the ASE, saw little need for Whitleyism, less organised workers in unskilled or semi-skilled occupations such as shop assistants believed that Whitleyism could enhance their bargaining position. While the NUR executive initially supported the Whitley principles in July 1917 as they were broadly in line with union policy, it concluded at its AGM in June 1918, following the release of the Final Report, that the Whitley Scheme did not "sufficiently safeguard the interests of Labour." This union was calling for a broader agenda of worker control that included equal representation in the management of the railway companies and their nationalisation.[39]

Beyond the employers and unions, there were supporters and critics of Whitleyism. The Industrial Reconstruction Council, which had an executive committee that included Labour MP Ben Tillet, publisher Ernest Benn and Conservative MP Sir Herbert Nield, and was primarily funded by industrialists, advocated Whitleyism as going "a long way to reconcile the divergent interests of Labour and Capital" and offered to assist the formation of JIC by providing speakers for crucial early meetings of unions and employers.[40] Sir William Ashley, Dean of the Faculty of Commerce

[38] Stitt, *Joint Industrial Councils*, pp. 120–1; TUC, *Report of Proceedings at the Fiftieth Annual Trades Union Congress. September 2nd to 7th 1918*, London, 1918, pp. 70, 88–93, 306–9.

[39] Philip Bagwell, *The Railwaymen: The History of the National Union of Railwaymen*, George Allen and Unwin, London, 1963, pp. 304, 372–3; NUR, *Agenda and Decisions of the Annual General Meeting, held on June 17th, 18th, 19th, 20th, & 21st, 1918*, London, 1918, pp. 26–7, MSS127/NU/1/1/6; NUR, *General Secretary's Report to and Decisions of Special Executive Committee Meetings, July 19th, 20th, and 21st July 1917, and 9th August 1917 and Quarterly Meeting, September 10th, 11th, 12th, 13th, 14th, and 15th, 1917*, London, 1917, p. 5, MSS127/NU/1/1/5, NUR Collection, Modern Records Centre, University of Warwick, UK (hereafter MRC); Stitt, *Joint Industrial Councils*, pp. 120–1; TUC, *Report of Proceedings at the Forty-Ninth Annual Trades Union Congress. September 3rd to 8th 1917*, London, 1917, pp. 226–35; TUC, *Report of Proceedings. September 2nd to 7th 1918*, p. 308.

[40] Stitt, *Joint Industrial Councils*, p. 126; The Industrial Reconstruction Council, *Trade Parliaments: Why they Should be Formed and How to Form One in Your Trade. An Explanation of the Whitley Report*, London, n.d., p. 12.

at the University of Birmingham, argued that Whitleyism would bring a "democratic spirit" into the workplace and give workers a feeling that they had a voice in determining their working conditions. This could assist improvements in the organisation of production through techniques such as scientific management and employee welfarism. Unless workers were consulted on these issues, there would be suspicion that improvements would be a matter of "speeding up" and undermining workers' conditions. At the request of the Ministry of Labour, Ashley took an active role in convening meetings of employers and unions in the Birmingham District in January 1918 to consider the application of Whitley committees to their industries.[41]

Guild socialists, including economist and historian George Douglas Howard Cole, who did not seek a permanent improvement in relations between capital and labour and advocated the abolition of the wage system and of capital, were particularly concerned with the impact of Whitley works committees on union organisation, noting that they provided for "the representation of non-unionists on an equal basis with unionists."[42] One of their fundamental criticisms of Whitleyism making works committees "mere adjuncts" to national JIC was "that it begins at the top with an endeavour to secure the discussion and settlement of questions on a national scale, instead of beginning at the bottom in the workshop and building up therefrom on a democratic basis."[43] They produced several pamphlets for the trade union movement warning against accepting Whitleyism.[44]

The German Works Councils

As in the UK with Whitley works committees, the German state played a crucial role in the introduction of works councils, which was mandated by legislation. The idea of works councils predates the Weimar Republic and can be traced back to the revolution of 1848 when the Industrial Commission of the revolutionary National Assembly in Frankfurt called for the establishment of factory committees consisting of elected employee representatives and the factory owner, which would issue works rules to

[41] Letters, Sir David Shackleton to Sir William Ashley, 8 Dec. 1917, Sir William Ashley to Sir David Shackleton, 9 Dec. 1917. Typescript, "Conference of Employers on the Whitley Report Held in the Council Room of the University of Birmingham January 28 1918", p. 2. Sir William Ashley Papers, Add MS 42250, British Library (hereafter WAP).

[42] National Guilds League, *Observations on the Interim Report of the Reconstruction Committee on Joint Standing Industrial Councils*, London, 1917, p. 6.

[43] National Guilds League, *Observations on the Interim Report*, p. 5.

[44] National Guilds League, *Notes for Trade Unionists. In Connection with the Adoption by the War Cabinet of the Interim Report of the Reconstruction Committee on Joint Standing Industrial Councils, Commonly Known as the Whitley Report*, London, 1918.

govern discipline in the factory. While the idea did not survive the revolution, it became an element of German labour's programme for reform.[45]

There was some related legislative activity in the decades prior to the First World War. The aspirations of labour were partially met in 1891, shortly after the fall of Bismarck, when the German parliament amended the Industrial Code to make the issuing of works rules compulsory for all businesses employing more than 20 workers. Though works committees were provided for in the legislation and were entitled to consult with employers, employers were not obliged to take any notice of works committees' recommendations. Prussia, the dominant German state, passed legislation to make workers' committees compulsory in all mining undertakings employing 100 or more workers in 1905.[46]

Some firms independently developed their own systems of worker representation. Siemens, the electrical engineering company, established a committee of worker representatives to cooperate with the management of pension funds. The company established workers' committees in 1903 to deal with all issues of interest to workers, including complaints and grievances about wages and conditions. While these committees comprised employee representatives appointed by management and elected by employees, in 1906 the firm stopped selecting worker representatives and allowed employees to elect all their representatives.[47]

The basis of the 1920 works council legislation lay in the works committees, which were established by the German government during the First World War to mobilise support for the war effort. The 1916 Auxiliary National Service Law provided for the conscription of all men between the ages of 17 and 60 for war service and drastic restrictions on the mobility of workers. Women, who did not yet have right to vote, were not covered by the legislation. While the legislation was draconian for workers, the labour movement obtained a number of major concessions such as gaining an important role in the administration of the legislation and having collective bargaining agreements given force of law in Germany. The legislation established joint committees of management and labour in firms with more than 50 workers, which were to settle disputes over wages and conditions of employment.[48]

Growing disillusionment with the war, declining real wages and shortages of food and coal also provided the basis for an upsurge in workplace

[45] Guillebaud, *The Works Council*, p. 1.
[46] Guillebaud, *The Works Council*, pp. 1–2.
[47] International Labour Office (hereafter ILO), *Studies on Industrial Relations I*, Geneva, 1930, pp. 12–13.
[48] Chickering, *Imperial Germany and the Great War*, pp. 79–80.

militancy from 1916 to 1918. German workers engaged in unauthorised strikes, such as that by 55,000 Berlin metalworkers in June 1916 over the radical Karl Liebknecht's imprisonment for treason for a May Day speech. As in the UK, they turned to workplace leaders willing to challenge trade union leaders and the government. City-wide networks of delegates, the Revolutionary Shop Stewards, developed among Berlin and Leipzig metalworkers. The government responded to major industrial unrest, such as that over bread rations in Leipzig and Berlin in April 1917, with military force. This heightened the appeal of the Independent Social Democratic Party (Unabhängige Sozialdemokratische Partei Deutschlands or USPD), which split from the SPD over the issue of war loans and supported worker demands for reform and immediate peace. The USPD encouraged the formation of works councils, which consisted of delegates elected by larger factories in the city and co-opted socialist and union leaders sympathetic to the movement. The councils grew from formal and informal networks of workers at different plants, including the Auxiliary Service Law joint committees. While these councils, unlike the Russian *soviets*, neither adopted radical goals nor represented revolutionary constituencies, leaders came from radical locals of the Metalworkers' Union (Deutscher Metallarbeiter-Verband or DMV), the Revolutionary Shop Stewards and the USPD. They mobilised radical popular action, most notably when 400,000 Berlin metalworkers struck on 28 January 1918 over a range of demands that included peace without annexation, improved food supplies, the repeal of the Auxiliary Service Law and democratic reforms. Berlin factory workers elected 414 delegates to an action committee, which the government initially refused to negotiate with and then dissolved. The strike spread quickly to other munitions centres and involved over 1 million workers, and was put down with considerable force by the army and police. Approximately 50,000 strikers were subsequently conscripted into the army. While Berlin shop stewards were the leaders of the strike and a special target of state repression, they continued to be active and played an important role in the events of November 1918. Their actions represented a challenge not only to the government and employers, but also to the socialist General Union Confederation or Allgemeiner Deutscher Gewerkschaftsbund (ADGB) and the SPD, which supported the government's wartime labour policy.[49]

The issue of workplace representation became prominent during the revolution that followed the November 1918 Armistice and led to the

[49] Stephen Bailey, "The Berlin Strike of January 1918", *Central European History*, vol. 13, no. 2, 1980, pp. 158–74; Chickering, *Imperial Germany and the Great War*, pp. 153–8; Guillebaud, *The Works Council*, p. 3; Haydu, *Making American Industry Safe for Democracy*, pp. 24–7.

abdication of the Kaiser. The success of the Russian Revolution led those on the far left to see *soviets* or councils of soldiers, workers and peasants as ways of transferring power from the state to the proletariat. The SPD rejected this approach and preferred a democratic parliamentary system. They gained support in their struggle with the revolutionaries from the military, the civil servants of the former imperial government and employers. Employers had joined with unions on 15 November 1918 to counter radicals through the corporatist Stinnes-Legien Agreement, which recognised unions, endorsed collective bargaining and called for "workmen's committees" in every workplace of 50 employees or more with responsibility for administering collective bargaining agreements. Similar to Whitleyism, they set up a central Joint Industrial Alliance at the national and industry level to deal with issues of demobilisation, which overturned existing ADGB policy against forming joint organisations with employers. The Provisional Revolutionary Government, which was dominated by the SPD, issued a decree on 23 December 1919, upholding the principles of the Stinnes-Legien agreement, but calling for workers' committees or councils in all undertakings with 20 or more workers to promote a good understanding between employers and workers. A worker revolt in Berlin in January 1919 was crushed by an alliance between the SPD and the Freikorps, an anti-communist paramilitary force of returned soldiers, resulting in the deaths of the noted revolutionaries Liebknecht and Rosa Luxembourg. A similar alliance ended attempts to form soviet-style republics in Bavaria, producing 557 deaths between April 30 and May 8 1919.[50]

Against this background of upheaval and continued industrial unrest, the movement towards moderate works councils continued. Several German states, including Bavaria, passed works council legislation. Two collective agreements were to have a significant effect on future legislation. An agreement for the Central German coal miners on 12 March 1919 following a strike required employers to provide works councils with all information relating to the management of the enterprise subject to secrecy in regard to confidential information. An arbitral award for the Berlin metalworking industry on 19 April 1919 contained a similar provision but also allowed works councils to scrutinise the recruitment and dismissal of all waged and salaried staff. Union leaders, who saw them as potentially subversive of

---

[50] Marcel Berthelot, *Works Councils in Germany*, ILO, Studies and Reports Series B (Economic Conditions) No. 13, Geneva, 1924, p. 8; Bessel, *Germany after the First World War*, pp. 56, 143; Guillebaud, *The Works Council*, pp. 4–13; Haydu, *Making American Industry Safe for Democracy*, p. 32; ILO, *Works Councils in Germany*, Studies and Reports Series B No. 6, Geneva, 1921, p. 5; Pinson, *Modern Germany*, pp. 378–91; Weitz, *Weimar Germany*, pp. 16–29.

authority, endorsed works councils as a basis for "industrial democracy" with management at the ADGB Congress in July 1919 on the understanding that they could only be established in cooperation with trade unions. To weaken the appeal of the revolutionaries, the Weimar Convention adopted Article 165 of the new German constitution on 31 July 1919, which gave workers the right to "cooperate with equal rights in common with employers" for the regulation of wages and working conditions and the development of production through works councils in each enterprise.[51]

The German works councils were introduced by legislation passed by the new Weimar Republic in February 1920 following consultation with unions and employers. The legislation aimed to strengthen the shop floor power of trade unions at the expense of the splinter revolutionary works council movement of communists and independent socialists. The legislation provided for elected works stewards in workplaces with between 5 and 19 regular employees, with a minimum requirement of ten regular employees for agriculture and forestry, and works councils of elected employee representatives in workplaces with 20 or more regular workers. There was a general works council for all employees, and separate councils for manual workers and salaried employees in the same workplace. They were required to cooperate with employers in promoting production efficiency and industrial peace, and to raise worker grievances with management. They could influence the introduction of new methods of work, dismissals, occupational health and safety, and industrial welfare. Workers could appeal to their works council; for example, Section 84 of the legislation provided for appeal if there was suspicion that an employee was dismissed on the basis of gender, political, military, religious or trade union activities.[52] While there was no requirement for eligible voters or employee representatives to be union members, the works councils were viewed as "auxiliary to the trade unions."[53] In the elections, workers over 18 voted in a direct and secret ballot for one list of candidates; each trade union or group presented a list and the number of seats won was determined by proportional representation.[54]

---

[51] Berthelot, *Works Councils in Germany*, pp. 15–17; Guillebaud, *The Works Council*, pp. 9–13; Haydu, *Making American Industry Safe for Democracy*, p. 33; Memo, The Undersecretary of State in the German Chancellery, 5 Apr. 1919. Bundesarchiv, Berlin, Germany (hereafter BB), R/904/447; Typescript, "Niederschrift der Verhandlung über Beilegung des mitteldeutschen Generalstreiks am 5 Marz. 1919", BB, R/3901/3481.

[52] Moses, *Trade Unionism in Germany*, pp. 467–503.

[53] Eduard Bernstein, "The German Works Councils Act and its Significance", *International Labour Review*, vol. 1, no. 2, 1921, p. 35.

[54] Letter, A.F.L. Gordon to Dr Steinmann, 10 Jun. 1927. BB, R/3901/504; Boris Stern, *Works Council Movement in Germany*, United States Department of Labor, Washington, DC, 1925, p. 24.

Works councils were expected to see that any collective agreements entered into with trade unions were observed. Where there was no collective agreement, the works councils were required to consult with trade unions before entering into agreements with employers that involved fixing wages for example. Trade union representatives were allowed to participate but not to vote at works council meetings if a quarter of the representatives requested it. It was believed that union involvement would ensure that works councils did not degenerate into "industrial particularism," which fostered a corporate spirit that could be "anti-social" by damaging the national economy.[55]

The Weimar works councils could impact upon corporate governance. They interacted with management on two levels – local management and the Supervisory Board of the company. The executive of the works council were delegated to discuss issues with local management at an alternative meeting. At the Krupp steelworks in Essen, the issues discussed at these meetings ranged from the settlement of a wildcat strike to the firm's performance in an internationally competitive market.[56]

In 1922 the government enacted legislation in face of considerable opposition, particularly from the banking sector, to allow the works council representatives on the Supervisory Board. At Siemens, for example, two works councils representatives had the right to attend and vote at all meetings of the Supervisory Board to raise workers' interests and discuss general management issues. Under the German two-board system of governance, the Supervisory Board was less important than the Executive Committee, which consisted of full-time executives, but it could play an important role in crisis management and selecting managers.[57]

The counter-revolutionary aspect of the works councils appeased employers, who were concerned that the legislation would weaken Germany's post-war economic recovery and ability to pay reparations through interfering with workplace managerial prerogatives, such as the dismissal of staff.[58] Some employers, such as confectionary and chocolate manufacturers, saw advantages in the legislation as it "soaks away lasting unrest and disputes

---

[55] Bernstein, "The German Works Council", pp. 28, 30–1.

[56] Meeting of the Working Committee, 21 Jul. 1921 (WA60/19), 18 Oct. 1922, 23 Oct. 1922. WA41/6-165, Historisches Archiv Krupp, Essen (hereafter HAK).

[57] Chandler, *Scale and Scope*, p. 425; Guillebaud, *The Works Council*, pp. 188–91; ILO, *Studies on Industrial Relations I*, pp. 20–1.

[58] Berthelot, *Works Councils in Germany*, pp. 21–3; Petition to Members of the German National Assembly, 26 Sept. 1919. BB, R/43/1/2064; Leaflet, *Erklärung über Betriebsräte vom Hauptausschuss des Deutschen Industrie- und Handelstags abgegeben am 5 Juli 1919*. BB, R/3901/3492.

with the workforce."[59] The Krupp steelworks management had encouraged the election of a workers' council among its workforce before the legislation as an alternative to the radical soldiers and workers councils.[60]

One concern employers had with the works councils was the legislation's provision for the disclosure of company information to works councillors. Section 71 of the legislation required the employer to provide the works councils with access to information relating to all the firm's transactions which "affected the contract of employment or activities of the employees" as well as wage books and balance sheets. Employers were also required to provide the works councils with quarterly reports of the company's business. Employers saw this as an erosion of their managerial prerogatives and a threat to their commercial secrecy. The German banks were particularly concerned about the impact on the privacy of their clients' accounts. The SDP appeased employers by inserting a provision that required members of the works councils to preserve the secrecy of confidential matters.[61]

There were mixed reactions to the legislation among workers. Some opposed the "mutilated" works council legislation and the exclusion of some workers, such as agricultural employees, from its provisions.[62] Communists and USPD supporters staged a major protest outside the Reichstag on 13 January 1920, and the police fired on the crowd, killing 45 protesters. The USPD joined with the Conservatives to vote against the legislation. The DMV criticised the legislation as an obstacle to the German social revolution and called for further trade union action to achieve the establishment of revolutionary works councils. While the ADGB had concerns that the works councils would challenge trade union authority, it nevertheless considered them one of the main achievements of the German Revolution. The Christian and Hirsh-Dunker unions were generally more positive about the legislation, viewing works councils as a way to achieve more equitable collaboration with management.[63]

---

[59] Letter, Vereinigung Deutscher Zuckwaren und Schokolade Fabrikanten to the Minister for Labour, 7 Oct. 1919. BB, R/3901/3493.

[60] H.A. Krupp FAH. Memo from Fried. Krupp Co., Essen, 21 Mar. 1919 (Bestands- und Einzelsignatur, z.B. FAH 3 E 5 oder FAH 21/659), HAK.

[61] Berthelot, *Works Councils in Germany*, p. 22; Bernstein, "The German Works Council," p. 34; German Cabinet direction for German companies, 20 Jan. 1920. BB, R/43-I/2065.

[62] Telegram, Bismarkhuette Workers' Committee to Minister of Labour, 15 Jan. 1920. Typescript, Schwerin Trade Unions, "Resolution", 17 Jan. 1920. BB, R/3901/3496.

[63] *Beilage zum Monatsbericht* (Berlin), 14 Feb. 1920, pp. 1, 3; Bernstein, "The German Works Council," p. 26; Berthelot, *Works Councils in Germany*, pp. 24–8; McPherson, "Collaboration between Management and Employees in German Factories", pp. 60–5; *Metallarbeiter-Zeitung*, 17 Jan. 1920, p. 1; Moses, *Trade Unionism in Germany*, p. 319.

Union-Management Cooperation

Unlike the three previous forms of workplace employee representation, trade unions were the instigators of union-management cooperation works committees in the US. The AFL faced declining union membership and aggressive anti-union campaigns by employers, which included the establishment of ERPs, following the First World War. Following major strikes in 1919 and 1920 and the whipping up of a "Red Scare," the AFL wanted to challenge perceptions that it was irresponsible, emphasising that it wanted to increase production through scientific means and cooperation with management. The AFL found an ally in the Taylor Society, which championed scientific management but had shifted towards a view that some form of cooperation between organised labour and management was needed to increase industry efficiency. There were precedents for union-management cooperation in the building and clothing trades. There were also hopes for increased participation in management among railway unions following their experiences with the United States Railroad Administration (USRA), the nationalised US railway system 1917–20, which was sympathetic to unions. Railway labour, like the NUR in the UK, lobbied unsuccessfully for permanent nationalisation of the railways. Their Plumb Plan proposed a board of directors with equal representation from labour management and the public. Advocates of the Plumb Plan, who believed that it could be applied to all industry, drew links to guild socialism. Despite their failure, there was increased interest among union leaders and members in participating in management decisions.[64]

Union-management cooperation was promoted by civil servants such as Otto Beyer in agencies like the military arsenals and the USRA during and immediately after the First World War. Beyer, a mechanical engineer, worked in the iron and steel industry and the railways, and took his first management position in 1913, when he became general foreman of heavy repairs at a locomotive workshop of the Rock Island System Railroad in Horton, Kansas. On the outbreak of the First World War, he entered military service and was assigned to the US Army's Ordinance Department, where he was commissioned captain in January 1918. He became the director of the Arsenal Orders Branch of the Ordinance Department, and remained

[64] Mark Hendrickson, *American Labor and Economic Citizenship: New Capitalism from World War I to the Great Depression*, Cambridge University Press, Cambridge, 2013, p. 142; Sanford Jacoby, "Union-Management Cooperation in the United States: Lessons from the 1920s", *Industrial and Labor Relations Review*, vol. 37, no. 1, 1983, pp. 18–24; Patmore, "Industrial Democracy", p. 365; David Vrooman, *Daniel Willard and Progressive Management on the Baltimore & Ohio Railroad*, Ohio State University Press, Columbus, 1991, pp. 38–9.

in that post until 1919. At the unionised Rock Island Arsenal, Illinois, where his programme originated, he introduced cooperative labour management committees to deal with working conditions, piecework rates and production methods. He intended to improve efficiency by working with unions rather than undermining them, and believed his ideas could be extended to other organised industries such as the railways. By the mid-1920s Beyer was working as an industrial relations consultant and technical advisor for AFL's Railway Employees Department. He was a member of the Taylor Society and strongly influenced by Whitleyism.[65]

While the AFL saw Whitleyism as an endorsement of unionism as a cornerstone of industrial relations, it had concerns. Samuel Gompers, AFL President, believed that committees at the workplace level would take action independently of the union, undermine union authority, exacerbate strife with employers and lead to "demoralization." Any workplace scheme involving union-management cooperation therefore had to be an extension of existing union organisation and not independently elected by employees at the workplace.[66] Beyer supported Gompers's view, arguing that if the committees were independent of unions, the scheme would lose its "vital essence" and take on the "anemic complexion" of an ERP.[67]

The Beyer Plan of union-management cooperation promoted unionism and collective bargaining. On the basis of a collective agreement, union representatives and managers met together on committees to discuss a range of issues that could eliminate waste, improve productivity and enhance safety. Wages and working conditions were left to the regular negotiations between the company and the unions. Under this scheme, management were to accept trade unions as necessary and constructive to the running of their enterprise, while unions agreed to go beyond their traditional concerns with collective bargaining and assist companies in the marketing of their services and the winning of government contracts. The committees also had other

[65] Otto S. Beyer, "Efficiency through Democracy in the Railway Industry of America", Typescript, 8 Apr. 1919. File – "Scientific Management", Container 64, Otto S. Beyer Papers, MS12633, Library of Congress, Washington, DC (hereafter BP); Hendrickson, *American Labor and Economic Citizenship*, p. 143; Gregory Field, "Designing the Capital-Labour Accord. Railway Labour, the State and the Beyer Plan for Union-Management Co-operation", *Journal of Management History*, vol. 1, no. 2, 1995, pp. 26–8; Joseph McCartin, *Labor's Great War: The Struggle for Industrial Democracy and the Origins of Modern American Labor Relations, 1912–1921*, The University of Carolina Press, Chapel Hill, 1997, pp. 211–12; Louis Wood, *Union-Management Co-operation on the Railroads*, Yale University Press, New Haven, 1931, pp. 81–4.

[66] *AF*, Oct. 1917, pp. 854–6; Letter, Samuel Gompers to Benita D. Berg, 23 Jan. 1920 in Peter J. Albert and Grace Palladino (eds.), *The Samuel Gompers Papers, Volume 11: The Postwar Years, 1918–21*, University of Illinois Press, Urbana and Chicago, 2008, p. 244.

[67] Otto Beyer, "B&O Engine 1003", *Survey Graphic*, vol. 4, no. 4, 1924, p. 313.

objectives, including the stabilisation of employment and sharing the gains of cooperation. Employees did not generally elect their representatives on these union-management committees directly. Given the AFL's concerns about unofficial rank-and-file action and ERPs, the current union workplace representatives served as the employee representatives on the cooperative committees. The work of the committees was done on company time with no impact on the wages of employee members and management provided the venue for the meetings. Beyond the workshops, there was provision under the Beyer Plan for regular meetings of union representatives and management on a regional- and/or company-wide basis to review the progress of the works committees and discuss issues of importance for the whole railway not covered by collective bargaining.[68] The AFL was reluctant to allow management to pay union representatives' expenses, including time lost, at these regional and company-wide meetings for, as in the ERPs, this would compromise the independence of the representatives, who would lose "full control" of the scheme.[69]

While the Beyer Plan for union-management cooperation stalled during the economic downturn that followed the First World War, Beyer gained the support of William Johnston, the President of the International Association of Machinists (IAM), a strong advocate of industrial democracy and the Plumb Plan, and Daniel Willard, President of the B&O, which had 59,000 employees in March 1921 and extensive employee welfare programmes. It also had precursors to the cooperative committees, which included safety committees, that dated from 1911, cooperative claim prevention committees to reduce loss or damage to freight shipments and open staff meetings. Willard, who had been a railway union member and had worked his way up through the management hierarchy, was sympathetic to unions. With the assistance of Justice Louis Brandeis of the US Supreme Court and Commissioner Mark Potter of the Interstate Commerce Commission, they commenced discussions about the introduction of union-management co-operation on the B&O in April 1922.[70]

While Willard was initially dubious about the proposal, even seeing the proposal initially as an attempt to establish a *soviet* in the B&O, assured that the unions did not want to challenge managerial authority but to help

---

[68] Otto Beyer, "Union-Management Cooperation in the Railroad Industry", *Proceedings of the Academy of Political Science*, vol. 13, no. 1, 1928, pp. 124–7; Wood, *Union-Management Co-operation on the Railroad*, pp. 106–9, 113–15.

[69] Letter, B.M. Jewell to J. Corbett, 27 Sept. 1927. File – "Correspondence, 1927", Container 70, BP.

[70] Hendrickson, *American Labor and Economic Citizenship*, p. 144; Typescript, "Report on the Activities of O.S. Beyer Jnr. and the Baltimore and Ohio Railroad". File – "Co-operative Plan. Development. Ca. 1921–1928", Container 97, BP; Vrooman, *Daniel Willard*, pp. 36–9.

Daniel Willard
(Courtesy of B&O
Museum Archives)

management, he saw the value of allowing workers to suggest improvements
that would increase the efficiency of the company.[71] Willard saw particular
problems in raising rates due to competition with other railroads such
as the Pennsylvania Railroad and believed that the B&O operated at a
disadvantage due to the mountainous terrain it covered. As he later noted,
the scheme "will eventually bring about economies in operation which ought
to be reflected in an enlarged net operating income ..."[72] Following the defeat
of the unions in the 1922 national Railway Shopmen's Strike, which showed
Willard in a positive light as he broke from other employers and signed
a union contract, the B&O workshop cooperative committees were first
introduced at the Glenwood railway workshops in Pittsburgh in February
1923. Willard became an active promoter of union-management cooperation
through public addresses and private correspondence.[73]

[71] Typescript, "Address by Mr. Daniel Willard, President, the Baltimore Railroad
Company before the National Civic Federation New York". File – "Willard, Daniel.
Statements. ca. 1923–1931", Container 105, BP.
[72] Letter from Daniel Willard to Otto Beyer, 21 May 1924. File – "Wage Increases.
1923–1929", Container 105, BP.
[73] Vrooman, *Daniel Willard*, pp. 9, 41–51.

Mount Clare
(Courtesy of B&O Museum Archives)

The union-management cooperation scheme came under attack from employers and within the labour movement. Noel Sargent, Secretary of the Employment Relations Committee of the NAM, questioned the sincerity of the AFL's desire to increase efficiency and production output, arguing in 1925 that organised labour disliked scientific management and that it had not rejected restrictive production practices. From the left of the labour movement, groups such as the Communist Trade Union Educational League and the IWW, came accusations that union leaders were involved in class collaboration and the betrayal of workers. There were concerns that the scheme's preoccupation with efficiency would undermine the bargaining position of skilled workers. Of particular concern was the AFL's opposition to allowing rank-and-file workers to direct representation through election onto the works committees, which led to complaints that union-management cooperation was a top-down approach imposed on workers.[74]

[74] *Bulletin of the Taylor Society*, vol. 10, no. 3, 1925, pp. 49–51; Jacoby, "Union-Management Cooperation", pp. 25–6, 30; Wood, *Union-Management Co-operation on the Railroads*, pp. 106–7, 128–30.

Conclusion

In examining the origins of these various schemes of employee representation, there is support for the argument that employers have adopted a cyclical approach to representation, driven by their perceptions of economic, political and industrial threats to their authority. The Whitley works committees arose against a background of wartime industrial unrest and growth of workplace rank-and-file movements that also challenged unions and the state. Similar wartime pressures arose in Germany with the added prospect of an overthrow of capitalism following the November 1918 Revolution. While the ERPs arose from the particular circumstances of CF&I, the Rockefeller family faced the threat of adverse public relations and federal government intervention in CF&I's labour relations following the Ludlow Massacre. Union-management cooperation differs from the other schemes in that it was union-initiated, but reflects the crisis the AFL was facing following the First World War in terms of public sympathy and growing employer hostility.

While the ERPs were specifically designed to avoid union representation, works councils and works committees were parallel structures to union organisation, with non-unionists participating in the election process and potentially winning positions on the works councils/committees. The union-management cooperation works committees did not in principle provide for direct elections and were an extension of existing union workplace representation. While the German works councils were required by law, the British government encouraged works committees on a voluntary basis, with the exception of railways. The ERPs were employer initiatives and union-management cooperation committees were union initiatives without state intervention. Employers met the costs of all these schemes in terms of the representatives' lost wages and the location of the meetings. While employers were represented on Whitley works committees and ERPs, they did not sit on the German works councils. These various dimensions of the concepts are summarised in Table 3.1.

While none of the schemes challenged fundamental managerial prerogatives, the German works councils had access to confidential company information and oversight over management's policies regarding the termination of employees. They could all assist management in improving workplace efficiency. While those schemes that supplemented union organisation were not allowed to engage in matters covered by collective bargaining between unions and employers, the ERP could in principle cover all issues relating to wages and conditions given the absence of an external collective agreement.

Table 3.1 ERPs, Whitley Works Committees, German Works Councils and Union-Management Cooperation Committees

Form	Mandated or voluntary	Employer funded	Relationship to unions	Participation of non-unionists	Employer reps.	Direct election
ERPs	Voluntary	Yes	Avoidance	Yes	Yes	Yes
Whitley works committees	Voluntary (with the exception of railways)	Yes	Supplements	Yes	Yes	Yes
German works councils 1920 legislation	Mandated	Yes	Supplements	Yes	No	Yes
Union-management cooperation works committees	Voluntary	Yes	Supplements	No	Yes	No

Source: Patmore, "Unionism and Non-Union Employee Representation", p. 534.

The next five chapters will examine the extent and impact of these schemes in the US, UK, Germany, Canada and Australia respectively. None of the schemes lived up to the expectations of their promoters; the Wagner Act outlawed ERPs in the US and the Nazis revoked the works council legislation in Germany. Some organisations persisted with some schemes and their variants through the interwar period despite their general demise. There was general interest in looking at all these concepts, irrespective of their national origins.

4

The US

This chapter examines the extent and impact of ERPs and union-management cooperation committees in the US in the period from 1914 to the country's entry into the Second World War. While union-management cooperation committees only gained limited support from employers, ERPs spread dramatically and by 1934 were challenging unions in terms of coverage. While ERPs were an important anti-union device for employers, there is evidence that they could give workers a voice and allow them to gain concessions from management even though the latter had the right of veto. Later, legislative changes to US labour law in the 1930s led to the virtual demise of ERPs and reduced union interest in promoting union-management cooperation committees.

ERP – The Extent

The Rockefeller Plan spread to other companies. In the decade after the Ludlow Massacre, JDR Jr. promoted his Plan through publications and public speaking. He also encouraged the extension of ERPs to companies in which the Rockefeller family had substantial interests, such as Standard Oil of New Jersey, which had two major violent strikes at its Bayonne refinery in 1915 and 1916. Clarence Hicks, who had played an important role for Rockefeller in implementing the ERP at CF&I, transferred to Standard Oil to implement the ERP there. The Standard Oil ERP adopted in 1918 was part of an elaborate programme of personnel management that included extensive company welfare benefits and the assumption of many of the supervisors' powers by industrial relations specialists. Although a Standard Oil executive, Hicks acted as a consultant to other oil companies interested in introducing similar ERPs. Progressive employers borrowed and modified the Rockefeller Plan. Arthur Young, a former employee of CF&I, and Mackenzie King drew up a modified ERP for International

Harvester. William Dickson, Vice-President of the Midvale Steel Company in Pennsylvania, consulted with CF&I management before borrowing the ERP with modifications in September 1918. That same year, Bethlehem Steel employed Mackenzie King and Ivy Lee, Rockefeller's former publicity agent, to develop and promote an ERP. The SCC, which was linked to Rockefeller interests and included companies such as Bethlehem Steel, International Harvester, Goodyear Rubber Tire and Rubber, General Electric and GM, saw ERPs as the cornerstone of their industrial relations philosophy.[1]

The US' entry into the First World War in April 1917 assisted the spread of ERPs. War production and a decline in net immigration led to labour shortages. There was labour unrest due to inflation and a deterioration of shop floor conditions. Labour turnover doubled, strikes dramatically increased and union membership grew, with the AFL undertaking major organising drives. President Wilson established the National War Labor Board (NWLB) in 1918 to settle industrial disputes that could hamper war production. It upheld workers' right to organise trade unions without interference from employers. However, it only compelled management to negotiate with shop committees consisting of company employees and not independent trade unions. Wartime government agencies such as the Shipbuilding Labor Adjustment Board, the USRA and the US Fuel Administration also encouraged shop committees. The wartime sentiment that favoured making the world "safe for democracy" led to an increase in public opinion favouring industrial democracy at home. Management wanted to obtain employee goodwill and minimise the intervention of the state and trade unions. Management's reliance on the drive system was no longer effective. Business also feared the growing appeal to workers of radical alternatives such as IWW and the success of the Russian Revolution.[2] Cyrus McCormick Jr., the President of International Harvester, noted in 1919 that the American people were concerned that their "country is about to deliver

---

[1] Stuart Chase, *A Generation of Industrial Peace: Thirty Years of Labor Relations at Standard Oil Company (N.J.)*, Standard Oil Company, 1947, pp. 9–10; Raymond Fosdick, *John D. Rockefeller, Jr.: A Portrait*, Harper & Brothers, New York, 1956, chap. 9; Hicks, *My Life in Industrial Relations*, pp. 52–9; Haydu, *Making American Industry Safe for Democracy*, 67–8; Hogler and Greiner, *Employee Participation*, pp. 37–9; Hogle, "The Rockefeller Plan", p. 310; Jacoby, Employing Bureaucracy, pp. 180–1; Kaufman, "Accomplishments and Shortcomings", pp. 22–9; Nelson, "Employee Representation", p. 376; Robert Ozanne, *A Century of Labor-Management Relations at McCormick and International Harvester*, University of Wisconsin Press, Madison, 1967, p. 117.

[2] Gerald Eggert, *Steelmasters and Labor Reform*, 1886–1923, University of Pittsburgh Press, Pittsburgh, 1981, pp. 108–9; Fairris, "From Exit to Voice", pp. 505–7; Kaufman, "Accomplishments and Shortcomings", p. 23; Sumner Slichter, "The Current Labor Policies of American Industries", *The Quarterly Journal of Economics*, vol. 43, no. 3, 1929, pp. 395–6.

itself to Bolshevism" and argued that ERPs were a "saner method by which the legitimate desires of the workmen for self-expression may be granted without at the same time completely ruining our present industrial fabric."[3]

ERPs flourished during 1918–19. Of the 225 plans surveyed in 1919 by the NICB, 120 were created through the intervention of the federal government and 125 were voluntarily introduced by companies. Employers saw ERPs as a welcome substitute for collective bargaining with unions. Midvale Steel introduced its plan after the IAM began organising its employees in April 1918. It rejected a proposed union contract and intervention by the NWLB. The federal government also applied pressure through Secretary of the Navy Josephus Daniels, who was "surprised and somewhat disturbed" that Midvale Steel had refused to cooperate with the NWLB. The Midvale plan, which was ultimately sanctioned by the WLB, thwarted the IAM organising campaign and frustrated any attempt by the NWLB to force the company to negotiate with the union. Labour concerns over the Midvale plan were heightened in August 1919, when a convention of 93 Midvale employee representatives in Atlantic City condemned worker demands for shorter hours and higher wages to meet the high cost of living as "uneconomic and unwise." Major employers made their stand clear at two national industrial conferences to consider the post-war world, organised by President Wilson in October and December 1919 against the background of a major steel strike organised by the AFL, when they rejected the right of unions to organise and collectively bargain, preferring no organisation at all or ERPs.[4]

The end of the First World War did not inhibit the further growth of ERPs during the 1920s. As Table 4.1 indicates, while the number of companies with ERPs or a company union declined in the late 1920s, the number of employees covered by the ERPs continued to increase and ERPs' significance was greater than their coverage. Although state intervention in US industrial relations was wound back and the trade union challenge diminished, employers continued to see ERPs as a valuable union-avoidance device and a way of maintaining communication with employees

---

[3] Cyrus McCormick, "Employees' Representation: Cooperation and Industrial Progress", in *National Safety Council, Advance Copy of Papers to be Presented before the Employees' Represen-tation Section of the National Safety Council Eighth Annual Safety Congress. Cleveland. October 1–4, 1919*, National Safety Council, 1919, p. 4.

[4] David Brody, *Labor in Crisis: The Steel Strike of 1919*, J.B. Lippincott, Philadelphia, 1965, pp. 115–27; United States Department of Labor, *Proceedings of the First Industrial Conference (Called by the President) October 6 to 23 1919*, Government Printing Office, Washington, DC, 1919, pp. 155–62, 250–2, 266–8, 283: Eggert, *Steelmasters*, pp. 103–27; Hogler and Greiner, *Employee Participation*, pp. 29–31, 36–9; McCartin, *Labor's Great War*, pp. 191–4; Philip Taft, *The A.F. of L. in the Time of Gompers*, Harper & Brothers, New York, 1957, pp. 399–400; *The Amalgamated Journal* (hereafter *AJ*), 18 Sept. 1919, p. 8.

Table 4.1 Employee Representation in the US, 1919–32

	1919	1922	1924	1926	1928	1932
Companies with ERPs	145	385	421	432	399	313
Total employees Covered	403,765	690,000	1,240,704	1,369,078	1,547,766	1,263,194
Average number of employees per ERP	2,785	1,792	2,947	3,169	3,879	4,036

Source: NICB, *Collective Bargaining through Employee Representation*, New York, 1933, p. 16.

in large-scale organisations. There was a radical shift in the relative strength of the ERPs compared to trade unions. ERP employee coverage as a percentage of trade union membership grew from 10 per cent in 1919 to 45 per cent in 1928. They were concentrated in strategic sectors of the economy, particularly large manufacturing firms in mass-production industries, and of the labour movement, particularly the strike-prone metal trades. They were more common in larger firms. In 1929, 2.5 per cent of firms with less than 250 employees and 9 per cent of firms with more than 250 employees had ERPs. As Table 4.1 highlights, the average number of employees covered by ERPs grew from 2,785 in 1919 to 3,879 in 1928.[5]

The onset of the Great Depression was a setback for ERPs as companies tried to reduce costs. As Table 4.1 indicates, between 1928 and 1932 there was an 18 per cent decline in the number of workers covered by ERPs and a 22 per cent fall in the number of ERPs. The remaining ERPs lost funding or became inactive. The Industrial Assembly at Goodyear did almost nothing in the five years after 1929. At International Harvester, funding was cut and meetings degenerated into lengthy discussions on trivial issues. Despite these financial stringencies, ERPs remained useful for employers in ratifying wage reductions, work time-sharing or rationing and even retrenchment. There were also legal setbacks in the railroads when the US Supreme Court upheld the Railway Labor Act in the *Railway Clerks* case of 1930, in which a company union was disestablished on the Texas and New Orleans Railway.[6]

[5] Haydu, *Making American Industry Safe for Democracy*, p. 79; Jacoby, *Employing Bureaucracy*, p. 191; Patmore, "Employee Representation Plans", p. 48.

[6] Jacoby, *Employing Bureaucracy*, p. 221; NICB, *Collective Bargaining through Employee*

The economic stimulus provided by President Roosevelt's NIRA in June 1933 encouraged a resurgence of ERPs, however. The NIRA recognised that workers had the right to bargain and organise collectively through their own representatives without employer interference. Unionism took off and employers rushed to set up plans to stop unions organising in their workplaces. Employers, such as Walter Teagle, the President of Standard Oil of New Jersey, and employer organisations, such as the American Institute of Iron and Steel, argued that ERPs were legitimate under the NIRA and superior to AFL unions. US Steel established ERPs in all its mills and mines in June 1933 with no worker involvement in their formulation or introduction. James Rose found that the first elected employee representatives at US Steel's Duquesne plant did not represent a "cross section of the mill's workforce," as they tended to be highly paid workers such as skilled tonnage men, skilled tradesmen and clerical workers and to have close ties to management. The representatives did not reflect the racial diversity of the mill as no Afro-Americans ever served on the ERP. While a rudimentary form of collective bargaining developed in the ERPs at US Steel, critics condemned these plans as "sham organizations" that impeded economic recovery. The number of workers covered by ERPs grew from 1.8 million in 1934 to 2.5 million in 1935.[7] ERPs reached their peak by 1934 when, according to Brody, "they covered probably three million workers, more than did the unions ..."[8]

There were variations on the Rockefeller Plan. The Leitch Plan mirrored the US political system. Workers elected delegates to a House of Representatives. Management appointed a Senate from the ranks of supervisors and a Cabinet, which consisted of executive officers. The Cabinet could veto initiatives coming from the Congress, but a two-thirds majority in both houses could overturn the veto, which may have been unlikely given the composition of the Senate. In contrast to the Rockefeller Plan, the Leitch Plan allowed workers to hold separate meetings rather than joint meetings. The Bethlehem Steel Corporation ERP also allowed worker representatives to meet separately as a group as well as serving on joint committees with

Representation, pp. 14–18; Patmore, "The Origins of Federal Industrial Relations Systems", pp. 163–4.

[7] American Iron and Steel Institute, *Collective Bargaining in the Steel Industry*, New York, 1934; Berstein, *The New Deal*, chap. 4; Kaufman, "Accomplishments and Shortcomings", pp. 24–6; Patmore, "The Origins of Federal Industrial Relations Systems", p. 164: James Rose, *Duquesne and the Rise of Steel Unionism*, University of Illinois Press, Urbana and Chicago, 2001, chap. 4: Walter Teagle, *Employee Representation and Collective Bargaining*, no publisher, 1933, pp. 8–9.

[8] David Brody, *Labor Embattled History, Power, Rights*, University of Illinois Press, Urbana and Chicago, 2005, p. 52.

management. One major US company that adopted the Leitch Plan in 1919, Goodyear, viewed the plan as a means of creating an "Industrial Republic."[9]

There were generally restrictions on who could stand for the committees in annual elections, including age, length of service, American citizenship and journeyman status, which favoured long-standing employees who were known to management.[10] These requirements were justified by the "supposed parallel between employee representation and civil government" and reflected the "wave of antipathy toward everything foreign" and enthusiasm for "100 per cent Americanism so widespread during and shortly after the World War."[11] A typical example is the International Harvester Plan, which specified that "only employees who are citizens of the United States, twenty-one years or over, and have been continuously in the Works' service for one year immediately prior to nomination" were eligible for election to the committee.[12] These rules could be tightened if management perceived a threat to its authority. In the middle of a dispute over wage reductions at CF&I, management obtained permission from employee and management representatives in December 1921 to change the eligibility rules for employee representatives from three to twelve months' employment. The employee representative now also had to be a US citizen and over 21. This reduced the threat of outside agitators becoming employee representatives.[13]

While there was interest in Whitley and German works councils,[14] employers and commentators generally dismissed them as inappropriate for US conditions. Influential US economist Waddill Catchings[15] argued that Whitleyism was an extension of the British labour movement and inappropriate for the US industry, where large numbers of workers were unorganised and there was a desire in firms such as Standard Oil New Jersey to "develop a common enterprise."[16] Cyrus McCormick from International

---

[9] Department of Manufacture, Chamber of Commerce of the United States, *Employee Representation or Work Councils*, Washington, DC, 1927, pp. 14–19; Hogler and Greiner, *Employee Participation*, pp. 17–18; Paul Litchfield, *The Industrial Republic*, Goodyear, Akron, Ohio, 1919; *The Iron Age*, 14 Jun. 1923, p. 1692.

[10] David Fairris, *Shopfloor Matters: Labor-Management Relations in Twentieth-Century American Manufacturing*, Routledge, London, 1997, p. 34; Carrol French, *The Shop Committee in the United States*, Johns Hopkins Press, Baltimore, 1923, pp. 40–1; Jacoby, *Employing Bureaucracy*, p. 188.

[11] Ernest Burton, *Employee Representation*, Williams & Wilkins, Baltimore, 1926, p. 113.

[12] International Harvester Company, Harvester Industrial Council, Chicago, 1919, p. 7.

[13] Patmore, "Employee Representation Plans at the Minnequa Steelworks", p. 854.

[14] E.g. *AF*, Feb. 1921, pp. 116–21; Bureau of Industrial Research, *The Industrial Council Plan in Great Britain*, Washington, DC, 1919; *NYT*, 22 June 1919, p. 53

[15] Hendrickson, *American Labor and Economic Citizenship*, p. 130.

[16] Waddill Catchings, *Our Common Enterprise: A Way Out for Labor and Capital*, Pollack Foundation for Economic Research, Newton, 1922, p. 20.

Harvester went even further and argued that Whitleyism had "organised British industry into two opposing camps, whereas the American system of employee representation is based solely on mutual cooperation" and proclaimed that "class prejudice has no place in this country."[17] JDR Jr. praised Whitleyism for uniting organisations of "Labor and Capital by a bond of common interest in a common venture," then drew favourable comparisons with the non-union ERPs at Standard Oil of New Jersey and C&FI.[18] Walter Gordon Merritt, a notable corporate labour lawyer, praised the German works councils for creating goodwill and a "desire for successful cooperation" between labour and capital, but noted that "it was a great tribute to the genius of the American people, with their spirit of individualism and independence" that ERPs developed in the US without government guidance and intervention as in Germany and elsewhere.[19] Despite Merritt's claim, the US federal government was interested in German works councils and the American Consul General in Berlin forwarded a report on works councils to the US Department of Labor in January 1933.[20]

ERP – The Impact

What did these ERPs do? Some were little more than advisory bodies with little or no authority. As Kaufman notes, "meetings in the less successful ones degenerated into forums for making announcements or consideration of minutiae."[21] Others had a final say over dismissals and seats on the board of directors. At the Union Construction Company, a shipbuilder in Oakland, California, the works committee formed by management in 1920 discussed working hours, the banning of pedlars in the workplace, the cleaning up of the garbage dump, the formation of a hospital committee and social events such as a "smoker." While the works committee was empowered to settle grievances between workers and their supervisors, management gave it no role in the decision to cut wages undertaken in 1921. Some companies, such as Bethlehem Steel and International Harvester, used their ERPs to reduce costs by suggesting ways of saving labour time and materials through, for example, the relocation of tool rooms and increasing the value of scrap by adopting better sorting methods.[22]

---

[17] McCormick, "Employees' Representation", p. 11.

[18] Rockefeller, *Representation in Industry*, pp. 18, 20.

[19] Walter Gordon Merritt, *The Four C's of Industry*, League for Industrial Rights, New York, 1923, pp. 10–11.

[20] Raymond H. Geist, "Employees' Councils in Germany", typescript, Berlin, 1933. HD 5655 G3U5, United States Department of Labor Library, Washington, DC (hereafter DLL).

[21] Kaufman, "Accomplishments and Shortcomings", p. 31.

[22] Kaufman, "Accomplishments and Shortcomings", pp. 31–2; Sumner Slichter, "The

The committees at the CF&I Pueblo steelworks dealt with a range of issues. A joint conference of 36 employee representatives and 36 management representatives was held in February 1918. CF&I President Jesse Floyd Welborn chaired the meeting and a management representative acted as secretary. The issues discussed included the employment of returned soldiers, the company magazine and concerns about the conduct of the recent election for representatives from the wire mill. Some workers were taking ballot papers from immigrant workers to multiple vote for their preferred candidates. In March and April 1918 there were four specialist joint committees: industrial cooperation and conciliation; safety and accidents; sanitation, health and housing; and recreation and education. They met separately once a month and were chaired by a management representative. The industrial cooperation and conciliation committee dealt with issues such as lockers, drinking water systems and mail. In the context of the First World War, one representative was concerned about the disloyal sentiments of particular employees. While the manager requested that employees inform him of any disloyal acts, he advised against hasty actions that could have unjust consequences for fellow employees. While the safety and accidents committee dealt with issues such as lighting, safe handling practices and dangers such as falling coal, the sanitation, health and housing committee dealt with the water supply, housing, medical services and laundry facilities. The recreation and education committee dealt with education programmes, the steelworks band and sporting activities. The ERP did generally improve working conditions in the plant through the construction of large modern washhouses with toilet facilities and the installation of drinking fountains.[23]

The ERP became a mechanism for changes in wages and conditions at the Pueblo steelworks. Its relative isolation weakened industrial militancy and encouraged an acceptance of the ERP in the absence of an independent union. The steelworks' average payroll peaked in 1920 at 7,783 employees. Pueblo had comparatively fewer immigrant workers than other US steel plants and American-born workers formed a slight majority of workers at the plant between 1915 and 1920. CF&I particularly employed immigrant workers as unskilled labour. From 1915 to 1920, there was a surge in Mexican workers at the plant, growing from 8 per cent of the workforce in 1915 to 39.4 per cent in 1920. The category "Mexican" in the plant's data is misleading as 10 per cent were born in the US. Given that at

---

Current Labor Policies", pp. 401–2; Union Construction Co. Weekly Letter to Craft Representatives, 13 Feb. 1920. Works Committee Minutes, 3 Feb. 1920, 20 Feb. 1920. HD 5653 U5, DLL; *Way and Works* (Union Construction Co.), 16 Jul. 1921, p. 1, 30 Apr. 1921, p. 1.

[23] Patmore, "Employee Representation Plans at the Minnequa Steelworks", p. 851.

Pueblo Steelworks
(Courtesy of Steelworks Center of the West, Pueblo Colorado)

least 60 per cent of these workers did not speak English, their voice was
limited in an ERP that communicated in English. Mexicans remained
an important component of the Pueblo workforce, constituting a third of
the total workforce in January 1927. CF&I began to develop its welfare
strategy with the YMCA opening a clubhouse at the steel plant in March
1920 which included a bowling alley, cafeteria, swimming pool, library,
gymnasium and soda fountain. There was a separate building for African
American workers called the "Colored Y," which also became the focal
point of Pueblo's African American population.[24]

Following frequent requests by employee representatives over several years
and conferences between company officials and employee representatives,
the shift at CF&I was reduced from 12 to eight hours on 1 November
1918, which led to increases in productivity, and the hourly tonnage and
piece rates were increased by 10 per cent. Though CF&I steelworkers' and
miners' wages were linked under the ERP to CF&I's competitors, the
miners had the advantage that their rates were determined by collective
agreement negotiated between the UMWA and major coal companies while
the steelworkers' wages were determined by reference to the non-unionised
United States Steel Corporation.[25]

---

[24] Patmore, "Employee Representation Plans at the Minnequa Steelworks", pp. 847–8.
[25] Patmore, "Employee Representation Plans at the Minnequa Steelworks", pp. 851–2.

In the wake of the 1919 steel strike and the defeat of the unions at Pueblo and elsewhere, David Brody generally noted that steel companies in the US, "having booted out the agitators, were eager to restore good feelings."[26] CF&I senior management took a more sympathetic view of their employees and the ERP, believing that with the defeat of unionisation the representatives had no alternative but to support the ERP. In February 1920, it allowed a joint committee of representatives and management to visit steel plants in the eastern states to investigate wage increases as a prelude to granting wage increases. This met a long-standing criticism of the representatives that they could not contribute to the adjustments of wage rates at the plant because they did not know what was going on elsewhere. Senior management also showed a greater willingness to reverse the decisions of supervisors following complaints by the employee representatives.[27] Social researcher Mary Van Kleeck,[28] investigating the Pueblo ERP, noted in February 1921 that, despite the union defeat, the 1919 steel strike "put more power into the hands of the workers and they are expressing it through the plan."[29]

While workers made some gains through employee representation at Pueblo, management still asserted its authority on crucial issues such as general pay and promotion. In January 1920, the company asked the Pueblo workers to accept a 20 per cent wage cut due to the recession. Employee representatives argued that this was too severe and requested a 15 per cent cut, which management accepted. The representatives said that they could make up the other 5 per cent by increased efficiency and elimination of waste. Two employee representatives did argue that the workers in their sections of the Pueblo plant believed that there should be no cuts in their wage rates, but accepted the majority view. There were further cuts of 15 per cent in August 1921 following more discussions with employee representatives and 10 per cent in January 1922. Employee representatives initially rejected the 10 per cent cut. Only after management began to issue dismissal notices and threatened to place the remaining staff on short time, did the employee representatives agree. As noted previously, management also tightened the eligibility rules for employee representatives during this dispute to reduce the threat of outside agitators becoming employee representatives.[30] Hogle

[26] David Brody, *Steelworkers in America: The Nonunion Era*. Harper & Row, New York, 1969, p. 264.

[27] Patmore, "Employee Representation Plans at the Minnequa Steelworks", p. 854.

[28] Hendrickson, *American Labor and Economic Citizenship*, pp. 154–60.

[29] Letter, Van Kleeck to Glenn, 27 Feb. 1921. MVKRP, Box 19, Folder 9.

[30] Patmore, "Employee Representation Plans at the Minnequa Steelworks", p. 854.

notes, "Without a union, they could not strike. They had no independent treasury or strike fund."[31]

Senior CF&I management also insisted that promotion be by merit rather than seniority. In March 1924, the six employee and six management representatives on the Joint Committee on Cooperation, Conciliation and Wages unanimously ranked one first helper over two others based on strict seniority. His supervisor, however, considered this worker less efficient than the others. CF&I President Welborn considered this ruling to have gone far beyond what management had considered appropriate for adjudication by the joint committees and ruled that the "direction of working forces" rests "unquestionably" with "managing officers."[32]

By 1927, the ERP at the CF&I steelworks was institutionalising conflict between employees and management rather than producing mutual understanding. Despite management's objections, representatives also began to meet independently of management on a regular monthly basis to consider issues as a "body."[33] They elected their own chair, vice-chair and secretary and invited management to discuss important issues. As noted previously, the ERP never assumed that the employee representatives would act collectively. The *Industrial Bulletin* published the minutes of these meetings as well as those of the joint committees. While management did edit out questionable material in the published minutes of all meetings, the airing of employee representatives' grievances before they were heard by the joint committees exacerbated the criticism of management, who did not have right of reply. In contrast to the mining camps, there was "legalistic wrangling" over the meaning of the ERP and employee representatives threatened to appeal against plant management to Welborn and Rockefeller. Local management believed it did not have the backing of senior management in dealing with the representatives and that the representatives could "wear down" local management in long and exhausting meetings. However, local management continued to emphasise that the ERP was subordinate to managerial prerogative and the requirements of steel plant operations.[34]

Tensions between the representatives and CF&I further flared during the economic downturn of the Great Depression, which hit the company severely. It went into receivership from August 1933 until July 1936. Renamed the Colorado Fuel and Iron Corporation, it emerged from the receivership with a reduced debt. Employment dropped to an average payroll of 2,924 in

[31] Hogle, "The Rockefeller Plan", 280.

[32] Minutes of meetings between Arthur Young, Dr Elton Mayo and R.J. McCutcheon on 15 Oct. 1928 and subsequent days. Box 3B, Folder 18. EMP.

[33] Letter, Elton Mayo to Arthur Woods, 20 November 1928. Box 3B, Folder 19. EMP.

[34] Patmore, "Employee Representation Plans at the Minnequa Steelworks", p. 857.

1932. The company newspaper, *The Blast*, published letters praising the ERP for assisting the company's economic survival by encouraging workers to raise grievances and allowing management to settle those complaints that had merit. The receiver's economy measures included shutting the YCMA clubhouse building, discontinuing employee group insurance and cutting company pensions. Andrew Diamond, chair of the employee representatives at the Pueblo steelworks and employed in the rod mill, was angered that the representatives learnt about the receivership in the press despite management's promise that they would be kept informed. Diamond had publicly supported the Rockefeller Plan, arguing that employee representation created better morale among employees and cooperation by fostering closer contact between workers and management. At a meeting of steel representatives with the receiver on 10 August, Diamond claimed that JDR Jr. would not "stand for" the closure of the YMCA building and would intervene to stop it. He appealed directly to JDR Jr. and his father concerning the YMCA clubhouse, group insurance and pensions. The Rockefeller family believed that such "sacrifices" were necessary to save the company from bankruptcy.[35] JDR Jr. rejected Diamond's request to personally fund the YMCA building and the pension fund. He had already forgone dividends from CF&I to allow these schemes to operate and argued that philanthropy was unwise as it could prevent employees from thinking "all the more of the extraordinary advantages they have."[36]

Surviving data for ERPs generally indicate that there was a high level of settlement in favour of employees, but at least one confidential internal company study indicates that caution has to be exercised in assessing these outcomes. At the Bethlehem, Steelton, Lebanon and Maryland plants of Bethlehem Steel, the plan settled 71 per cent of 2,365 grievances in favour of the employee between October 1918 and June 1923. Of the total grievances, 26 per cent related to employment and working conditions and another 24 per cent to earnings. The CF&I ERP delivered favourable responses to worker grievances. During 1920, employees at the steelworks and lime quarries raised 118 issues with management. Of these issues, 44.9 per cent related to working conditions, 13.6 per cent to living conditions such as company housing, 9.3 per cent to medical treatment and 7.6 per cent related to wages; employees received favourable outcomes in at least 83 per cent, 75 per cent, 73 per cent and 67 per cent of cases respectively. Management figures were

[35] Patmore, "Employee Representation Plans at the Minnequa Steelworks", pp. 857–8; "Pueblo Payroll from 1915 to 1940", Typescript, n.d. MSS 1057, Box 6, File 130, CFIC, CHS; Scamehorn, *Mill & Mine*, pp. 140–1.

[36] Letter, JDR Jr. to C.J. Hicks, 7 Sept. 1933. Box 14. Folder 114. Record Group III2C. RFA RAC.

flawed, however. CF&I's internal report of 1924 found that management manipulated the data concerning favourable outcomes to include cases where workers had made considerable concessions to management to gain an improvement. Further, the significance of the issues that management accepted or rejected is not clear. Management may have granted many minor requests that had minimal impact but rejected requests that had significant implications for costs or managerial authority. A more conservative estimate can found in the employee committees of the Pennsylvania Railroad, which handled 45,930 cases between 1921 and 1924 inclusive. Here 47.7 per cent of cases were adjusted or compromised in favour of the employees, 29 per cent were withdrawn or rejected and 23.3 per cent appealed to the next higher office.[37]

David Fairris, in a reappraisal of US company unions using abstract industry data, notes that company unions or ERPs were beneficial for both shop floor safety and productivity. He argues that these schemes "marked a definite improvement for the worker as well as the firm" in the 1920s through reducing labour turnover, fostering worker loyalty and giving workers a voice in the determination of shop floor conditions.[38] Fairris's findings clashed with an unpublished internal study of the CF&I ERP in 1924 which suggested that the economic benefits of the plan for management were disappointing. It certainly improved "morale," but did not necessarily reduce costs or increase productivity. Ernest Burton further argued in a major study of ERPs in the US in 1926 that these schemes did not necessarily lead to greater output, increased efficiency or improved morale. Impediments that reduced the willingness of employee representatives to cooperate with management included the failure of the latter to provide satisfactory wages and conditions relative to competitors, managerial inefficiencies and management's unwillingness to share information about the company with employee representatives.[39]

While the ERPs did provide certain benefits for employees and management through providing worker voice, they were a union-avoidance device. While there are examples of management with ERPs tolerating union membership, they did not recognise unions as bargaining agents and fought against union efforts to organise their particular plants. Management introduced a works committee at the Union Construction Company in 1920

---

[37] Burton, *Employee Representation*, p. 227; Patmore, "Employee Representation Plans at the Minnequa Steelworks", p. 855; Slichter, "The Current Labor Policies", p. 414; *The Iron Age*, 14 Jun. 1925, pp. 1694–5; *The Nation*, 11 Apr. 1934, p. 406.

[38] Fairris, "From Exit to Voice", p. 524.

[39] Burton, *Employee Representation*, p. 262; "Report on Industrial Relations in the Colorado Fuel and Iron Company", p. 21. Box 7-1.5, File 3, BHSA.

because its dealings with unions were "unsatisfactory" and "conservative workmen" had lost control of their unions to officials that did not represent them. The worker representatives elected to the works committee were reminded of the common interests of capital and labour, that collective bargaining was unsatisfactory and that "better results" could be obtained through cooperation. In a major study of US ERPs in 1922, Earl Miller came to the conclusion that the majority of plans were introduced to either undermine existing unions or avoid the possibility of union organisation and collective bargaining, though he recognised that there were other motivating factors. Miller found that union membership fell from 80 to 20 per cent following the adoption of a works council at the Walworth Manufacturing Co., which had a factory in South Boston, and from 90 to 2 per cent at the Virginia Bridge and Iron Co. of Roanoke, Virginia.[40]

The experience at CF&I highlights the tensions that arose between unionism and ERPs. While JDR Jr. and Mackenzie King did not publicly condemn trade unions, the ERP was a substitution for collective bargaining with the UMWA. JDR Jr. was, however, particularly sensitive about allegations of victimisation of union members. He felt strongly "that the cause of industrial peace is hindered rather than advanced by the indiscriminate, revengeful and unthinking attacks which are so often made upon unionism by capitalists and employers" and "deplored" the open shop movement.[41] In February 1916, CF&I officials were concerned that allowing union organisers to visit CF&I facilities would encourage employees to believe that the company was willing to enter into a contract with the union.[42] JDR Jr. made it clear to Welborn, CF&I President, that if the policy of allowing visits by union organisers were compromised then the company would be open to the "charge of insincerity" and "would be an hundred fold more harmful to the success of the Plan than the worst condition which could be imagined as possibly resulting from a rigid adherence to the plan."[43] He even drew up notices for the company to issue to employees which explicitly indicated that they had the right to hold meetings on company property outside working hours and that union membership would have no effect on

---

[40] Earl Miller, "Workmen's Representation in Industrial Government", PhD thesis, University of Illinois, 1922, pp. 162–4; Union Construction Co., Service Manager, Memo, 14 Jan. 1920. Letter from President of Union Construction Co. to Carr, 19 Jan. 1920. HD 5653 U5, DLL.

[41] Letter, JDR Jr. to E.A. Van Valkenburg, 8 Jun. 1921. Box 13. Folder 108. Record Group III2C. RFA. RAC.

[42] Letter, J.F. Welborn to JDR Jr., 3 Feb. 1916. Box 15. File 127. Record Group III2C. RFA. RAC.

[43] Letter, JDR Jr. to J.F. Welborn, 10 Feb. 1916. Box 15. Folder 127. Record Group III2C. RFA. RAC.

an employee's interests in CF&I. Rockefeller was critical of a proposal that managers should follow union organisers around CF&I camps as it has "a little the appearance of detective work" and would undermine worker respect for company management. In December 1919 and January 1923 JDR Jr. asked Welborn to explain reports that mine superintendents were undermining the policy of no victimisation of unionists.[44] Alongside the ERPs, CF&I nevertheless employed spies to gather intelligence on union organisation and identify union activists.[45]

Within the AFL there was hope during the war that ERPs could be a springboard for union organisation and the UMWA initially accepted the CF&I ERP, believing that the clause banning discrimination against union members would eventually lead to full recognition. Union members participated in the plan. Ultimately, however, the union saw that the plan undermined its chances of gaining a contract with the company and UMWA District 15, which covered all of Colorado, and banned ERP participation in 1918. Three unionists from the ERP resigned in 1920 because of the ban and the union expelled another who refused to resign in 1921. There was widespread hostility to the ERP: meetings organised by the US Department of Labor of CFI miners, both union and non-union, indicated virtually unanimous opposition in August 1919.[46] Rees argues that the UMWA "essentially gave up organising CF&I just as its workers began to realise the limitations of the plan."[47] While the AFL and affiliated unions rejected the ERPs, they continued to discuss ways of defeating them by capturing them from within and using them as a base for union organising or "boring from within" during the 1920s.[48] As will be seen later, this could be a successful strategy under certain circumstances in the 1930s.

The AFL steel organising campaign of 1918–19 and the 1919 steel strike, which was the only major strike at the Pueblo steelworks before the Second World War, tested Pueblo employees' support for the ERP and management's willingness to accept unions. The AFL had declared "war" on ERPs

[44] Letters, A. Adams to J.F. Welborn, 16 Jan. 1923, Box 13, Folder 105, JDR Jr. to E.H. Weitzel, 8 May 1916, Box 15, Folder 127, JDR Jr. to J.F. Welborn, 10 Feb. 1916, Box 15, Folder 127, JDR Jr. to J.F. Welborn, 23 Dec. 1919, Box 15, Folder 128, J.F. Welborn to JDR Jr., 3 Feb. 1916, Box 15, File 127. Record Group III2C. RFA. RAC.

[45] Rees, "'X,' 'XX' and 'X-3'".

[46] Hogle, "The Rockefeller Plan", pp. 126–7; Daniel Nelson, "The AFL and the Challenge of Company Unionism, 1915–1937", in Bruce Kaufman and Daphne Taras (eds.), *Non-Union Employee Representation: History, Contemporary Practice and Policy*, M.E. Sharpe, Armonk, 2000, pp. 61–2, 64; Rees, *Representation and Rebellion*, pp. 111–12, 126–9.

[47] Rees, *Representation and Rebellion*, p. 129.

[48] *AF*, Oct. 1925, pp. 873–4; Robert Dunn, *Company Unionism*, Vanguard Press, New York, 1927, pp. 194–8.

at its 1919 convention,[49] declaring them to be a "delusion and a snare" for workers.[50] Unionists at the company's Pueblo steelworks who were also representatives organised employees during the AFL's steel campaign of 1918–19 spontaneously upon hearing of the initial organising successes in the east. Unlike many other steel plants, skilled English-speaking workers rather than non-anglophone immigrants took the lead in organising.[51] The Amalgamated Association of Iron, Steel and Tin Workers (AAISTW) hailed the formation of a lodge among nail and wire workers at Pueblo in November 1918 as a defeat for "Rockefeller's 'union.'"[52] The union established three additional lodges by June 1919. The employees of the coke department formed a lodge of the International Union of Mine, Mill and Smelter Workers. Overall, 16 steelworker unions were organised at the plant and federated into the Allied Steel Council of Pueblo, which became the central union organisation for Pueblo steelworkers. Ironically, the ERP's rejection of discrimination against union members allowed union activists to organise during working hours. While some supervisors wanted to dismiss union activists, they felt they lacked authorisation because of the ERP.[53]

An important factor encouraging steelworkers to join unions was the success of railway employees at the steel plant in negotiating a collective agreement following a short strike in December 1918. The railway employees worked for the Colorado and Wyoming Railway Company, a CF&I subsidiary, and handled freight within the steel plant and between the steel plant and the various CF&I mines. Long-standing grievances included promotion and supervisors' arbitrary behaviour. With the end of the First World War in November 1918, the workers approached the Brotherhood of Railway Trainmen and the Brotherhood of Locomotive Firemen and Enginemen for assistance. Management countered by offering the railway workers participation in the ERP, which they rejected. When the company rejected a union contract, the railway workers went on strike on 9 December and the plant faced closure given its strategic role in shifting raw materials and completed products around the plant at a time of peak production. The ERP representatives at the steelworks intervened and tried to mediate to keep the plant open. A union agreement was signed on 11 December and the strike ended. CF&I tried to undermine the agreement by creating a

---

[49] Nelson, "The AFL and the Challenge of Company Unionism", p. 62.

[50] AFL, *Report of the Proceedings of the Thirty-Ninth Annual Convention*, Washington, DC, 1919, p. 303.

[51] Brody, *Labor in Crisis*, p. 75; Selekman, *Employees' Representation in Steel Works*, p. 166.

[52] *AJ*, 28 Nov. 1918, p. 27.

[53] Selekman, *Employees' Representation in Steel Works*, pp. 166–7, 171; *AJ*, 13 Feb. 1919, p. 3, 5 Jun. 1919, p. 3.

new division for railway employees in the ERP, but the latter refused to participate in the January 1919 elections for employee representatives. The agreement departed from CF&I's insistence on the ERP and encouraged union organisers to believe that a similar tactic could be successful for all steelworkers at Pueblo to obtain union contracts and end the ERP.[54]

The organising was so successful at Pueblo that the plant was initially shut down by management during the 1919–20 national steel strike. Ninety-eight per cent of union members voted for the strike if all other means failed to obtain an agreement between the unions and CF&I. Only 300 of the 6,500 employees reported for work on 22 September 1919. Dissatisfaction with the ERP was a major reason for the strong worker support for the strike. The strike demands included the right to collective bargaining and the abolition of "company unions," which CF&I rejected. The dispute was peaceful until the company began to resume operations on 17 December 1919. Welborn claimed that Austrian women picketers threw rocks at men entering the plant. On the evening of 26 December, shots were fired at F.E. Parkes, manager of the Pueblo steelworks, as he returned home from work. He was not injured, but his car was hit several times. This led the Colorado Governor to order the National Guard into Pueblo the following day to prevent further disorder. During the dispute, a number of dissident strikers formed a "Back to Work League," which circulated petitions calling for a resumption of work under the old conditions of the ERP. While the AAISTW claimed that the strike was a "death blow" for the ERP at Pueblo, management defeated the union and a number of union activists were not rehired. Management also asked rehired steelworkers to sign cards stating that they knew that the plant was an open shop under the ERP. These cards reinforced management's policy against dealing with unions at the Pueblo steelworks. The unions did not formally end the strike until 8 January 1920.[55]

Despite requests from both the Mayor of Pueblo and the strike committee, JDR Jr. refused to intervene during the 1919 strike, simply giving his support to Welborn. Despite JDR Jr.'s public support for the right to join labour unions, he ignored this strong push by the Pueblo workers for unionisation and the rejection of the ERP. CF&I management had believed that the Pueblo steelworkers would not join the strike and was surprised when

[54] Selekman, *Employees' Representation in Steel Works*, pp. 175–6, 197–214.

[55] Brody, *Labor in Crisis*, p. 112; Hogle, "The Rockefeller Plan", pp. 126–7, 276–7; Nelson, "The AFL and the Challenge of Company Unionism", p. 64; *Pueblo Chieftain*, 28 Dec. 1919, p. 1; Letter, J.F. Welborn to JDR Jr., 29 Sept. 1919. Box 15. Folder 128. Telegram, J.F. Welborn to Starr J. Murphy, 10 Oct. 1919. Box 17. Folder 143. Record Group III2C. RFA RAC; Selekman, *Employees' Representation in Steel Works*, pp. 165–70, 190–6; *AJ*, 25 Sept. 1919, p. 1.

presented with the strikers' demands on September 18 1919. Management believed that the demand for the right to collective bargaining was met by the ERP and that the sole objective of the strike was to gain union recognition.[56] While CF&I admitted that the ERP did not stop Pueblo steelworkers from joining the strike, "conditions outside the company" induced the men to strike and it was not the fault of Pueblo management nor the ERP. The company claimed that the strike was a national or international movement, not local, and "was organized by men representing the extreme radical section in labour union politics."[57]

The 1919 strike at Pueblo and other steel plants with ERPs, such as Bethlehem Steel, reinforced the views of employers critical of the ERPs. Some large companies, such as US Steel, rejected ERPs and favoured share ownership or grievance procedures for individual workers, believing that representation of any kind would ultimately lead to a closed shop. Judge Elbert Gary of US Steel argued that the employee walkout at the CF&I steel plant during the 1919 Steel Strike showed that ERPs failed to prevent labour unrest.[58]

During a major confrontation between CF&I and the IWW at the company's coal mines in 1927 the ERP representatives at Pueblo provided assistance to the company. IWW support was built on discontent with the ERP in the coal mines and the strike over demands for increased wages. A meeting of the ERP representatives at the steelworks unanimously passed a motion calling for the dismissal of all IWW members at the steelworks. The Pueblo representatives also met with the coal mine representatives during the strike to help resolve the dispute as approximately 2,500 steelworkers had been stood down due to a coal shortage. Despite claims that these meetings had nothing to do with management and that no information would be passed on, one of the steel representatives recorded the discussions and sent the minutes to senior management for review. The steel representatives encouraged the miners to "say what they thought." While such loyalty to CF&I was impressive, the company contributed to employee commitment by employing labour spies to monitor IWW activities and sympathisers in its mines and at the Pueblo steelworks. The strike eventually involved 5,500 miners and led to a report by the Colorado Industrial Commission

---

[56] Letter, J.F. Welborn to JDR Jr., 29 Sept. 1919. Box 15. Folder 128. Telegram, M. Sudzinski to JDR Jr., 23 Sept. 1919. Telegram, J.F. Welborn to Starr J. Murphy, 24 Sept. 1919. Telegram, J.F. Welborn to JDR Jr., 24 Sept. 1919. Box 17. Folder 143. Record Group III2C. RFA RAC.

[57] Letter, JDR Jr. to A.C. Bedford, 5 Nov. 1919. Box 17. Folder 143. Record Group III2C. RFA RAC.

[58] Brody, *Labor in Crisis*, p. 177; Brody, *Steelworkers in America*, p. 269; Jonathan Rees, *Managing the Mills: Labor Policy in the American Steel Industry during the Nonunion Era*, University Press of America, Lanham, 2004, p. 172.

that indirectly criticised the CF&I ERP for not allowing miners their organisation of choice and for fuelling support for the IWW.[59]

While trade unions faced a challenge from ERPs, supervisors and middle managers expressed concerns about the implications of ERPs for their status and authority within their organisations and the time lost in ERP activities. Most ERPs included a grievance procedure whereby workers could protest about their supervisors if they treated them unfairly or breached company rules. Certain weaknesses of the ERPs hindered this provision. Representatives were often unwilling to take up the grievances of their fellow workers and some ERPs required the workers to take their concerns directly to the supervisor in question before they would consider them which, as Jacoby argues, "made workers reluctant to voice any complaints, even though the foreman's decision could be appealed to a higher level."[60] Management was also reluctant to overrule supervisors, and some companies promised line managers that no provision in the ERP would encroach upon their powers. Management also found that ERPs required considerable time and expenses, what with the provision of meeting facilities and employees taking time away from work to attend. ERPs could indeed generate more work for managers in terms of the additional issues and grievances raised by employee representatives.[61]

While cost data for ERPs are difficult to find, the expenditure relating to social and industrial betterment schemes at CF&I totalled $1,480,466.01 between 30 June 1915 and 31 December 1923 of which $67,867.09 related to employee representatives' expenses, $3,056.85 related to industrial representation meetings and $3,450.61 related to ERP printing and translation costs. The cost of these schemes rose from $3.61 per employee for the year ending June 30 1916 to $29.05 for the year ending 31 December 1921, before falling to $18.74 per employee for the year ending 31 December 1923.[62]

At CF&I, supervisors and senior management not only had to contend with the ERP, but also deal with JDR Jr., who monitored the operations of the ERP closely through reports, correspondence with CF&I officials, press articles and occasional visits to Colorado. During the early 1920s, JDR Jr. was concerned with CF&I's poor economic performance and in November 1923 encouraged Welborn to allow external consultants to undertake reviews of CF&I. A report was produced on general management at CF&I and

---

[59] Patmore, "Employee Representation Plans at the Minnequa Steelworks", p. 857; Rees, *Representation and Rebellion*, pp. 160–73.

[60] Jacoby, *Employing Bureaucracy*, p. 188.

[61] Jacoby, *Employing Bureaucracy*, p. 188; Daniel Nelson, "The Company Union Movement, 1900–1937: A Reexamination", *Business History Review*, vol. 56, no. 3, 1982, pp. 352–3.

[62] "Report on Industrial Relations in the Colorado Fuel and Iron Company", Table V. Box 7-1.5, File 3, BHSA.

another comprehensively evaluated all aspects of CF&I labour practices at both the mines and the steel plant, including the ERP, and criticised the accuracy of data relating to the success of the ERP and its impact on productivity. JDR Jr. visited the Pueblo steel plant in July 1924 and June 1926 while on holiday in Colorado.[63] During the latter trip, he met employee representatives to talk "about everything under the sun."[64]

There was resistance to the ERP from supervisors at Pueblo who saw it as taking away their authority without providing them with any privileges. Some supervisors were also concerned that senior management had not consulted them when the ERP was introduced and there had been no meeting to explain the plan to them. Rockefeller initially excluded supervisors from the ERP: employees elected their representatives and management appointed the superintendents of the supervisors to represent them. The supervisors' hostility towards the ERP discouraged employees and representatives from taking up grievances, as they did want to anger them. To overcome this hostility, senior management granted the supervisors the right to elect their own representatives in 1919.[65]

Though senior management at the Pueblo steelworks were more supportive of the ERP by the mid-1920s, and some supervisors had decided to cooperate with the employee representatives in order to avoid having their decisions overturned by senior management, some supervisors were still opposed to the ERP. This led to a wide variation in the way the ERP functioned across the plant. In the rod mill, the superintendent and the employee representative had a good relationship. They were able to settle grievances and by 1928 no grievances were being referred to the Joint Committee on Co-operation, Conciliation and Wages from the rod mill. By contrast, a casting foundry employee representative complained in January 1924 that there was a lack of cooperation between management and labour. He had to follow up 90 per cent of grievances and there were long delays before replies were received from local management. In the by-product coke plant, Superintendent H.B. Carpenter suppressed the operation of the ERP because "we have practically 100% harmony." Carpenter was strongly opposed to the ERP, believing that its committees were "inefficient" and that workers showed "poor judgement" in electing their representatives, and he stopped his employee representatives from attending one joint conference. Senior CF&I management overruled Carpenter.[66]

---

[63] Patmore, "Employee Representation Plans at the Minnequa Steelworks", pp. 855–7.

[64] *Industrial Bulletin*, Nov. 1926, p. 22.

[65] Nelson, "The AFL and the Challenge of Company Unionism", pp. 63–4; Selekman, *Employees' Representation in Steel Works*, pp. 162–3, 225.

[66] Patmore, "Employee Representation Plans at the Minnequa Steelworks", pp. 854–5.

The ERP also faced a crisis at Pueblo when Carpenter became the General Superintendent of the Steelworks in May 1925. Carpenter tried to destroy the ERP by encouraging superintendents and supervisors to withdraw support. Active employee representatives such as Warren Densmore were threatened with dismissal and CF&I President Welborn intervened to stop one outspoken representative from the Open Hearth Department being fired. Carpenter also clashed with the CF&I President's Industrial Representative at Pueblo in front of the representatives. JDR Jr. personally met with Carpenter to discuss the deteriorating situation at Pueblo and Carpenter found it necessary to soften his stance against the ERP. One senior manager at the plant later complained that this intervention undermined Carpenter's authority in the plant and strengthened the position of the representatives in bringing forward employee grievances. Carpenter eventually resigned in May 1928.[67]

Cooperative Management – The Extent

Cooperative management spread beyond the B&O, but never achieved anything like the success of the ERP movement in the US. Three other major US railways adopted cooperative management with varying degrees of success and application. B&O President Daniel Willard succeeded in encouraging William Harahan, the President of the Chesapeake and Ohio Railway (C&O) to adopt cooperative management in C&O's Seventeenth Street workshop in Richmond, Virginia in July 1924.[68] AFL workshop craft unions were well established at C&O but cooperative management was never extended beyond the Seventeenth Street workshop despite union requests. Workshop employees became increasingly frustrated as many of their suggestions were not recorded in committee minutes or acted upon by management. Senior management reduced the length of the meetings and the detail of the minutes. Management made relatively few suggestions compared to the union representatives. Though meetings continued until at least February 1929, they became ritualised with no new business and all old business concluded.[69] One union official noted that the situation had "more of the elements of a burlesque than genuine cooperation."[70]

---

[67] Patmore, "Employee Representation Plans at the Minnequa Steelworks", pp. 854–5.

[68] Vrooman, *Daniel Willard*, pp. 66–7, 128.

[69] Letters, Daniel Willard to William Harahan, 4 Feb. 1925, G.H. Stewart to J.R. Gould, 19 Sept. 1926, N.M. Taylor, J.L. Spicer, H.E. Griffin, I.N. Wilcox, F.D. Carlisle and W.C. Burke to G.H. Stewart, 8 Feb. 1927, L.P. Murphy to Otto Beyer, 28 Jul. 1931. C&O, 17th Street Shop Cooperative Management Meeting Minutes, 27 Feb. 1927. Railway Employees' Department. AFL-CIO Records, Box 89, FF 4, Code # 36-8. Kheel Archives, Cornell University (Hereafter RED KA).

[70] Letter, G.H. Stewart to J.R. Gould, 17 Jan. 1927. Box 89, FF 4, Code # 36-8. RED KA.

Outside the railway companies, other firms adopted union-management cooperation. The Pequot Mills of the Naumkeag Steam Cotton Company of Salem, Massachusetts was a union textile shop facing increased competition from the South and declining profits in the late 1920s. In 1927 it adopted the B&O plan to improve operating efficiency. The Pequot plan provided for union recognition and the maintenance of "good" wages and working conditions. In return, the AFL-affiliated United Textile Workers agreed to cooperate in "effecting economies." Mill officials and members of the union executive attended monthly conferences to discuss questions of mutual interest, though these became less regular as time went by. Union members were also involved in production time studies and changes to plant layout.[71]

Another example was the small Chicago firm of Yeomans Bros., which adopted union-management cooperation with the IAM in July 1930. It sold electric pumps for use in water supply and sewerage and was the only union shop in its industry at the time. This plant was built around batch production rather than mass production, without any standardisation. This production method was not appropriate for the installation of bonus payment schemes or piecework as a way to increase efficiency. Charles Yeomans, the President of the company, was impressed with the operation of union-management cooperation on the B&O and the Canadian National Railways (CNR). He considered the relationship with his employees "satisfactory," but wanted to look at ways to reduce costs to overcome the unfavourable wage differential between his firm and non-union competitors. Yeomans believed that workers would gain in job security, the "satisfaction" of having a voice in management and the possibility of gaining a share of the gains resulting from cooperation "from time to time."[72] In return, he argued that "management gains increased morale, increased efficiency, and a lower cost of production."[73]

The AFL tried unsuccessfully to use union-management cooperation as part of a strategy to organise a number of large corporations, including General Electric, GM and Ford, and Southern textile mill owners. William Green, Gompers's successor as AFL President, repeatedly used the Taylorist argument that only a unionised firm could achieve the organised concept essential for increased productivity. During its Southern organising campaign

---

71 Richard Nyman, *Union-Management Cooperation in the "Stretch Out": Labour Extension at the Pequot Mills*, Yale University Press, New Haven, 1934, pp. 3–10; Vrooman, *Daniel Willard*, p. 71.

72 C. Aultz, "Union-Management Cooperation", MBA Honours Report, The University of Chicago, 1940, p. 37; Charles Yeomans, "Cooperation as an Incentive", *American Machinist*, 9 Apr. 1931, p. 584.

73 Yeomans, "Cooperation as an Incentive", p. 584.

aimed at textile workers in 1929–31, the AFL engaged Taylorist consultant Geoffrey Brown to explain to employers the benefits of union-management cooperation and offer them assistance in establishing such schemes. Between March 1930 and September 1931, Brown held over 200 conferences with managers and directors of Southern cotton mills, but only persuaded three small enterprises in Columbus, Georgia to adopt the scheme.[74]

The fledgling movement built around cooperative management faced a number of barriers. There were supervisors who resented the intrusion of the committees into their traditional areas of authority. At the Glenwood workshops of the B&O in 1924, for example, a boilermaker supervisor bullied employee representatives and forced three to resign. Supervisors' unwillingness to offer any suggestions destroyed the union-management cooperation committee at the C&O's Seventeenth Street workshop in Richmond, Virginia.[75]

There was also opposition among rank-and-file union members. The idea was introduced in a top-down manner and linked in some cases to wage cuts, layoffs and work intensification. There was restricted participation for union members on the B&O, who were encouraged to pass suggestions on to their union representatives. The Communist Trade Union Educational League encouraged this opposition through factions in key unions such as the IAM, which almost cost Johnson his re-election as President of the IAM in 1925. An example of a grassroots employee defeat of union-management cooperation can be seen in 1931 at the St. Louis Terminal Railway, which provided rail interchange services at a key railway hub in Missouri. Surrounded by railways with company unions, it was seen as a crucial beachhead for promoting cooperative management. Union members unanimously rejected the proposal. They referred to complaints from B&O workers and failed to see that any benefits had come out of cooperative management. Some workers described it as a "speed up system" that would lead to further dismissals in a period of economic depression.[76]

---

[74] Jacoby, "Union-Management Cooperation", p. 25; David Montgomery, *The Fall of the House of Labor*, Cambridge University Press, Cambridge, 1987, p. 424; Jean Trepp, "Union-Management Cooperation and the Southern Organizing Campaign", *Journal of Political Economy*, vol. 41, no. 5, 1933, pp. 616–19.

[75] Letter, P.D. Harvey to Otto Beyer, 12 Aug. 1924, File – "Cooperative Plan. Committees. ca. 1924–1928", Container 96, B.P.; Letter, N.M. Taylor, J.L. Spicer, H.E. Griffin, I.N. Wilcox, F.D. Carlisle and W.C. Burke to G.H. Stewart, 8 Feb. 1927. Box 89, FF 4, Code # 36-8. RED KA.

[76] Beyer, "B&O Engine 1003," p. 313: Jacoby, "Union-Management Cooperation", p. 27; Letter, J.M. Burns to members of Executive Council, Section No. 2, Railway Employees Department, 8 Oct. 1931, File – "St. Louis Terminal Railway, ca. 1931", Container 64, B.P: Montgomery, *The Fall of the House of Labor*, pp. 423–4.

Cooperative Management – The Impact

What did the union-management cooperative committees do? The meeting held at the back shop of the Glenwood Railway Workshops of the B&O on 24 July 1924 is typical. It lasted 2 hours and 20 minutes and there were six representatives of management and seven of employees. Equal numbers of employer and employee representatives were not required for the meeting to proceed. The Superintendent of Shops, an employer representative, chaired the meeting. The other management representatives included a representative from the Chief Efficiency Bureau, the tool room foreman and the Chief Clerk of the Stores Department; the employee representatives included union representatives of the local federation of railway crafts and union representatives from the blacksmiths, boilermakers, electricians, car men and machinists. There was also a visitor present, a Superintendent of Shops from the C&O. Among the 33 suggestions made were ways of reducing waste in packing pumps and improving the conditions of dyes for steam hammers, the repairing of leaky pipes, the installation of fixed ladders to an overhead fan in the spring shop to allow for easier maintenance, the use of petroleum jelly rather than grease for lubrication and stopping the practice of parking steam engines outside the back shop as it made entrance to the shop unsafe. Complaints were heard about managers ignoring cooperative items raised by employee representatives, and the chair promised to look into it.[77]

Surviving aggregate data suggest that the scheme delivered a number of useful suggestions for management to improve work practices and improve productivity. Suggestions under union-management cooperation related primarily to improvements in working methods and equipment. From March 1924 to December 1939, 30,673 suggestions were received and discussed by workshop cooperative committees of the B&O, of which 86.2 per cent were adopted. At Yeomans Brothers, between its first meeting in July 1930 and the seventy-fifth in March 1941, the cooperative committee received 418 suggestions, 299 of which were from employee representatives and 119 from management representatives. Of these, 71 per cent were adopted, 22 per cent were dropped and 7 per cent were still under consideration by March 1941. There are difficulties in comparing union-management cooperative plans with ERPs, as many of the suggestions made in ERPs related to grievances and working conditions, while under the union-management cooperative plans, unions and management handled these matters.[78]

[77] Back Shop Glenwood Cooperation Minutes, 24 Jul. 1924. File – "Cooperative Plan. Minutes. Glenwood. ca. 1924." Container 97, BP.

[78] Aultz, "Union-Management Cooperation", p. 57; Yeomans Brothers, Cooperative

One benefit for those companies that engaged in cooperative management was union assistance in marketing and gaining contracts. In the case of the B&O, this initially involved local union branches actively campaigning for patronage for the railway. As the economy improved after 1932, employee efforts to increase business for the B&O were formalised through the Cooperative Traffic Program (CTP), in which staff and local committees were modelled on the cooperative committees. Vrooman has estimated that the CTP may have increased B&O traffic by a small but significant 1.1 per cent in 1934.[79] In the case of Yeomans Brothers, union connections helped the company obtain contracts from municipalities where organised labour was influential. These connections helped the company gain at least five contracts during 1932–33 and assisted its survival through the depths of the Great Depression. Productivity gains and increased business derived from the cooperative management scheme were viewed by these companies as important offsets for the high wages of a union shop relative to their non-union competitors.[80]

While union-management cooperation brought benefits to partner firms in terms of marketing and contracts, there were limitations. While promoting one company at the expense of others may be of benefit to the firm that adopts union-management cooperation, other competitors that have also accepted unions but do not participate in this scheme will be disadvantaged. As Vrooman has noted, while the Pennsylvania Railroad was hostile to unions and had its own ERP, other competitors that recognised unions and engaged in collective bargaining, such as the New York Central Railroad and the Erie Railroad, were disadvantaged by union promotion of the B&O's services. This union support for the B&O could have weakened management's sympathy for unions on those other railroads.[81] There are also issues relating to unions' distortion of tendering processes by using their political connections to favour firms with union-management cooperation. This had the potential to damage the public standing of unions.

Did these schemes deliver benefits for employees in terms of increased wages and employment stabilisation? While Willard saw the efficiency benefits of the plan, he could not justify paying higher wages than his competitors. One benefit was the restoration of the time-and-a-half rule for Sunday and holiday work. In 1924 and 1925 the B&O assisted the stabilisation

---

Committee Meeting, 18 Mar. 1941. File – "Yeomans Brothers Company Minutes of Cooperative Meetings ca. 1930–1939", Container 46, B.P.

[79] Vrooman, *Daniel Willard*, p. 136.

[80] Aultz, "Union-Management Cooperation", p. 43; Letter, Charles Yeomans to R.T. Eastwood, 10 Dec. 1940. File – "Yeomans Brothers Company Correspondence ca. 1932–1936," Container 46, B.P.

[81] Vrooman, *Daniel Willard*, p. 128.

of its workshop jobs by diverting heavy upgrading work on locomotive and rolling stock from outside firms to its workshops.[82]

The benefits of cooperative management for the stabilisation of employment came into question with the onset of the Great Depression. Despite attempts to stabilise employment as the depression hit, by 1932 layoffs at the B&O had reached similar levels to its competitors. By contrast, Charles Yeomans claimed in July 1932 that the cooperative plan was largely responsible for avoiding reductions of employment in his company despite a decline in business.[83]

What impact did this scheme have on union membership? While there is no evidence of a direct impact, in January 1931 the workshop superintendent at the Mt. Clare workshops of the B&O organised a meeting of employees to encourage them to become financial members of their respective unions, highlighting the regular employment that the unions had achieved for them through the cooperation scheme in a period of economic depression.[84]

The Demise of ERPs and Union-Management cooperation during the 1930s

Both the ERP and union-management cooperation went into decline in the US in the 1930s. As previously noted, the Wagner Act of 1935 outlawed ERPs. The NLRB moved against the ERP after the Supreme Court upheld the legislation in 1937. In 1939, the Board won a major case against Newport News Shipbuilding and Dry Dock when the US Supreme Court ruled that any ERP in existence since 1927 was illegal. The ERP was illegal even though the employer no longer funded employee representatives' expenses and workers had voted for it in a secret ballot in preference to independent trade unions. The decision spelt the effective end of the movement inspired by the Rockefeller Plan.[85]

The various plans collapsed or were absorbed by AFL- and CIO-affiliated trade unions. A small number of ERPs evolved into independent local unions such as at Thompson Products, an aircraft engine parts manufacturer in Detroit, Michigan and Cleveland, Ohio.[86] In 1936 SWOC, which was

---

[82] Vrooman, *Daniel Willard*, pp. 56–7.

[83] Letter, Charles Yeomans to Frank Hayes, 7 Jul. 1932. File – "Yeomans Brothers Company Correspondence ca. 1932–1936", Container 46, B.P; Vrooman, *Daniel Willard*, pp. 99–100.

[84] Letter, W.J. McGee to B.M. Jewell, 27 Jan. 1931. File – "System Federation No. 30. Organization, ca. 1924–31", Container 104, B.P.

[85] Patmore, "Employee Representation Plans in the United States", pp. 43–4.

[86] Sanford Jacoby, "Reckoning with Company Unions: The Case of Thompson Products, 1934–1964", *Industrial and Labor Relations Review*, vol. 43, no. 1, 1989, pp. 19–40.

a joint venture between the CIO and the AAISTW, set out to "capture" ERPs. SWOC encouraged members at the Lackawanna plant of Bethlehem Steel to run in the ERP elections to "Capture the ERP – Then Bury It."[87] Where there were no SWOC sympathisers on the ERP, unionists would use it to submit a large number of grievances which management would not be willing to resolve. This would discredit the ERP and highlight the need for a "bona fide" union. Generally, SWOC explicitly targeted plan representatives to organise union members through "friendly contact" and encouraged disaffected plan representatives to organise bargaining committees that represented a number of steel plants. At the Duquesne plant of the Carnegie-Illinois Company, Elmer Maloy won a seat on the ERP in June 1935 and tried to force changes on issues such as occupational health and safety and the distribution of work hours. Increasingly frustrated with management's responses to the ERP's demands, Maloy became an in-plant paid SWOC organiser in 1936. In December 1936, he chaired a meeting of employee representatives from 42 steel plants at Pittsburgh that declared support for the CIO and called on representatives to use their influence to enrol steelworkers. This campaign, plus fear of a government-imposed closed shop, led US Steel to recognise SWOC on 2 March 1937.[88]

Some recent positive reassessments of the ERPs have highlighted that some workers supported their retention. Representatives from the Industrial Assembly at the Goodyear Tyres plant in Akron, Ohio and the Cooperative Association at Leeds & Northrup gave evidence against the NLRA before Congress. Carnegie-Illinois employees sympathetic to their representation plan formed a defence committee which obtained company endorsement, retained legal counsel and published an anti-union publication. At the Gasden, Alabama plant of Goodyear Tyres, management had established an Industrial Assembly in 1933. The Assembly leaders waged a war against union organisers and members that included beatings. Following the Supreme Court decisions, the Assembly leaders created an "independent union," the Etowah Rubber Workers' Association, which continued the anti-union campaign into the 1940s.[89]

[87] SWOC, Bethlehem Campaign Headquarters, *Memorandum # 20*, 8 Feb. 1939, Harold T. Curtiss Papers, Box 5, File 14, Pennsylvania State University Libraries Labor Archives, State College (hereafter CP).

[88] Hogler and Greiner, *Employee Participation*, pp. 50–5; Rees, *Managing the Mills*, p. 234; Rose, *Duquesne*, pp. 113–37; SWOC, Bethlehem Pennsylvania Lodge 1409 Minutes, 22 Mar. 1939, CP, Box 2, File 24; *AJ*, 17 Sept. 1936, p. 3, 1 Oct. 1936, p. 12, 8 Oct. 1936, pp. 1, 9, 29 Oct. 1936, p. 14, 24 Dec. 1936, pp. 1, 8, 23 Dec. 1937, p. 3.

[89] Nelson, "Employee Representation in Historical Perspective", pp. 382–3; Nelson, "The Company Union Movement", pp. 355–7.

Kaufman has noted that significant numbers of workers voted to retain the plans in preference to trade unions. During 1933–35, one-third of workers voted to keep ERPs in elections conducted by the National Labor Board and the NLRB. From 1935 to 1941, company unions and derivative independent trade unions won 50 per cent of the NLRB-supervised elections against AFL and CIO unions. The extent to which these votes are an accurate reflection of worker opinion is difficult to determine. Employers were willing to dismiss union activists or transfer them to isolated locations, to use spies and deploy company police to prevent unionisation. In April 1940 there were SWOC allegations that only candidates sympathetic to management and the ERP at the Bethlehem plant of Bethlehem Steel were able to electioneer on company time and property and to serve as scrutineers of the counting of the vote. The Bethlehem plant ERP also attempted to win worker sympathy by organising social events such as a performance by swing legend Duke Ellington and his orchestra on the same night as a union-organised dance. It also claimed that a vote for the plan was a vote for "American freedom and independence."[90]

The favourable climate for trade unions coincided with changes at CF&I. Though Rockefeller interests continued to dominate the company, JDR Jr. was losing interest in the company. In October 1933, CF&I miners voted for collective bargaining through the UMWA and against the ERP by 877 votes to 275. While CF&I officials recognised the miners' wishes, they regretted the defeat of the ERP. They concluded that passive resistance was preferable to overt resistance, which "would lead to serious labor disturbances and probably bloodshed."[91] JDR Jr. took the view that the ERP at CF&I was "eminently satisfactory." However, if the National Industrial Recovery Act directed them to deal with unions in issues of wages and hours, they had to comply. He hoped that the ERP could continue to deal with "other matters of common interest."[92]

---

[90] Letter, H. Curtis to F.W. Birnbach, 1 May 1939, CP, Box 2, File 24; H. Curtis, "Supplementary Statement. To report on New Card-Signing Campaign – Bethlehem Plant", typescript, 12 Dec. 1939, CP, Box 2, File 5; Milton Derber, *The American Idea of Industrial Democracy 1865–1965*, University of Illinois Press, Urbana, 1970, p. 326; "ERP Election Fraud", Press Release to *Philadelphia Record*, 30 Mar. 1940. United Steelworkers of America, CP, Box 4, File 6; Hogler and Greiner, *Employee Participation*, pp. 54–5; Kaufman, "The Case for the Company Union", p. 337; Plan of Employees' Representation at the Bethlehem Plant of the Bethlehem Steel Company, *Attention!*, n.d., CP, Box 3, File 10.

[91] Letter, A. Roeder to Colonel A. Woods, 31 Oct. 1933. Box 15. Folder 122. Record Group III2C. RFA, RAC; Patmore, "Employee Representation Plans at the Minnequa Steelworks", pp. 847, 858.

[92] Letter, JDR Jr. to A. Woods, 24 Jul. 1933. Box 14. Folder 114. Record Group III2C. RFA, RAC.

Despite JDR Jr.'s views concerning the mining of CF&I, the ERP remained in operation longer at the Pueblo Steelworks. CF&I's management believed that the ERP could continue there because the steelworks were not organised to any great extent and the NIRA recognised ERPs. The CF&I newspaper *The Blast* published articles that supported the ERP and management credited the ERP with providing steelworkers one week's vacation on full pay in July 1936 and wage increases in December 1936. *The Blast* highlighted the advantages of the ERP by carrying news of other steel plants where workers supported ERPs in preference to "outside unions" in collective bargaining. It also claimed that unions were forcing steelworkers to join them. When *The Blast* covered ERP elections, it highlighted their fairness and the high voter turnout. Management continued to employ spies to monitor any labour organising in Pueblo and further ensure the survival of the ERP.[93]

While CF&I management saw the ERP as preferable to unions, tensions between the representatives and local management remained. There was a tied vote between employee and management representatives for the Joint Committee on Cooperation, Conciliation and Wages over the reinstatement of an employee named Anderson. Management had fired him because he had allowed a furnace bottom to burn out. The employee representatives wanted arbitration, while the management representatives upheld the decision. Employee representatives called for a revision of the ERP to remove the requirement for CF&I's consent before any question was referred to arbitration. With the threat of unionisation looming, the company agreed to amend the ERP in 1936 to allow the referral of any deadlocked matter for final arbitration to a board comprising an employee representative, management representative and a third person selected by mutual agreement at the request of either management or employee representatives.[94]

Management faced the threat of growing unionisation. SWOC began organising the plant in 1937 and chartered a lodge in Pueblo on 3 August 1938. During its campaign for recognition, SWOC alleged that supporters of the ERP had assaulted union organisers and that the local media and public authorities were biased and sympathised with CF&I. In February 1938, the company asked its employees to ratify the ERP and designate its

---

[93] Letter, A. Woods to JDR Jr., 18 Jul. 1933. Box 14. Folder 114. Record Group III2C. RFA, RAC; Patmore and Rees, "Employee Publications", pp. 268–9; Spy report on IWW dance/meeting, 14 Mar. 1936, Box 1, RG 2.1.1, BHSA.

[94] In the Matter of the Colorado Fuel and Iron Corporation and International Union of Mine, Mill and Smelter Workers, Local 442. In the matter of the Colorado Fuel and Iron Corporation and Steel Workers, Organizing Committee, 22 NLRB, no. 14, 1940, pp. 200–3.

representatives as their collective bargaining agents. The subsequent vote was 2,426 in favour and only 198 against the ERP. Many of the employees who voted for the ERP believed that the continuation of their insurance, pension and medical plans depended on a positive vote. The company changed the name of the ERP to the Employees' Representation Organization (ERO) to indicate a break with the past, but most of the officers administering the ERP remained to administer the ERO, under Diamond as President. Despite the vote and the changes, the NLRB ruled on appeal in March 1940 that the ERP was company-dominated and directed CF&I to withdraw recognition. At the first representation ballot in March 1941 the employee representatives made a strong appeal in the local newspaper for workers to vote against any outside representation. ERP lawyer A.T. Stewart compared the union's organising campaign with Hitler's invasion of Norway during one local radio broadcast and warned of "bloodshed" and a loss of earnings if the union replaced the ERP. The supporters of the ERP were victorious: 2,670 workers voted for no representation and 1,783 voted for the CIO out of 4,838 votes cast. CF&I meanwhile petitioned the Tenth Circuit Court of Appeal for a review of the NLRB direction, but the court upheld the NLRB direction in June 1941.[95]

The ERO was reorganised again and became ERO Inc., which the company identified as the collective bargaining agent for its employees on 1 December 1941. In June 1942 the Tenth District Court of Appeals ordered the company to withdraw its recognition of ERO Inc., ruling that there was an insufficient break with the disestablished ERO and that ERO Inc. was not a truly independent labour organisation. During the final representation election in July 1942, ERO Inc. tried to persuade workers to vote against the union by hinting that the CIO was led by communists and thus un-American. They were unsuccessful, however, in saving the final vestiges of the Rockefeller Plan and the result was 58 per cent in favour of the union. The major reason for the defeat of the ERP

[95] Joanne Dodds, *They All Come to Pueblo: A Social History*, Donning, Virginia Beach, 1994, pp. 195–6; National Labor Relations Board, Decision and Direction of Election, Case No. R-2190, 12 Feb. 1941, p. 3. The US National Archives, Rocky Mountain Region, Denver, R 276. Records of the United States Courts of Appeal. Tenth Circuit Denver, Colorado. Transcripts of Records on Appeal 1929–1954, Case 2097; "Proceedings of the Third Annual Convention, Colorado State Industrial Union Council, Pueblo, Colorado, September 20 and 21, 1940", Typescript, pp. 3–4. Frank and Fred Hefferly Collection (hereafter HC), Box 3, Folder 4, University of Colorado at Boulder Archives; Patmore, "Employee Representation Plans at the Minnequa Steelworks", pp. 859–60; Rees, *Representation and Rebellion*, pp. 193–202; A.T. Stewart, radio broadcast recording, KGHL Pueblo, 1941. HC, Box 8; George Zinke, *Minnequa Plant of Colorado Fuel and Iron Corporation and Two Locals of United Steelworkers of America*, National Planning Association, Washington, 1951, pp. 29–31.

was a major influx of new employees as steel mill production expanded to meet wartime demand.[96]

Management-union cooperation also lost its impetus in the early 1930s. The 1930s depression generally weakened cooperative management. The Chicago & Northwestern Railroad dropped the scheme in February 1932, later claiming that the reduction of the workforce and the curtailment of repair work meant that the scheme's continuation could not be justified. Deteriorating economic conditions, wage cuts and an the increasing number of machines to be supervised by workers led to a strike and the collapse of the scheme at the Pequot Mills in May 1933.[97]

The new labour legislation in the US that eliminated ERPs also weakened union enthusiasm for cooperative management. There were concerns that the union-management cooperative committees were now redundant and could even weaken the US trade union movement. Jacoby claims that by 1933 the AFL had "quietly dropped its official support for cooperation."[98] Alexander Whitney, President of the Brotherhood of Railroad Trainmen, argued in a letter to Otto Beyer in March 1938 that if workers had any ideas they could submit them to their superintendents through the union. He noted that there were "well-founded suspicions" that labour's attention would be divided and moved away from their central objective of improving wages and conditions. The traditional approach to collective bargaining was resurrected.[99]

Despite these setbacks, several firms persisted with union-management cooperation and there were continued attempts to expand the movement. Willard died in July 1942, but cooperative management was continued at the B&O until 1962, and the Yeomans scheme was still in operation in 1949. Cooperative management was introduced on the bankrupt Rutland Railroad, which was primarily located in Vermont, and the Enterprise Foundry Company of Belleville, Illinois. In the latter case, the AFL unions persuaded the owner to accept cooperative management in 1939 as an alternative to relocating to the South. The Tennessee Valley Authority (TVA), established by the US federal government in 1933 to develop water resources in the Tennessee River Valley, adopted union-management cooperation for union employees in 1942 and this was still in operation in 1955. Beyer, who was the

[96] Dodds, *They All Come to Pueblo*, p. 196; Patmore, "Employee Representation Plans at the Minnequa Steelworks", p. 860; Rees, *Representation and Rebellion*, pp. 202–5; Zinke, *Minnequa Plant*, pp. 31–33.

[97] Aultz, "Union-Management Cooperation", p. 25; Nyman, *Union-Management Cooperation*, pp. 119–43.

[98] Jacoby, "Union-Management Cooperation", p. 31.

[99] Letter, A. Whitney to Otto Beyer, 11 Mar. 1938. File – "Brotherhood of Railway Trainmen ca. 1932–1942", Container 49, B.P.

TVA's labour relations consultant from 1935 until his death in 1949, played a crucial role in its introduction by the TVA.[100]

Beyer also continued to lobby the AFL to persist with union-management cooperation. Following a speech in favour of union-management cooperation by Beyer, then a member of the US National Mediation Board, at the AFL Convention at New Orleans in November 1940,[101] several workshop craft union officials, concerned with growing possibility of the US entering the Second World War, successfully obtained the passage of a resolution calling for "the extension of the practice of union-management cooperation throughout industries as rapidly as union organisation will warrant ..."[102] They saw union-management cooperation as an aid that would increase industry efficiency, improve living standards and assist rearmament for defence if required.[103]

There was, however, strong support for the traditional approach to collective bargaining among the AFL leadership. At a subsequent AFL Executive meeting called to discuss the resolution in February 1941, there was opposition from George Harrison, an AFL Vice-President and President of the Brotherhood of Railway Clerks, who saw the railroad cooperation schemes as "nothing but a vitality sapping arrangement for the labor movement."[104] He argued that "it is the function of our organisations to represent the interests of workers and our unions grow and thrive on opposition within the industry and economic injustice."[105] While the AFL Executive referred the matter for further discussion by AFL officers at a future meeting, it was not followed through.[106]

[100] Aultz, "Union-Management Cooperation", p. 25; Harry Case, *Personnel Policy in a Public Agency: The TVA Experience*, Harper & Brothers, New York, 1955, p. 62; Letter, Otto Beyer to W.E. Navin, 21 Oct. 1941. File – "Rutland Railroad Company Minutes ca. 1940–42", Container 64, B.P; *Teamwork*, Jan. 1949, p. 1; *The Yeomans Guard*, Jan.–Feb. 1949, p. 3; Vrooman, *Daniel Willard*, pp. 159, 181.

[101] AFL, *Report of Proceedings of the Sixtieth Annual Convention of the American Federation of Labor held at New Orleans, Louisiana, November 18 to 29, Inclusive 1940*, Washington, DC, 1940, pp. 342–6.

[102] AFL, *Report of the Proceedings of the Sixtieth Annual Convention*, Washington, DC, 1940, p. 373.

[103] AFL, *Report of the Proceedings of the Sixtieth Annual Convention*, Washington, DC, 1940, pp. 372–3, 549–50.

[104] AFL, Executive Minutes, 18 Feb. 1941. George Meany Memorial Archives, Silver Spring, Maryland (hereafter GMMA), RG4-001.

[105] AFL, Executive Minutes, 18 Feb. 1941. GMMA, RG4-001.

[106] AFL, Executive Minutes, 18 Feb. 1941. GMMA, RG4-001.

Conclusion

While there was an awareness of alternative forms of workplace employee representation in the US, low levels of unionisation did not provide a favourable environment for either Whitley or German works councils, which recognised unions, and led to a preference among employers for the non-union ERP. Some employers may have seen ERPs as a way of improving communications with employees and heightening worker commitment to the firm. A major motivation for most US employers, however, was the avoidance of unions and state intervention in the internal affairs of their companies. While the Rockefeller Plan did not discriminate against union members, CF&I and other enterprises saw ERPs as a substitute for unions. The plans also tended to be found in large-scale industries with continuous or mass production, where communication problems were intensified and strategic groups of workers could create bottlenecks in the production process if alienated. There is evidence that some managers opposed ERPs as they potentially undermined their status and authority.

ERPs generally did not provide a long-term alternative to trade unions. Employers' commitment to ERPs generally depended on the economic and political climate. Following Ramsay's argument, cycles or waves of interest arose from the challenges of the First World War and the New Deal of the 1930s, and led employers to look for alternatives to trade unions. Some plans were tied to the fortunes of particular individuals within management, such as JDR Jr. in the case of CF&I. While some positive reassessments have highlighted workers' support for retention of the plans, it is difficult to determine whether the votes in representation elections after 1933 are an accurate reflection of worker opinion given employer intimidation and divisive tactics. In the end, the state banned ERPs with the Wagner Act, though some survived in the form of independent unions.

Could ERPs be a platform for trade union organising? The evidence suggests that this was very difficult except in exceptional circumstances. The unions required both a well-resourced organising campaign and a favourable political and legal climate. US steelworkers successfully used the plans as a springboard for unionisation in the late 1930s. There was also the determined campaign of SWOC and the fact that the Wagner Act underpinned the organisation of US Steel.

The union-management cooperative committees were never able to match the success of the rival ERPs. While the AFL was concerned that direct representation could undermine union authority and lead to the establishment of a rival ERP, rank-and-file members were opposed to union-management cooperation because it offered no direct representation. As in the case of

ERPs, there is evidence of management opposition to union-management cooperation.

Union-management cooperation committees did have some benefits in that they indirectly allowed workers a voice to improve their working conditions and increase efficiency. There is some evidence that the schemes did provide stabilisation of employment for permanent employees during the 1920s. They also had certain increased benefits for management in terms of sales and contracts. However, the unions' promotion of organised firms that adopted union-management cooperation could weaken competitors that also had union shops but refused to adopt union-management cooperation. Further, unions' use of political pressure to win contracts for firms that adopted union-management cooperation could also undermine competitive tendering processes and bring the unions into disrepute.

The union-management cooperative movement, like the ERPs, was weakened by the depression of the 1930s. Economic circumstances even led to the cessation of union-management cooperation in some firms. The movement was also a casualty of the Wagner Act in the US. Unions no longer saw the cooperative committees as helpful in gaining and maintaining recognition as agents for collective bargaining. However, union-management cooperation survived in some firms into the post-war period, and even won some new adherents, notably the TVA. Members of the AFL even attempted to have it adopted as a formal strategy for all industry in 1940 in the context of the growing possibility of the US entering the Second World War.

5

The UK

This chapter examines the extent and impact of ideas about workplace employee representation in the UK during the interwar years. Despite the promise of Whitleyism, Whitley works committees were not extensive and had limited impact. There were some employers, however, who persisted with Whitley works committees or variations on them, such as John Lysaght & Co., Rowntree Confectionary and ICI. There was also some interest in overseas developments, such as ERPs, union-management cooperation and German works councils.

The Extent of Whitley Works Committees

In the UK, attempts to develop Whitley committees at the workplace level had limited impact, while JICs did not develop at the industry level. Initially there was some degree of enthusiasm for JICs: 74 were created between 1918 and 1921 and it has been estimated that they covered over 3.5 million workers by the end of 1920. Whitleyism was irrelevant for much of private manufacturing, such as the iron and steel industry, where collective bargaining and trade unionism were well established. JICs tended to flourish in industries where unions were weak, but in the case of the wrought hollow-ware trade, which produced metal tableware and already had a statutory Trade Board, the JIC lapsed after increased powers conferred on the Trades Boards in 1918 led parties to believe the JIC to be superfluous. JICs generally fell into abeyance in the wake of the First World War, the Civil Service being a notable exception. Many JICs only met a few times or very infrequently. The construction JIC survived until 1922, and the paper industry JIC was active until 1924. Only 42 JICs still functioned in 1930 and only 20 survived to 1939. Employers feared that union militants would use the scheme for "class war" rather than "constructive collaboration," while unionists feared that employers would use the scheme to eliminate union presence in the workplace.[1]

There are a number of reasons why the JICs failed to develop during the interwar period. The post-war economic boom broke in 1920 and there followed a severe economic recession in 1921–22. The British economy remained sluggish throughout the 1920s and was hit severely by the Great Depression. Trade union membership declined and employers became more belligerent and determined to reassert managerial prerogative in the workplace and to do what was necessary to challenge overseas competition. The threat posed by militant shop stewards and shop committees also dissipated. The last major wartime challenge from the shop floor came in January 1919 and ended in disaster when the Clyde and Belfast District Committees of the ASE called strikes for a 40-hour week and 44-hour week respectively in protest against a national agreement which reduced hours to 47. The government declared martial law in Glasgow and police brutally attacked a meeting of strikers and arrested strike leaders. Where shop floor organisation survived the economic downturn, it was integrated into and subordinated to official union structures.[2]

There was also a decline in political support. During the general election of December 1918, Prime Minister Lloyd George weakened any push towards JICs by hardly referring to them in the campaign. The wartime coalition government did nevertheless organise a National Industrial Conference of employers and unions in February 1919 in the context of an upsurge of industrial discontent during the winter of 1918–19. Some elements within the government and among employers also hoped that an "industrial parliament" might meet the needs of the highly organised coal, iron and steel, railway and engineering sectors. While there was resounding support from all sides of the conference for industrial cooperation and discussion of forming an elected National Industrial Council of employers and unions to advise government on major industrial issues, there were virtually no positive results in terms of industrial reform. The Ministry for Reconstruction

[1] Charles, *The Development of Industrial Relations*, pp. 124–5; Letter, Robert Wilson to Sir William Ashley, 19 Jan. 1918; Letter, Harry Eyles to Sir William Ashley, 29 Oct. 1924. WAP; Patmore, "Unionism and Non-Union Employee Representation", p. 536; Sharpe, *Industrial Conciliation and Arbitration in Great Britain*, p. 330; Peter Sloman, *The Liberal Party and the Economy, 1929–1964*, Oxford University Press, Oxford, 2015, p. 39; Stitt, *Joint Industrial Councils*, p. 147; Chris Wrigley, *Cosy Co-operation under Strain: Industrial Relations in the Yorkshire Woollen Industry 1919–1930*, University of York Borthwick Paper No. 71, 1987, pp. 2–3.

[2] Clegg, *A History of British Trade Unions since 1889*, pp. 270–1; Gospel, "Employers and Managers", p. 163; Richard Hyman, "Foreword to the 1975 edition", in C.L. Goodrich, *The Frontier of Control*, Pluto Press, London, 1975, p. xv; Arthur Pugh, *Men of Steel: By One of Them*, Iron and Steel Trades Confederation, London, 1951, p. 292.

was quickly disbanded in 1919, and most of its duties were transferred to the Ministries of Labour and Health. While the Ministry of Labour did continue to promote JICs, the funding for allocated staff was cut at the Treasury's insistence in 1919 and there again during the government financial crisis of 1922, which saw the Industrial Relations Division of the Ministry, the heart of bureaucratic support for Whitleyism, reduced from 115 to 20 staff.[3] Stitt has noted that after this point the Ministry of Labour "provided advisors and monitors for the JICs that existed but moved away from any active attention to the creation of new JICs."[4] The Ministry became more focused on Trade Boards, which provided it with a more direct method of addressing industrial conditions than the JICs, which operated independently from the Ministry.[5]

The development of works committees under the Whitley Scheme was also disappointing. While it is difficult to estimate the number of works committees, the Ministry of Labour estimated in 1923 that over 1,000 had been formed in the UK, though this figure included works committees in industries where there were no JICs. Many of these committees had ceased to function by 1925, though some persisted where workers and managers had a strong commitment to their continuation. From 1925 the number of works committees remained stable with approximately 500 functioning in 1932. They were particularly found in large firms, where British managers, similar to their US counterparts, desired to maintain a means for the "more intimate and frequent contact" with employees found in smaller firms.[6]

Examples of this sympathetic approach by employers to works committees can be seen in the confectionary and chemical industries. In the confectionary trade, notable Quaker employers such as Cadbury and Rowntree were interested in setting up workplace committees. By 1920, Cadbury, based at Bourneville near Birmingham, employed 7,870, mainly unskilled and semi-skilled employees, 50 per cent of whom were women, in sugar

---

[3] Charles, *The Development of Industrial Relations*, p. 204; John Seymour, *The Whitley Council's Scheme*, P.S. King & Son, London, 1932, p. 38; Paul Johnson, *Land Fit for Heroes: The Planning of British Reconstruction 1916–1919*, University of Chicago Press, Chicago, 1968, p. 377; Keith Middlemas, *Politics in Industrial Society: The Experience of the British System since 1911*, André Deutsch, London, 1979, p. 139; Stitt, *Joint Industrial Councils*, pp. 137–41; Chris Wrigley, *Lloyd George and the Challenge of Labour: The Post-War Coalition 1918–1922*, Harvester Wheatsheaf, Hemel Hempstead, 1990, pp. 130–4.

[4] Stitt, *Joint Industrial Councils*, p. 141.

[5] Stitt, *Joint Industrial Councils*, p. 141.

[6] J. Henry Richardson, *Industrial Relations in Great Britain*, 2nd ed., Studies and Reports Series A (Industrial Relations) No. 36, ILO, Geneva, 1938, pp. 158–9; UK Ministry of Labour, *Report on the Establishment and Progress of Joint Industrial Councils 1917–1922*, HMSO, London, 1923, p. 8.

confectionary and paper box production. While the Quaker employers emphasised the Christian value of compassion, believed in the "brotherhood of man," developed extensive welfare programmes and recognised unions, they were also concerned with business efficiency to ensure economic survival. During the late 1920s, Cadbury undertook a programme of techno-logical change that was accompanied by a loss of more than 2,000 jobs by the end of 1930.[7]

Ernest Bevin, the national organiser of the Dock, Wharf, Riverside and General Union (DWRGWU) and later the first General Secretary of the Transport and General Workers' Union, approached Cadbury and other chocolate, cocoa and confectionery manufacturers in 1917 to encourage them to adopt the recommendations of the Whitley Committee. Bevin was also active in the National Alliance of Employers and Employed, which brought together employers and unionists to promote industrial peace and minimise industrial unrest through cooperation. However, the leading confectionary manufacturers were unable to persuade the Ministry of Labour to recognise a JIC for the industry because of the lack of organisation in the industry as a whole. Cadbury saw works councils as a means of ultimately initiating a JIC for the industry, which it considered a way of developing a new kind of industrial order based on cooperation, and adopted a three-tier scheme in 1918 with shop committees representing various trades, of which there were 130 by 1921, group committees with representatives of the shop committees and works councils. There were separate men and women's committees but there was a joint works council. Workers elected their representatives and the board of directors appointed its own delegates. The scheme was not allowed to contravene union custom and practices, while wages and conditions were dealt with through negotiations between management and unions rather than the councils. The councils could consider health and safety, discipline, the improvement of production methods, the elimination of waste, welfare, educational activities and suggestions for greater efficiency, but they could not make policy – this was management's prerogative.[8]

[7] Charles Dellheim, "The Creation of a Company Culture: Cadburys, 1861–1931", *The American Historical Review*, vol. 92, no. 1, 1987, pp. 16, 22, 29, 40–1.

[8] Cadbury Ltd., *A Works Council in Being: An Account of the Scheme in Operation at the Bourneville Works*, Publication Department, Bourneville, 1921, pp. 2–7; Clegg, *A History of British Trade Unions*, p. 573; Dellheim, "The Creation of a Company Culture", pp. 36–8; Chris Smith, John Child and Michael Rowlinson, *Reshaping Work: The Cadbury Experience*, Cambridge University Press, Cambridge, 1990, pp. 67–9: Chris Wrigley, "Trade Unionists, Employers and the Cause of Industrial Unity and Peace", in Chris Wrigley and John Shepherd (eds.), *On the Move: Essays in Labour and Transport History Presented to Philip Bagwell*, Hambledon Press, London, 1991, pp. 156–70.

The board of directors at the Rowntree factory in York began considering a scheme for works councils in 1916 and, following consultation with workers' shop leaders and trade unions, adopted a constitution in December of that year – before the establishment of the Whitley Committee. It then began to roll out the scheme; the Almond Paste Department and its sections held meetings from March 1917. The works councils were elected by employees in each section and each department and given considerable powers to alter working conditions. As at Cadbury, Rowntree had a central works council or "Cocoa Works Parliament," which held its first meeting on 6 January 1919. In 1922, the works council comprised 27 management representatives, some elected by fellow managers and some appointed, and 28 worker representatives elected by the worker representatives on the department councils. While Rowntree's employees were roughly equally divided between men and women, there were only nine female worker representatives and eight female management representatives on the council. The works councils voted for the abolition of Saturday work in 1919 and established an appeal committee to hear worker grievances. Union shop stewards and works councils existed alongside each other. Rowntree allowed non-unionists to be elected to the works councils despite union objections. Like Cadbury, increasing emphasis was placed on efficiency, particularly against the background of the sluggish British economy of the 1920s, and the unions at Rowntree cooperated in the introduction of scientific management practices such as time studies. Rowntree's management emphasised consultation and disclosure of company information with workers and their unions, but retained its executive power and right of veto over the works councils. Both Rowntree and Cadburys also operated a profit-sharing scheme alongside works councils. The works councils at Cadbury and Rowntree were active throughout the period examined.[9]

In the chemical industry, ICI and the companies that merged to form it in 1926 encouraged works committees. Unlike the confectionary industry, the Ministry of Labour saw chemicals as sufficiently organised to allow for a JIC. Employers were reluctant to engage directly with trade union leaders. In March 1918, Roscoe Brunner, Chair of the Chemical Employers

    [9] Ian Bradley, *Enlightened Entrepreneurs: Business Ethics in Victorian Britain*, Lion Hudson, Oxford, 2007, pp. 156–7; W. Fieldhouse, "Works Councils", Typescript, 24 Nov. 1969. R/WC/3, Rowntree & Co. Collection, Borthwick Institute for Archives, University of York, UK (hereafter RBIAY); Fitzgerald, *Rowntree and the Marketing Revolution*, Cambridge University Press, Cambridge, 1995, p. 253; B. Seebohm Rowntree, *The Human Factor in Business*, 3rd ed., Longmans, Green and Co., London, 1938, pp. 9–10; Ben Selekman and Sylvia Selekman, *British Industry Today: A Study of English Trends in Industrial Relations*, Harper & Brothers, New York, 1929, pp. 134–61; *The Cocoa Works Magazine*, Mar. 1922, vol. 2, no. 3, pp. 72–6.

Federation, described union officials as "amateurs" in business matters due to the chemical industry's technical and commercial complexity, particularly in regard to research.[10] Despite these concerns, the first meeting of the chemical trade JIC was held on 16 August 1918; Brunner was elected Chair and Bevin from the DWRGWU was elected Vice-Chair. The JIC sponsored the formation of district councils, which became the organising platform for works committees. The works committees were prohibited by the JIC executive in April 1919 from discussing wage issues, but were allowed to absorb the existing workplace safety committees. The chemical trade JIC was still active at the outbreak of the Second World War and was dominated from 1926 to 1936 by the merged ICI, which employed over half the wage earners in the industry and adopted increasingly progressive labour policies that led to strains within the JIC. ICI left the JIC in 1936 after it decided to give all workers a common basic wage irrespective of the district they worked in.[11]

Against this background, several of the firms that had merged to form ICI in 1926 had established works committees. Brunner, Mond & Co. established a General Works Council in July 1918 and works committees chaired by local managers were founded a month later. The works committees in the Cheshire towns of Middlewitch and Sanbach suggested the establishment of a co-partnership scheme in 1920, but this proposal was turned down by the directors due to deteriorating economic conditions. However, two directors and members of the Brunner family were willing to sell 10,000 shares to set up a Stock Purchase Scheme. The works committees also supervised various welfare provident societies such as a benevolent fund whereby a company donation matched employee contributions, and were placed in charge of a branch of the new hospital fund from 1921. Castner-Kellner Alkali Co., near Liverpool, held an inaugural meeting of its works committee in June 1920.[12]

Sir Alfred Mond, who came from Brunner Mond & Co. and was the first chair of ICI, built on the existing works committees of the merging companies by establishing works councils throughout the company. While Mond was a strong critic of socialism, particularly guild socialism, he

[10] Great Britain Ministry of Labour (hereafter GB MOL), Memo, "Heavy Chemicals No. 4. Joint Industrial Councils. (Whitley Report.)", 4 Apr. 1918. LAB 2/265/HQ12029/2/1918. PRO.

[11] Charles, *The Development of Industrial Relations*, pp. 126–7, 178–9; GB MOL, Chemical Trade JIC Minutes, 16 Aug. 1918, LAB 2/265/HQ12029/16/1918, Chemical Trade JIC executive minutes, 3 Apr. 1919, LAB 2/265/JIC/116/2/1918, PRO.

[12] Brunner, Mond & Co., *The 50th Anniversary: 1873–1923*, 1923, p. 36; Fitzgerald, *British Labour Management & Industrial Welfare*, pp. 119–20; Ray Markey and Greg Patmore, "Employee Participation and Labour Representation: ICI Works Councils in Australia, 1942–75", *Labour History*, no. 97, 2009, p. 59.

believed that it was possible for capital and organised labour to cooperate. With Ben Turner, Chair of the TUC General Council, he initiated the Mond-Turner talks in January 1928, a dialogue between some prominent employers and the TUC over improving industrial relations in the wake of the union defeat in the 1926 General Strike. The initial report, which was ultimately rejected by employers, recognised trade unions, opposed victimisation of union activists, proposed a system of conciliation boards and called for the efficient rationalisation of British industry.[13]

Mond wanted to be able to maintain a "personal touch" with the 40,000 employees of his company. ICI established a central labour department to ensure uniform labour standards and in 1929 established a company-wide system of 71 works councils. Initially there were works councils for each of the factories, group councils with representatives from each works council in each group of companies and a central works council with representatives from each of the group councils. The councils consisted of equal numbers of employee and management, but a management representative served as chair. They met monthly and discussed safety and ways of improving productivity. Management would consider any "reasonable" requests but had the right of veto over council decisions. The work councils provided an important means for management to communicate any changes in the workplace and employee conditions. Mond also introduced a share ownership scheme, a company magazine and special staff status for employees, which gave ICI's employees greater job security and benefits at the directors' discretion after five years' service.[14]

In the British railways, works committees or Local Departmental Committees (LDCs) persisted until the outbreak of the Second World War. After 1921, the British railway networks were dominated by four giant private companies with extensive welfare programmes and developed labour administration. The London Midland and Scottish Railway Company (LMS), for example, had shareholder capital of £414 million in 1937, compared to ICI's £74 million, 19,926 miles of track and 232,000 employees. Unlike in other industries, Whitley works committees had a statutory basis in the rail sector through the 1921 Railways Act for occupations covered by the NUR, the Associated Society of Locomotive Engineers and Firemen

[13] G.W. McDonald and Howard Gospel, "The Mond-Turner Talks, 1927–1933: A Study in Industrial Cooperation", *The Historical Journal*, vol. 16, no. 4, 1973, pp. 807–29; Alfred Mond, *Industry and Politics*, Macmillan & Co., London, 1927, pp. 334–5; Reader, *Imperial Chemical Industries*, pp. 58–60.

[14] ICI Press Release, "Inaugural Meeting of the Central Works Council of the Imperial Chemical Industries, 18th April 1929, London", D600/1000/202/1, ILO Archives, Geneva, Switzerland (hereafter ILOA); Reader, *Imperial Chemical Industries*, pp. 60–3; *The Times* (London), 8 Oct. 1927, p. 7, 18 Oct. 1927, p. 18, 7.6.1929, p. 16.

(ASLEF) and the Railway Clerks' Association. The legislation provided for Central and National Wages Boards with equal representation, which the Ministry of Transport had offered to the railway unions in November 1919. While the NUR accepted the proposal, the scheme was advantageous for the government in diverting the unions' attention away from the nationalisation of the railways.[15]

The LDCs were established at any station or depot where the number of employees exceeded 75 and had a maximum of four elected employee representatives, including the LDC secretary, and four railway management representatives. Their major role was to provide a means of communication between employees and local railway officials, and to give the workers a broader interest in the conditions of their employment, including efficiency, welfare, safety, hours of attendance, holiday arrangements and suggestions for improvements in railway work and organisation, but they could not deal with matters covered by wage agreements. If the LDC disagreed, then the matter could be referred to the relevant Sectional Council.[16] Railway management saw these committees as an acceptable alternative to the possibility of legislation requiring worker directors on company boards, which the Labour Party had supported during the passage of the 1921 Railways Act.[17] They warned that the "inclusion of subordinate officers or wages grade men" was "impossible as no General Manager could accept orders from a Board so constituted."[18] Despite this, management largely ignored the LDCs for they considered them to undermine management authority.[19]

Against the background of the economic downturn of the early 1920s, the railway unions accepted the Whitley councils and LDCs as an alternative to board representation and were critical of management's delays in introducing them into the industry. Concemore Cramp, Industrial General Secretary of the NUR, claimed in February 1922 that experience gained by railway workers on these committees would assist them when they eventually gained control of the railways through nationalisation. While management resisted railway union calls for the committees to play a more active role in labour

[15] Susan Armitage, *The Politics of Decontrol of Industry: Britain and the United States*, London School of Politics, London, 1969, pp. 81–9; Fitzgerald, *British Labour Management & Industrial Welfare*, pp. 25–43; Patmore, "Unionism and Non-Union Employee Representation", p. 537; *The Economist*, 2 Jul. 1938, p. 2.

[16] LMS, *Scheme For Establishment of Local Departmental Committees, Sectional Railway Councils, and Railway Councils*, LMS, London, 1924, pp. 10–11.

[17] Armitage, *The Politics of Decontrol*, p. 89.

[18] Great Britain Ministry of Transport, "Note of Meeting between Officers of the Ministry of Transport and General Managers Held on 11-12.10.1920", MT 49/2, PRO.

[19] Patmore, "Unionism and Non-Union Employee Representation", p. 537.

relations, they did agree to an extension of the scheme to railway workshops with shop committees and works committees in August 1927.[20]

There are a number of reasons why works committees generally failed to take off. Only some JICs showed enthusiasm at the outset and very few persisted with them. The pottery JIC did try to organise works committees through special campaigns and to keep up ongoing interest by organising quarterly conferences of existing workplace committee representatives. While 100 pottery work committees were organised by August 1929, only approximately half of them survived and it was estimated that not more than six were "really functioning." Works committees did not take root where the collective bargaining machinery was weak, as in the silk and hosiery industry and quarrying for example. Some employers believed that works committees were inappropriate for their workplaces because of the small numbers of employees. The Cliffe Hill Granite Company quarry in Leicester, for example, informed the Ministry of Labour that their works were too small as they employed only 15 people; Bests Brewery in Stockwell similarly rejected the idea of a works council on the grounds that they had 26 employees. Where employers were suspicious of trade unions, such as in the soap and candle trades, they did not encourage works committees.[21] The Secretary of the London Brewers Council noted in June 1920 that he was not in favour of Whitley works committees because they encouraged "employees to join trade unions."[22] Colliery owner opposition to the imposition of works or colliery committees in the coal mining industry by legislation led the government to abandon the proposal. While the MFGB had also opposed the idea initially, it had dropped its objections by December 1921 following defeat in the 1921 lockout, wage cuts and a deteriorating economic climate for the coal industry.[23] Colliery managers threatened to resign "on the ground that they would not accept the dictation of the men."[24] As the ILO observed of Great Britain in general, "few employers are willing to surrender any part

---

[20] Fitzgerald, *British Labour Management & Industrial Welfare*, p. 43; Patmore, "Unionism and Non-Union Employee Representation", p. 537; *The Times*, 20 Feb. 1922, p. 5; Weekly Report, London, 19 Dec. 1921, p. 4. C25/* 25/2/1/2, ILOA.

[21] Charles, *The Development of Industrial Relations*, p. 204; Great Britain Ministry of Labour, Industrial Councils Division, Works Committee Section, "Report for Week Ending 12th June, 1920", p. 1; "Report for Week Ending 11th September, 1920", p. 1. JIC186/1920/PSTSII, PRO; Patmore, "Unionism and Non-Union Employee Representation", p. 536; Seymour, *The Whitley Council's Scheme*, p. 85; *The Ministry of Labour Gazette*, Aug. 1929, p. 278.

[22] Great Britain Ministry of Labour, Industrial Councils Division, Works Committee Section, "Report for Week Ending 12th June, 1920", p. 1. JIC186/1920/PSTSII, PRO.

[23] Clegg, *A History of British Trade Unions*, pp. 321–5; Patmore, "Unionism and Non-Union Employee Representation", pp. 536–7; *The Times*, 11 Aug. 1921, p. 7, 1 Mar. 1922, p. 10.

[24] Weekly Report, London, 24 Jul. 1920, p. 4. C25/* 25/2/1/1, ILOA.

of their control not only over the works but over the workshop."[25] British employers were also generally reluctant to share information with employees due to a "tradition of secrecy" that was "firmly ingrained."[26]

In the engineering trades, both labour and management preferred the existing system of union shop stewards and shop committees. Shop stewards could take grievances to their supervisor and then to the manager if not satisfied. The matter would then be taken to a union official and committee of shop stewards if still not settled and hopefully it would be resolved through a conference with the local employers' association. As one engineering union official in Birmingham noted, "the whole thing was already there in the engineering industry": and he "was not clear that anything in the Whitley Report would improve their system."[27]

There were also concerns among engineering employers that Whitley works committees would lead to workplaces becoming debating clubs, which would undermine rather than enhance production. As Thomas Mitton, an executive member of the Engineering Employers Federation and founder of the Birmingham brass founding firm Hunt and Mitton, noted in January 1918 in reference to the Russian Revolution, "Russia was a warning against" workplaces becoming debating clubs.[28] While there was little interest in the private engineering sector, there was interest in the works committees in some government engineering workshops, such as those of the Admiralty.[29]

There were union concerns about the works committees and government support for the extension of works committees declined. Unions objected to non-unionists voting for works committee representatives and running for positions on them. The understanding developed that while non-unionists could vote for the committees, they were ineligible for election to office. Some unions saw works committees as "inadvisable" if they did not have significant presence in a workplace. Similarly, when the Ministry of Labour was directly encouraging the formation of works committees in 1920, it refused to provide assistance to employers where there was insufficient union organisation. The financial cuts imposed upon the Ministry of Labour also weakened the push towards work committees as staff focused on the encouragement of works committees were either dismissed or transferred to other government departments with vacancies in December 1920. Though

---

[25] Weekly Report, London, 30 Oct.1920, p. 11. C25/* 25/2/1/1, ILOA.

[26] Selekman and Selekman, *British Industry Today*, p. 109.

[27] Typescript, "Report on a Conference of Trade Unionists at Birmingham in the Metal, Engineering and Connected Trades, January 19, 1918", p. 5. WAP.

[28] Typescript, "Conference of Employers on the Whitley Report Held in the Council Room of the University of Birmingham January 28 1918", p. 5. WAP.

[29] Patmore, "Unionism and Non-Union Employee Representation", p. 536.

the Committee of Industry and Trade, or the Balfour Committee, which was appointed by Labour Prime Minister Ramsay McDonald in July 1924 to investigate the decline in the UK's economy since the First World War and included Cramp from the NUR, did present a report favouring works committees on a voluntary basis in March 1929, there was no revival of the earlier interest shown by the Ministry of Labour.[30]

JICs remained a feature of the Civil Service and there is some evidence of activity by office committees, the Civil Service equivalent of workshop committees. While the Civil Service was not considered in the original report, some Civil Service unions recognised the benefits of Whitleyism in enhancing their role in the determination of wages and conditions. The Second Report of the Whitley Committee, published in October 1917, which recognised that its recommendations covered state and municipal authorities, weakened initial government opposition to union support for the extension of Whitleyism into the Civil Service. Civil Service Whitley Councils were essentially joint conciliation boards with broad terms of reference including wages and conditions, but without an independent chair. There was a National Whitley Council, which held its first meeting on 23 July 1919, departmental councils, district committees and office committees. The functions of the office committees were not spelt out and were subject to the discretion of the departmental councils. By March 1928 there were 68 departmental councils and ten Whitley Industrial Councils, which covered blue-collar workers such as engineers in government workshops and established works committees, in the British Civil Service.[31]

While there are no data available on the number of office committees in the British Civil Service, office committees were active in several notable Civil Service departments. In the Admiralty the office committees operated in most of its headquarters. But, as Leonard White noted, many of them were "without real vitality" and operated "under very real handicaps" as they did not deal with many major issues; a lack of business led to the frequent suspension of meetings.[32] When the Kew Ministry of Labour office in London attempted in October 1938 to vitalise its office committee

---

[30] Great Britain Ministry of Labour, Memo, Establishments Officer, 31 Dec. 1920. JIC 186/15 1920 A465/12, PRO; Patmore, "Unionism and Non-Union Employee Representation", pp. 536–7; *The Ministry of Labour Gazette*, Mar. 1929, p. 82; *The Times*, 12 Mar. 1929, p. 9.

[31] Alan Clinton, *Post Office Workers: A Trade Union and Social History*, George Allen & Unwin, London, 1984, pp. 90–3; Great Britain, *Report of the National Provisional Joint Committee on the Application of the Whitley Report to the Administrative Departments of the Civil Service*, HMSO, London, 1919; UK Treasury, Typescript, "List of Departments having Departmental Whitley Councils", 6 Mar. 1928. T275/39, PRO; Leonard White, *Whitley Councils in the British Civil Service*, University of Chicago Press, Chicago, 1933, pp. 3–15.

[32] White, *Whitley Councils in the British Civil Service*, p. 89.

by requiring that all labour matters raised by unions be brought through the committee, union protests noted that the Whitley scheme in the Civil Service did not prevent them from raising issues directly with management and the relevant minister. There were also active office committees in the Post Office, those in Birmingham in 1927 preventing the employment of women in branch offices for a time. However, problems arose within the Post Office (Administrative) Whitley Council relating to union representation in July 1928. The Union of Post Office and the Civil Service Clerical Association rejected representation from the "secessionist" National Federation of Postal and Telegraph Clerks, even though it was recognised by management, who wanted them on the Post Office (Administrative) Whitley Council. This dispute resulted in the suspension of the Post Office (Administrative) Whitley Council and its local office committees until May 1932.[33]

While the JICs did not achieve their promise, there were attempts to extend them further by giving them legal powers to prevent unorganised employers undercutting the wages paid by employers loyal to the JIC agreements. The Association of Joint Industrial Councils and Interim Reconstruction Committees (AJICIRC), founded in March 1921, lobbied for legislation to allow the JICs' statutory enforcement of agreements if they wanted to exercise them. The main support for the AJICIRC came from the pottery JIC, since Fred Hand was secretary of both organisations. While the TUC did give support to the idea at its 1925 conference, it later had reservations about the application of penalties to unions and workers who broke agreements, and the movement was weakened by a lack of support among JICs, the tinplate industry JIC arguing that it had a long and successful history without the need for legal powers. Between 1924 and 1935, there were six unsuccessful attempts to have a Bill passed in Parliament to give the JICs the necessary powers.[34]

[33] Clinton, *Post Office Workers*, pp. 452–3; *The Times*, 22 Feb. 1928, p. 16, 31 May 1928, p. 8, 16 Aug. 1928 p. 12, 6 Feb. 1932 p. 9, 22 Sept. 1932, p. 7; UK Treasury, Whitley Bulletin No. 67, Jul. 1928. T 199/199, PRO, Letters, J.R. Simpson to H. Parker, 22 Nov. 1938, Letter, W. Taylor to H. Parker, 23 Dec. 1938. T215/14, PRO; White, *Whitley Councils*, pp. 70–85.

[34] AJICIRC, Memo, 27 Jul. 1934. UK Treasury, T 162/604/E1067/1, PRO; Charles, *The Development of Industrial Relations*, pp. 205–10; Letter, General Secretary to J. Gilmour, 2 Dec. 1936. MSS.292/221/1, TUC Collection, MRC; Sharpe, *Industrial Conciliation and Arbitration in Great Britain*, pp. 333–4; Stitt, *Joint Industrial Councils*, pp. 145–53; *The Times* (London), 18 May 1927, p. 11.

The Impact of Whitley Works Committees

What did the Whitley works committees do? Most of them were joint committees, but there was a tendency not to insist on equal representation with employers and to emphasise cooperation and consultation rather than a "tug of war" based on two sides with a conflict of interest. Works committee representatives were allowed, with management's consent, to move around the workplace to consult with constituents and look out for any problems in areas such as safety. Elections of worker representatives were usually held annually and meetings were generally held on a regular monthly basis. At least one company, R.A. Lister, an agricultural machinery manufacturer in Dursley, Gloucestershire, in 1928, gave the company's directors the right to veto nominations for employee representatives they believed would not represent the "best interests" of the majority of employees or who did not have regard for the "seriousness" of their duties. Unlike the original Rockefeller Plan in the US, employee representatives were generally allowed to meet separately before full committees to determine their group perspective on issues. They were paid for all the time spent on committee business, generally at the average wage earned on the job. The secretary of the works committee was usually the employment manager and committees were found in companies that had well-organised employment departments with a centralised personnel function. Minutes were taken, for which purpose the rules of the Whitley Works Committee of Best & Lloyd, a light fitting manufacturer in Birmingham, required a shorthand typist to be present to take notes. Some works committees, such as that at John Trapp & Son, a wine bottlers and warehouse in London, operated on an informal basis, with no written constitution. Trapp & Son's works committee was an extension of its profit-sharing scheme committee with additional representation by supervisors.[35]

The powers of the works committees were mainly consultative and advisory, the final power remaining in the hands of management. Cadbury's management for example repeatedly rejected its works council's request to share the responsibility for the dismissal of the employees with management. Generally, there was no formal vote: management relied on the consent of the worker representatives. They ensured that wages and working conditions complied with industry collective agreements but left the negotiation of

[35] Letters, R.A. Lister & Co. to TUC General Council, 30 Aug. 1928, J.H. Trapp to Secretary, Research and Economic Department, TUC, 30 Aug. 1928. MSS.292/221/5, TUC Collection, MRC; Richardson, *Industrial Relations in Great Britain*, pp. 160–4; Selekman and Selekman, *British Industry Today*, pp. 112–18; Typescript, Best & Lloyd, "Rules of the Whitley Works Committee", p. 2. MSS.292/221/5, TUC Collection, MRC.

these issues to unions and employers' associations. The works committees also handled grievances and concerned themselves with safety, training and welfare issues. Some went further and focused on production costs, such as suggesting ways of reducing wastage of scrap metal. At Belle Vue railway depot near Manchester, an LMS LDC in March 1939 discussed a wide range of issues including the enforcement of speed restrictions on trains, the showing of educational films, an anti-waste campaign, the condition of the railway shed turntable and better arrangements for the payment of employees' wages. Management generally also found the works committees to be a valuable means of communication with employees about a variety of issues such as production, raw materials and competitors' prices.[36] In 1927, the greatest value of the works committee at the Stanton Ironworks near Nottingham, in management's view, was "that they enable the managing director to maintain personal touch with large bodies of workers."[37] The Stanton works committee had been established in 1919 and met monthly in the boardroom. It was not encouraged by management to discuss financial issues but did frankly discuss workers' grievances.[38]

Few extensive examples of Whitley works committee minutes survive that provide long-term insights into their operations. One exception to this is the Orb Works, an iron and steel plant that produced galvanised sheets at Newport in Wales, founded in 1898 and employing 3,500 workers by 1928. Forty-eight mills were rolling sheets up to 72 inches wide in 1928 and it was claimed then that the Newport mills were the largest of their type in the world with an annual output of 200,000 tons. The market for its products was growing with the rise of the automobile industry, the power generation sector and domestic appliances, such as refrigerators and washing machines, both in the UK and overseas, and output was shipped from its wharf on the east bank of the River Esk. The Orb Works was initially owned by John Lysaght & Co., which was based in Bristol. While the majority interest in the latter was purchased by the Berry Group in 1919, and then by Guest, Keen and Nettlefolds in 1920, the Lysaghts retained managerial control. The plant was organised by the Iron and Steel Trades Confederation (ISTC), which was recognised by management and had 95 per cent coverage of

---

[36] Letter, H.F. Morcombe to Walter Citrine, 8 Jan. 1926. MSS.292/221/6, TUC Collection, MRC; Richardson, *Industrial Relations in Great Britain*, pp. 164–6; LMS, Belle Vue LDC Minutes, 15 Mar. 1939. File – "London, Midland and Scottish Railway Company, 1938–1939", Container 58, BP; Selekman and Selekman, *British Industry Today*, pp. 114–15, 118–19; Seymour, *The Whitley Council's Scheme*, p. 84; UK Ministry of Labour, *Report on the Establishment and Progress of Joint Industrial Councils*, pp. 73–84.

[37] *The Times*, 14 Jan. 1927, p. 9.

[38] Stanley Chapman, *Stanton and Staveley: A Business History*, Woodhead-Faulkner, Cambridge, 1981, p. 173.

eligible employees by November 1919. The company also had plants at Bristol and Scunthorpe in North Lincolnshire and they developed similar works committees. While John Lysaght Limited played an active role in the Sheet Trade Board, which determined wages and conditions in the industry, it withdrew from the Board in July 1938 over the latter's lack of "uniformity" on determining wages and conditions and because of other employers' willingness to ignore and undermine industry standards. The surviving minutes of its Whitley works committee cover the period 1919–39 and the committee was active until at least 1956.[39]

The Orb Works Whitley works committee, the first in the British iron and steel industry, was initiated in 1918 and from 1919 generally met on a monthly basis.[40] Managing Director William Royse Lysaght[41] hoped that the works committee would be the "public opinion" of the works and become the "avenue for a mutual interchange of ideas between" employers and workers.[42] Management believed that the committee would provide an orderly forum in which to resolve grievances as employees would take their complaints to worker representatives rather than take wildcat action such as strikes. The committee had an equal number of management and employee representatives, but still functioned if there were unequal numbers at a particular meeting. There was also a chairperson, who was an employee representative, a vice-chair and a secretary. By April 1919, there also was a president and a vice-president, who were drawn from management and employees respectively. The minutes were printed and circulated among members and posted up in the Works Assembly Hall for all employees to read. The president and secretary of each union lodge in the plant also were encouraged to attend the meetings.[43]

Changes were made to the form of the committee over time. To ensure that the views of white-collar workers were covered, the committee decided in August 1919 to allow the chair and secretary of the local branch of the National Union of Clerks (NUC) to be present at meetings and that senior

[39] John Lysaght Ltd., *The Lysaght Century 1857–1957*, Bristol, 1957, pp. 18, 29–31, 61; Letter, William Lysaght to John Brown, 20 Jul. 1938, MSS36 M6OC 6a, Orb Works Whitley Committee Minutes, 3 Mar. 1919, 3 Nov. 1919, 2 Feb. 1920, 12 Apr. 1920, 2 Jul. 1927, MSS.36/016, ISTC Collection, MRC; *The Times*, 24 Nov. 1934, p. 14.

[40] Typescript, "Reminiscences of J.R. Wardell", n.d. MSS36/2003/90, ISTC Collection, MRC.

[41] *South Wales Argus*, 5 Mar. 1928, p. 3.

[42] Orb Works Whitley Committee Minutes, 6 Jan. 1919. MSS.36/016, ISTC Collection, MRC.

[43] Orb Works Whitley Committee Minutes, 6 Jan. 1919, 3 Feb. 1919, 3 Mar. 1919, 7 Apr. 1919, 2 Jun. 1919, 11 Aug. 1919, 12 Apr. 1920, 2 May 1920, 1 Oct. 1923, 6 Jul. 1925, 7 Feb. 1927. MSS.36/016, ISTC Collection, MRC.

staff, not represented by the NUC, be allowed to elect a representative. Following a suggestion by the solicitor for the ISTC who was concerned at the increasing number of accidents in the industry and aware of the activities of safety-first committees in the US, the committee expanded its jurisdiction to cover safety in May 1920. When the company formed a Foreman's Safety First Committee in November 1927 to gain exemption from Factory Act provisions regarding workplace safety, employee representatives of the Whitley committee were co-opted onto the Safety Committee, the latter reporting to the former and prohibited from overriding the Whitley committee's decisions. A further expansion occurred in July 1925, when the Chair and Secretary of the Canteen Committee were given direct representation on the Whitley works committee. At various points there was also a Workmen's Committee, which consisted of employees' representatives.[44]

The emphasis was on consensus and when votes were taken, they were unanimous, but there were tensions. In September 1921, worker representatives alleged that one of their number had been victimised for his comments and activities on the Whitley committee and they threatened to reconsider their continued participation on the committee. The President, a management representative, dismissed the complaint, arguing that the trade unions in the plant were strong enough to ensure that any victimisation of worker representatives did not take place. The worker representatives continued to participate on the committee. During the 1926 General Strike, which involved ISTU members at the plant, J.R. Wardell, the employee chair of the committee, warned that the committee could collapse due to management comments to union members about the misuse of union funds during the dispute. While William Royce Lysaght reminded committee members that he supported the ISTU, he criticised the TUC for calling out the iron and steelworkers on an "illegal" strike.[45]

The Orb Works Whitley committee dealt with a wide range of issues. Table 5.1 indicates the types of new issues raised at meetings. In 1919, against a background of general industrial unrest, exactly 50 per cent of the issues dealt with by the committee related to industrial issues such as wages, hours and union membership. Employment issues were also important in 1919 as a result of the re-employment of returned soldiers. The committee also became an important forum for dealing with issues relating to workplace safety after the expansion of its jurisdiction in 1920 and produced regular reports on accidents and compensation payments. Over half the new issues

[44] Orb Works Whitley Committee Minutes, 11 Aug. 1919, 12 Apr. 1920, 2 May 1920, 6 Jul. 1925, 7 Nov. 1927, 5 Dec. 1927. MSS.36/016, ISTC Collection, MRC.

[45] Orb Works Whitley Committee Minutes, 5 Sept. 1921, 3 May 1926, 10 May 1926. MSS.36/016, ISTC Collection, MRC.

Table 5.1 Orb Works Whitley Works Committee –
Issues in Selected Years

Issues	1919	1924	1929	1934	1938
Committee governance %	8	9	4	0	0
Employment %	17	0	5	0	0
Improvements to plant and machinery %	3	2	5	10	0
Industrial relations%	50	15	9	3	3
Labour discipline %	3	2	0	3	0
Production %	8	9	2	0	3
Repairs %	0	2	12	8	0
Welfare %	11	9	16	3	3
Workplace safety %	0	52	54	74	91
Issues per annum total	36	46	57	39[*]	34[+]
No. of meetings	12	12	12	7[*]	9[+]
Issues per meeting	3	3.8	4.8	5.6	3.8

[*] The minutes of the May, July, October and November 1934 meetings are missing and there was no meeting in August 1934.
[+] The minutes of the October and December 1938 meetings are missing and there was no meeting in August 1938.
Source: Orb Works Whitley Committee Minutes, 11 Aug. 1919, 12 Apr. 1920, 2 May 1920, 6 Jul. 1925, 7 Nov. 1927, 5 Dec. 1927. MSS.36/016, ISTC Collection, MRC.

at the committee meetings in 1924, 1929 and 1935 were related to workplace safety and by 1938 it dominated the agenda. There were already concerns in March 1926 that the Whitley committee was "drifting" into a Safety-First Committee and ignoring other issues, such as worker housing. The emphasis on safety highlights the dangers of working in the iron and steel industry: in November 1937 alone, for example, there were 1,244 accidents at the Orb Works, which included 922 cuts, 118 burns, 87 bruises and one amputation. One major safety issue pursued by the Whitley committee was adequate lighting of the workplace to prevent accidents. Despite the focus on safety, there was a continued interest in the company's welfare policies. The committee established a canteen for the Workmen's Club, which opened on 2 October 1919, a Thrift Society in 1921, a Joint Benevolent Fund in 1923 and a subsidised employee housing scheme. The concerns of the works committee went beyond the Orb Works: it discussed and produced a subcommittee report in 1922 on the wages and living conditions of former employees who had migrated to a new John Lysaght plant in Newcastle, Australia, which was shut down in February 1922 due to a drop in demand for the product and the employees' rejection of a wage cut. Governance issues relating to meeting procedures and the election of officers virtually disappeared during the 1930s as the committee was by then well established.[46]

As with other works committees, the Orb Works committee increasingly became a means of communication for management to present reports to employee representatives on issues such as financial performance and the economic climate of the industry. In March 1919, William Royse Lysaght noted that the position of the steel sheet trade was "most serious" due to increasing prices and the growing preference of overseas customers to manufacture their own requirements. He was also concerned that miners' current demands for wage increases would have an adverse impact on industry costs. Management reports on the "state of trade" became a regular feature of the committee's meetings.[47]

While the focus of the Orb Works Whitley works committee became workplace safety, this was not the case at Rowntree, where the management's interest in scientific management and industrial psychology promoted a greater focus on production issues such as the time and motion study of particular tasks. The Cream Packing Department, which packed the cream chocolates at the York factory, employed 149 male and 1,132 female workers in September 1924. While there was an overwhelming predominance of female workers, there were also a large number of workers under 18, representing 22 per cent of the female workers and 91 per cent of male workers. There were representation issues for the younger workers as males under 21 and females under 16 were not eligible to vote in Departmental Council elections. Women also generally left employment upon marriage, which explained 47 per cent and 34 per cent of women's departures in 1922–23 and 1923–24 respectively, reducing their ability to participate in the works councils for lengthy periods. In the Cream Packing Department, departures due to marriage were even higher: 96 per cent of the 51 women leaving in 1923–24.[48]

---

[46] Orb Works Whitley Committee Minutes, 13 Oct. 1919, 6 Dec. 1920, 6 Mar. 1922, 1 May 1922, 22 May 1922, 5 Nov. 1923, 3 Dec. 1923, 8 Mar. 1926, 2 Mar. 1936, 3 Jan. 1938, MSS.36/016, Typescript, Report by the Whitley Committee of the Orb Works, 4 Oct. 1922, MSS36 L31a/1-65, ISTC Collection, MRC.

[47] Orb Works Whitley Committee Minutes, 3 Mar. 1919, 8 Jan. 1934. MSS.36/016, ISTC Collection, MRC.

[48] Rowntree & Co. Ltd., "Labour Report 1924", Typescript, pp. 59–60, 85–6, R/DL/L/2/1, "Memorandum to the Employees of Rowntree & Co. Ltd. York with Regard to Works Councils. 1st September 1916. First Revision, 1st February, 1917. Second Revision, 1st March, 1918", p. 7, R/WC/3, RBIAY.

Table 5.2 Cream Packing Departmental Council, Rowntree, York
– Issues, 1924–27

Issues	1924	1925	1926	1927
Committee governance %	3	5	5	7
Employment %	3	15	29	13
Improvements to plant and machinery %	4	13	5	0
Industrial relations%	9	18	10	7
Labour discipline %	4	3	0	9
Production %	47	18	29	57
Repairs %	2	0	5	0
Welfare %	22	28	19	4
Workplace safety %	6	3	0	4
Issues per annum total	68	39	21	46
No. of meetings	10	9	6	8
Issues per meeting	6.8	4.3	3.5	5.7

Source: Rowntree & Co., Cream Packing Departmental Council Minutes, 1924–1927. R/WC/DC/1, RBIAY

As Table 5.2 indicates, the Cream Packing Department Council, which was merged with the Cake Packing Department Council in 1928, discussed a wide range of issues, including production. Production discussions ranged from time study to quality control issues, such as the removal of foreign objects from chocolates and the eradication of moths and their grubs, which could spoil chocolate, particularly for the export trade. Disciplinary issues related to problems such as workers' failure to clock in on arrival at the factory, while employment issues particularly related to short-time, the reduction of working hours in response to fluctuation in demand for Rowntree's chocolates.[49]

The few works committees associated with the Whitley Scheme had benefits for unions. They proved a valuable ally in promoting union membership. There were some union concerns about non-unionists getting elected to works committees and undermining union membership, but generally works committee representatives were union activists. At the Orb

[49] Rowntree & Co., Cream Packing Departmental Council Minutes, 8 Sept. 1925. R/WC/DC/1, RBIAY.

Works, the employee representatives won the sympathy of management in 1919 with their efforts to remove unionists and obtain a closed shop. Management also only recognised the ISTC and opposed efforts by other unions to organise the plant. The works committee resolved in May 1919 that all new employees must be members of the ISTC. Management was initially reluctant to force the issue on existing unorganised employees in the plant, but by July 1924 it had dismissed several non-unionists at the request of union representatives.[50]

In the railways, the unions dominated the LDCs and the shop committees in the workshops. Non-unionists were rarely elected and the NUR organised lists of its members for election to the committees. The main concern for the NUR was not non-unionists, but candidates from rival unions such as the ASLEF and unofficial union candidates. Some NUR members criticised the use of candidate lists for restricting their freedom of choice in the committee elections. The NUR was so concerned that unofficial candidates would split the union vote in competition with other unions that in 1937 it took the step of adopting a policy of expelling unofficial candidates from the union. By June 1939 the Executive of the union had expelled four members on these grounds. The NUR representatives also reinforced the value of union membership by refusing to take up the grievances of non-unionists.[51]

Despite Sir Alfred Mond's sympathy towards unions and assurances, the labour movement in the UK was concerned that the ICI works councils could challenge representation of workers in the chemical industry. ICI management saw the works councils and the other labour practices as increasing commitment to the company and discouraging union membership. Unions opposed the scheme, but they could do very little to fight these initiatives because they were weak within the chemical industry and the scheme was developed without the involvement of the chemical trade JIC. Lloyd Roberts, an ICI labour manager, took the view that where unions were well organised then union nominees would be elected, but they would have to do "missionary work" in the other workplaces to ensure they won seats on the Council. To redress union concerns, in 1928 Mond established a Labour Advisory Council, which comprised six senior ICI executives and union delegates representing the five major unions

[50] Orb Works Whitley Committee Minutes, 3 Feb. 1919, 3 Mar. 1919, 12 May 1919, 2 Jun. 1919, 7 Jul. 1924. MSS.36/016, ISTC Collection, MRC.

[51] NUR, *Agenda for Annual General Meeting to be Held on July 3rd, 1939 and the Following Days*, pp. 58–9, MSS.127/NU/1/1/27, NUR, *General Secretaries' Report to the Annual General Meeting 1928*, pp. 19–20, MSS.127/NU/1/1/16, NUR Collection, MRC; *The Railway Review*, 1 Sept. 1921, p. 7.

in ICI. Despite these concessions, the concern that the works councils unfairly bypassed the unions in communication with factory management remained.[52]

In the UK there was some interest among employers in using works committees to undermine union membership. While the London Brewers rejected the Whitley Scheme, they set up informal works committees in 1920 that did not recognise trade unions. The Admiralty tried unsuccessfully to establish works committees for non-unionists at its dockyard workshops following the 1926 General Strike. There was strong union opposition to the proposals, unions reminding management of the positive role they had played in the Whitley works committees and threatening their withdrawal from the Whitley system.[53] One union claimed that the proposals' effect would be to "smash the trade unions in the Dockyard."[54] In the face of union opposition, the Admiralty did not proceed with the proposals. The one major example of a works committee developing into an ERP with the aim of reducing union power was the Dunlop Rubber Company, which will be discussed in the next section of the chapter.[55]

Looking beyond the UK

There was interest in other ideas of employee participation in the UK during this period. Private and government employers both visited the US to examine the latest developments in management practice. In September 1926, Rowntree sent labour manager Dr Clarence Northcott and G. Hawksby, the chief shop steward to the US to investigate 20 firms, including Ford, Gillette and Eastman Kodak, focusing on technology, industrial welfare and scientific management practices. A British government mission investigating industrial relations in the US and Canada in 1926 visited the Mt. Clare workshops of the B&O to examine the operation of union-management cooperation.[56] Its report praised the adoption of union-management

---

[52] Chemical Trade JIC Minutes, 17 Jan. 1929. UK Ministry of Labour, LAB 2/265/IR114/1929, PRO; Reader, *Imperial Chemical Industries*, pp. 63–6, 298–302.

[53] Admiralty, Conference Minutes, 14 Feb. 1929. Deputation from the Trade Union Side of the Admiralty Industrial Council, 27 Jun. 1929. ADM 116/2626, PRO; UK Ministry of Labour, Industrial Councils Division, Works Committee, "Negotiations during Week Ending 29 May, 1920", p. 1. JIC186/1920/PSTSII, PRO.

[54] Admiralty, Deputation from the Trade Union Side of the Admiralty Industrial Council, 27 Jun. 1929. ADM 116/2626, PRO.

[55] Admiralty, Memo, 10 Jul. 1929. ADM 116/2626, PRO; Gospel, *Markets, Firms and the Management of Labour*, p. 99; *The Times*, 7 Dec. 1927, p. 9.

[56] *Baltimore and Ohio Magazine*, Dec. 1926, p. 74; Fitzgerald, *Rowntree and the Marketing Revolution*, p. 274; Rowntree & Co., "Notes on the American Tour of Messrs. Northcott and

cooperation on the CNR and was "greatly impressed by its results, both in increased efficiency and in satisfaction to the employees in the short period since its introduction,"[57] but noted that the ERP at CF&I had "created a better situation for industrial relations."[58]

There was trade union concern that ERPs would accompany the adoption of US manufacturing practices in the UK. Bevin, who had actively promoted Whitley works committees and was a member of the 1926 government delegation to the Canada and the US, believed that company unionism combined with "specious welfare schemes" would undermine trade union membership.[59] He supported the Mond-Turner talks, arguing that employers' recognition of trade unions was crucial to preventing the spread of company unionism in the UK, and even claimed that the Mond-Turner talks "acted as the greatest check on company union growth that has taken place in this country."[60]

There was some interest among employers in forming ERPs after the defeat of unions in the 1926 General Strike but these plans generally went nowhere. One firm that did move successfully towards an ERP was the Dunlop Rubber Company in Birmingham, which employed approximately 12,000 workers in 1929 in the production of rubber items such as automobile tyres and golf balls. Prior to the 1926 General Strike Dunlop, had collective agreements with unions. After 1926, skilled metalworkers remained organised, but other workers were covered by an ERP built on the foundations of the Rockefeller Plan. Dunlop established a Joint Factory Council which comprised management members appointed by the company and employee representatives elected by a secret ballot of the workers, and had the objective of securing an agreement between management and labour over wages and conditions. The council provided a grievance procedure for employees and promoted company welfare programmes. The scheme had developed from works committees established in 1919 and was adopted overwhelmingly by

Hawksby September 1926", Typescript. R/DH/CP/7, RBIAY; *The Times*, 31 Jan. 1968, p. 10; United Kingdom Ministry for Labour, *Report of the Delegation Appointed to Study Industrial Conditions in Canada and the United States of America*, HMSO, London, 1927.

[57] UK Ministry for Labour, *Report of the Delegation Appointed to Study Industrial Conditions*, p. 49.

[58] UK Ministry for Labour, *Report of the Delegation Appointed to Study Industrial Conditions*, p. 21.

[59] TUC, *Report of Proceedings at the Sixty-First Annual Trades Union Congress. September 3rd to 8th 1928*, London, 1928, p. 448; Chris Wrigley, "Labour Dealing with Labour: Aspects of Economic Policy", in John Shepherd, Jonathan Davis and Chris Wrigley (eds.), *Britain's Second Labour Government, 1929–31: A Reappraisal*, Manchester University Press, Manchester, 2011, pp. 38–44.

[60] TUC, *Report of Proceedings at the Sixty-First Annual Trades Union Congress*, p. 448.

a ballot of employees.[61] Management argued that their employees believed that unions did not truly represent them, and Sir Eric Geddes, the chair of the company, claimed that through promoting cooperation between management and workers the scheme had contributed to improved efficiency and financial performance. Dunlop had extensive welfare schemes, such as the contributory pension scheme introduced in 1938, and the ERP was still in operation at the outbreak of the Second World War.[62]

There was also some interest and experimentation with union-management cooperation. The TUC was aware of the union-management cooperation programmes on the B&O and the CNR. The LMS, which had LDCs, adopted a form of union-management cooperation in 1927. While the LMS scheme did not persist beyond the 1930s depression, management claimed that by February 1931 they had received 13,000 suggestions, of which 10 per cent were of "practical value" and had saved management an estimated £40,000 per annum. Union-management cooperation continued to attract interest in the UK up to the outbreak of the Second World War. In April 1939, the NUR contrasted this approach favourably to the "blunt industrial oppression" of British employers.[63]

The Liberal Party, facing electoral decline, adopted German works councils as a cornerstone of its industrial relations policy in 1928. Lloyd George, who replaced Asquith as leader of the Liberal Party and had taken a more sympathetic view of workers during the 1926 General Strike than Asquith, focused on developing new policies to revitalise its fortunes, particularly in opposition to the Labour Party. He established the Liberal Industrial Inquiry (LII), which was chaired by Walter Layton, the editor of *The Economist* and a former Cambridge economist, to develop policy and enlisted a team of talented businessmen, politicians and economists, such as Seebohm Rowntree and John Maynard Keynes, to assist policy formulation.[64]

---

[61] Richardson, *Industrial Relations in Great Britain*, pp. 262–3; Selekman and Selekman, *British Industry Today*, pp. 158–9; *The Times*, 7 Dec. 1927, p. 9; TUC, *Report of Proceedings at the Sixty-First Annual Trades Union Congress. September 2nd to 6th 1929*, London, 1929, p. 181.

[62] *The Times*, 7 Dec. 1927, p. 9, 6 Apr. 1938, p. 22.

[63] Letter from O.S. Beyer to H. Cassidy, 8 Nov. 1927. File – "Correspondence 1927," Container 115, B.P; LMS, Board of Directors minutes, 27 Oct. 1927, 26 Apr. 1928. PRO, RAIL 418/6; LMS, *Report of Proceedings at the Eighth Ordinary General Meeting of Proprietor held at Euston Station, London, NW I on Friday 27th February*, 1931, London, 1931, p. 34. PRO, RAIL 418/158; Memo, F. McDonald to Milne Bailey, 27 Nov. 1929. MSS.292/221/5, TUC Collection, MRC; *The Railway Review*, 14 Apr. 1939, p. 2.

[64] Chris Cook, *A Short History of the Liberal Party, 1900–1984*, 2nd ed., Macmillan, London, 1984, pp. 106–9; Sloman, *The Liberal Party and the Economy*, p. 43; Thorpe, "The 1929 General Election and the Second Labour Government", p. 19.

The LII undertook a detailed investigation of the German works council system in May 1927 with assistance from the German Ministry of Labour in Berlin and travelled throughout Germany, including the Ruhr and Bavaria. Archibald Gordon, who carried out the inquiry, was very interested in the progress of works councils, which struck him as "particularly satisfactory."[65] A proposal for works councils was included in the LII policy document entitled *Britain's Industrial Future* (the "Yellow Book") in February 1928, whose authors included Rowntree and Keynes. The "Yellow Book" advocated an expansive state role in restoring the health of the British economy and at the micro level proposed that works councils be mandatory for all factories or workshops with 50 or more employees (20 under the German legislation). While these works councils would have a consultative role, they have would have considerable oversight regarding the power of employers to dismiss employees and its assent was required for any changes in factory rules. Trade unions would still have an important role but in a much less adversarial system of wage determination. The Liberal interest in works councils was shared by the TUC and employers engaged in the Mond-Turner talks, who both listed works councils as a subject for discussion and investigation, but did not pursue it further. The Annual Meeting of the National Liberal Federation Council held at Great Yarmouth in October 1928 adopted statutory works councils as Liberal Party policy.[66]

While the Liberals failed to achieve success in the May 1929 election, which saw Labour win the largest number of seats and from a minority government, the Liberal Party continued to promote works councils. Liberal parliamentarian Geoffrey Mander, with the support of other Liberal parliamentarians, unsuccessfully brought a Works Council (No. 2) Bill before the House of Commons in March 1930. Mander was the Chair of Mander Brothers, a varnish and paint factory in Wolverhampton, where a joint works committee had been in operation since 1921 with the support of trade unions. Mander believed that the works committee had created an "atmosphere of mutual trust" in the factory. Mander's Bill followed Liberal policy in urging mandatory works councils in factories and workshops with 50 or more employees with oversight over dismissal. The Labour Cabinet took the view that the Bill had no chance of passing and believed that it was unnecessary for government representatives to enter into any discussion relating to the

[65] Letter, A.F.L. Gordon to Dr Steinmann, 10 Jun. 1927. BB, R/3901/504.

[66] National Liberal Federation, *Proceedings in Connection with the 45th Annual Meeting of the Council Held at Great Yarmouth on October 10th to 12th, 1928*, The Liberal Publication Department, London, 1928, p. 49; Sloman, *The Liberal Party and the Economy*, pp. 43–5; *The Times*, 3 Feb. 1928, p. 9; TUC General Council Industrial Committee Minutes, 28 Feb. 1928. MSS.292/262/1, TUC Collection, MRC.

Bill. At a Liberal Party function in Birmingham in February 1934, Sir Herbert Samuel, the Liberal Parliamentary Party leader, again called for the establishment of works councils in every large industrial establishment. Mander unsuccessfully repeated his earlier attempt to introduce Works Council Bills in the House of Commons in March 1935 and December 1937.[67]

Conclusion

As the cycle approach would suggest, the general wartime interest in Whitley works committees was not sustained as the British economy stagnated, particularly in the export staples industries. The Department of Labour withdrew resources from establishing the committees and employers lost interest as the threat of wartime shop floor unrest faded. Management was generally unwilling to undermine its prerogative in the workplace or share information with workers. Unions, who had been divided over the establishment of Whitley works committees, absorbed the surviving wartime shop committees into their official workplace structures.

Some employers did persist with Whitley committees. Innovative medium to large firms maintained Whitley workplace committees in confectionery, chemicals, steel products and the railways, the latter being underpinned by statutory provisions for the LDC. The Civil Service, which found the Whitley system valuable for regulating labour relations with its employees, also implemented office committees with varying success. While these committees were in unionised sectors and not allowed to negotiate on matters relating to collective agreements, they could deal with a wide range of issues that reflected their workplaces; the Orb Works Whitley works committee increasingly focused on work safety and the Cream Packing Department at Rowntree's York factory explored production issues such as time study. Generally, despite the fears of the AFL in the US, unions found that works committees could play a valuable role in assisting union organisation, particularly if they played an active role in organising official union candidates in works committee elections for representatives, as in the case of the NUR.

The Whitley workplace committees' lack of impact led British employers and unions to look at the experiences of other countries. Dunlop Rubber transformed its works committees into an ERP, which reinforced union fears that works committees could undermine union organisation, but this

---

[67] Cook, *A Short History of the Liberal Party*, p. 110; *The London Times*, 19 Mar. 1930, p. 5, 23 Nov. 1931, p. 8, 19 Feb. 1934, p. 17, 1 Mar. 1935, p. 16, 2 Mar. 1935, p. 7, 3 Dec. 1937, p. 7; UK Cabinet Office papers. Cabinet Minutes, 6 May 1931, CAB/23/4, 22 Dec. 1937, CAB/23/90A, PRO; UK House of Commons, *Works Councils (No. 2) A Bill*, HMSO, London, 1930.

lead was not followed by other employers due to the strength of organised labour in the UK. The LMS developed a hybrid of union-management cooperation and Whitley workplace committees, but abandoned it under the financial constraints of the Great Depression. Some employers and the Liberal Party considered the possibility of adopting a statutory equivalent of German works councils and a Bill was placed before the House of Commons on several occasions, even after, as we shall see in the next chapter, the Nazi government abolished works councils in Germany.

6

Germany

This chapter explores the German experience with works councils. It will assess the extent of the works councils in Germany during the interwar period and German interest in alternatives such as ERPs and union management. The chapter will explore issues such as the disclosure of information to works councillors, access to the board of directors and the role of works councils in dismissals, welfare, safety, collective agreements, the promoting of productivity and engagement in broader political issues. It will also examine the impact of works councils on trade unionism, women and management. Like their ERP counterparts in the US, the German works councils were legislated out of existence. The chapter will conclude with a discussion of their demise.

The Extent of German Works Councils

Unfortunately there are no surviving data on the number of works councils in Germany between 1920 and 1933. Using dated data from the last German industrial census of 1907, Guillebaud estimated in 1926 that there had been 108,789 agricultural, industrial and commercial establishments employing 8,379,200 workers that could have had works councils. At the industry level, in 1922 there were 32,565 wage-earning and 7,219 salaried employees who were works stewards or members of works councils in 11,557 establishments in the highly organised metal industry. In the same year, there were also 25,239 works councillors in 7,219 textile factories.[1]

The number of workplaces with works councils fluctuated with economic conditions. Following the hyperinflation of 1923, the move towards stabilising the German economy led to dismissals and increased unemployment, which weakened the power of trade unions and works councils. These circum-

[1] Guillebaud, *The Works Council*, pp. 118–20.

stances made employees reluctant to stand for positions on works councils due to fears of victimisation and an unwillingness to be involved in the dismissal of fellow employees. With the resurgence of the economy, and thus trade unions, in 1925 and 1926, there was a revival of interest in works councils among employers.[2]

Significant numbers of eligible workplaces did not have works councils. The decline in fortune of works councils in 1923–24 can be seen in the context of growing numbers of eligible workplaces without works councils. Chemnitz, Saxony, was home to 228 establishments with no works councils in 1923 and 603 in 1924. Factory inspectors found that the number of Leipzig workplaces with only salaried employees that had works stewards and works councils fell from 23 to 12 per cent between 1923 and 1924. The corresponding figures for industrial concerns in Leipzig with waged employees were 53 per cent in 1923 and 50 per cent in 1924. Factory inspectors continued to report problems with compliance and found that only 26 per cent of eligible workplaces in the Prussian city of Königsberg had works councils. An inspector for Weimar and Meiningen reported that the factories with works councils in that district fell from 80 per cent in October 1925 to 60 per cent in October 1926. By contrast, the well-organised metal trades had councils in 85 per cent of workshops in 1927 and 90 per cent in 1930.[3]

Generally, mandatory works councils were less likely to be found in eligible workplaces that were small and poorly organised and consisted mainly of salaried or female employees. Small employers believed that works councils were unnecessary and too complicated for their businesses and preferred that the legislative requirement be increased to 50 employees for a works council and a mandatory single works steward. There was also the issue of worker apathy towards works councils in smaller workplaces, where they had direct personal contact with employers.[4]

In larger enterprises, the organisation of works councils was complex. In September 1929, Siemens had a total workforce of 138,179, of whom 111,549 worked in Germany.[5] Its largest plant was Siemenstadt, "a picture of unusual architectural homogeneity and beauty,"[6] located ten kilometres north of Greater Berlin and employing 76,679 salaried and waged employees,

---

[2] Guillebaud, *The Works Council*, pp. 128–9, 224–6.

[3] Guillebaud, *The Works Council*, p. 129; McPherson, "Collaboration between Management and Employees", pp. 281–2.

[4] Raymond H. Geist, "Employees' Councils in Germany", typescript, Berlin, 1933. HD 5655 G3U5, DLL; Guillebaud, *The Works Council*, p. 129; Letter, A.F.L. Gordon to Dr Steinmann, 10 Jun. 1927. BB, R/3901/504; McPherson, "Collaboration between Management and Employees", p. 282.

[5] ILO, *Studies on Industrial Relations I*, p. 6.

[6] ILO, *Studies on Industrial Relations I*, p. 6.

Siemens, Siemensstadt, Berlin, 1930 (Courtesy of Siemens)

of whom approximately 3,000 lived in Siemenstadt. There was a works council at each individual Siemens plant, of which there 24 in Greater Berlin alone in 1921, the largest attaining the statutory maximum of 30 members. There were also a salaried workers' council and a wage earner's council in each of those plants. At the company level, there was the United Works Council with 30 representatives from the various plant works councils. An executive committee of five members of the United Works Council was the final voice of the workers in dealing with management. In 1930, there were 398 works councillors at Seimens's plants in Berlin and Nuremberg, of whom 171 were salaried employees and 227 were wage-earning workers.[7]

Another example of the elaborate organisation of works councils was the German Federal Railways, one of the largest employers in the world, with 452,000 waged staff and 566,000 salaried staff in 1922. As at Siemens, there had been works committees on various state railways before the Works Council Act and their merger into the German Federal Railways. As a state enterprise, it received special status under the legislation as the Federal Minister for Transport governed workers through Administrative Orders. The Administrative Order issued on 3 March 1921 was based on the Works Council Act but there were differences in terms of the structure

---

[7] ILO, *Studies on Industrial Relations I*, pp. 6, 14–15; Typescript, "Bericht des Gesamt-betriebsräte", Box 3, Erich Lübbe Collection, Frederich-Ebert Stiftung Archive, Bonn (Hereafter ELC, FSA).

and organisation of works councils. There were local works councils and stewards, district works councils, and the Central Works Council for the whole railway system. The local works councils covered wage earners only and workplaces included all industrial railway undertakings including power stations and railway workshops. The district works councils corresponded to each of the 26 District Railway Directorates and the Central Works Council comprised 25 wage-earner representatives. Workers had direct representation on both the district works council and the Central Works Council and their representatives were elected annually. The local works councils could refer matters to the district works councils, which could not, however, refer matters to Central Works Council if the District Board of Management failed to act on their representations. Despite this, the Central Works Council had direct access to the Minister of Transport and represented the interests of nearly 25,000 works councillors by 1924.[8]

While works councils spread through the German workplace, particularly in larger firms, German firms did look at alternatives forms of employee voice. German employers, unions and bureaucrats were fascinated by US industrial practices, seeing them as potential ways of revitalising their economy. Numerous employer delegations went to the US.[9] Siemens's management took a great number of trips to the US and Homburg notes that from 1923 "almost every Siemens plant manager subsequently visited the United States in the 1920s."[10] Hans Beiersdorf, a Siemens director, visited the Pittsburg plant of Westinghouse in 1926, reporting that in the absence of a workers' committee or collective agreement with a union, the plant engineer in each department met with individual workers on a monthly basis to discuss their performance and adjust their earnings accordingly. Beiersdorf praised the "sober business sense" of Americans and believed that a lot could be learnt from them.[11] There was an ADGB tour to the US in 1925 and the *Metallarbeiter-Zeitung*, the newspaper of the DMV, published an article on the B&O plan in 1925. Otto Beyer corresponded with Germans about union-management cooperation. The German Ministry of Labour also collected information on ERPs in Canada and the United States, and the German General Consul provided the ministry with reports and copies of ERPs in firms such as Standard Oil of Indiana and International Harvester in April 1924. While the focus was on North America; the German Ministry of

---

[8] Berthelot, *Works Councils in Germany*, p. 124; Guillebaud, *The Works Council*, pp. 197–200; Letter, A.F.L. Gordon to Dr Steinmann, 10 Jun. 1927. BB, R/3901/504.

[9] Nolan, *Visions of Modernity*, p. 8.

[10] Homburg, "Scientific Management and Personnel Policy", p. 149.

[11] Typescript, "Bericht des Herrn Direktor Beiersdorf über seinen Aufenthalt in Amerika vom 3. Oktober bis 26. November 1926", Box 3, ELC, FSA.

Labour also looked at Whitleyism, sending a representative to the UK in May 1930 to explore the role of JICs in industrial relations, and the ADGB published an overview of Whitleyism, including works committees, in its journal in October 1931.[12]

The Impact of German Works Councils

What did the works councils do? Unfortunately no long runs of works council minutes have survived; the Siemens records, for example, were destroyed during the Second World War. There are, however, overviews and scattered documents relating to works councils sufficient to provide an insight into their impact.

One of the hopes of the works council legislation was that management would be forced to disclose information relating to the company to workers. The Minister of Labour, for example, ruled in January 1921 that wage records of individual workers, whether covered by collective agreements or not, should be submitted by the employers to the works councils. The works councils, however, could not obtain access to workers' personal files held by employers. Further, as the relevant section of the legislation did not specifically refer to the earnings of salaried employees, a Federal Labour Court ruling in May 1930 meant that works councils could not obtain information regarding individual salaries but were only entitled to see total salary data relating specific classifications of salaried workers.[13]

Despite efforts to placate their concerns about the confidentiality of information provided to works councillors, employers continued to resist the legislation by providing limited information to the works councils. As McPherson has noted, "employers sought by every conceivable means to let their employees know as little as possible about the financial conditions of their establishment."[14] Some employers gave their quarterly reports orally in the belief that the councillors would find it more difficult to remember the information. The German Ministry of Labour upheld oral presentation of reports on the grounds that the legislation did not specify the form of

---

[12] *Gewerkschafts-Zeitung*, Oct. 1931, pp. 701–2; Letter, A. Borsig to Otto Beyer, 12 Nov. 1927. File – "Union Gains from Cooperation. ca. 1923–31", Container 104, B.P.; Letter, Fritz Kummer to Otto Beyer, 6 Oct. 1925. File – "Correspondence 1925", Container 115, B.P.; Letter, Secretary, Research and Economic Department, TUC to Fred Hand, 16 May 1930. MSS.292/221/2, TUC Collection, MRC; Memos, German General Consul to German Ministry of Labour, Chicago, 11 Apr. 1924, 30 Apr. 1924. BB, R/3901/3489; Nolan, *Visions of Modernity*, p. 20; Typescript, "Kanada. Schaffung von Betrieberäten in der Stahlindustrie", 9 Feb. 1924. BB, R/3901/3489.

[13] McPherson, "Collaboration between Management and Employees", pp. 80–1.

[14] McPherson, "Collaboration between Management and Employees", p. 95.

presentation. Works councils found it necessary to demand the quarterly reports, whether written or oral, from employers, which generally adopted a pessimistic tone about the enterprise and highlighted financial difficulties. Similarly, while works councillors in enterprises with more than 300 persons or 50 salaried employees could demand annual balance sheets or profit and loss accounts, employers constructed the balance sheets in such a way as to hide significant facts and took advantage of Germany's inflation and currency devaluation in the early 1920s to make unrealistic valuations of stock. In enterprises with individual plant works councils and a Central Works Council, employers were generally only obliged to present the balance sheet to the Central Works Council. Some employers found the secrecy provisions of the legislation useful in that troublesome works councillors could be prosecuted for breaching a requirement of confidentiality if the information was circulated beyond the works council. Works councillors could be fined or imprisoned. Despite these difficulties, the works councillors usually obtained sufficient information to ensure that collective agreements were observed, provide useful suggestions for business improvements and feel a greater affinity to the firm. Employers also used the information to put an end to potentially harmful rumours and gossip circulating among workers and to obtain worker sympathy for their managerial problems.[15]

The works council legislation and subsequent legislation enacted in February 1921 also aimed to give works councillors greater access to information relating to the working of their firm by allowing them places on the Supervisory Boards of German companies, which made strategic decisions on investment and product ranges. German employers were hostile to the legislation and some companies responded by modifying their company rules to limit the rights of the Supervisory Board and establishing special management subcommittees to cover issues such as staffing from which works councillors were excluded. Management were particularly reluctant to have worker directors on committees that dealt with the appointment and performance of managers, as they believed that this would undermine management authority. This approach was subject to legal challenge so employers accelerated a trend to reduce the number of meetings of the Supervisory Board to as few as one or two per annum, of a duration of as little as ten or 15 minutes, and to force the Board to deal with a large number of items in a short period of time. There were limitations

---

[15] Guillebaud, *The Works Council*, pp. 185–6; McPherson, "Collaboration between Management and Employees", pp. 95–7; William McPherson, *Works Councils under the German Republic*, University of Chicago, Chicago, 1939, pp. 8–10; Typescript, "On Sachen Lenzing and Genossen gegen Siemens & Halske A.G. Blockwerk, Siemenstadt, den 28 August 1922", Box 3, ELC, FSA.

on what the one or two works council representatives could do anyway as the Supervisory Boards were overwhelmingly dominated by management representatives who had a greater expertise in business issues and the secrecy provisions of the relevant legislation silenced the worker directors. Traditionally, management had also been reluctant to take the Supervisory Board into its confidence and could refuse to supply certain information. The greater tendency of German industry to form holding companies after the First World War also weakened the influence of works councils since these holding companies did not require a Supervisory Board. While many works councillors were initially disappointed with the level of insight they obtained into business operations, over time the situation improved, employee directors gaining a greater understanding of the business and employers becoming less hostile.[16]

The works councils had oversight of management's right to dismiss employees, including works councillors. Prior to the enactment of the works council legislation, the German employers' power to dismiss employees was regulated by a range of Civil, Commercial and Industrial Codes. With the exception of certain serious offences, such as assault or wilful damage of the employers' property, employees only could be dismissed with two weeks' notice according to the Industrial Code, if no notice period was set in the collective agreement. While employees could do little if dismissed with proper notice, they had the right to appeal to a labour tribunal if dismissed without notice.[17]

The works council legislation expanded the rights of workers regarding unfair dismissal and allowed workers to appeal to the works council if they had a grievance. The works council could either dismiss the appeal or try to persuade the employer to reinstate the worker or provide monetary compensation. If the works council was unsuccessful here, it could take the case to the local labour tribunal. One area of significant impact was employers' retrenching groups of workers on economic grounds: management was obliged to consult works councils in advance when drawing up lists of employees for dismissal and in some cases voluntarily handed over the whole process to the works council to avoid an unpleasant task. Through the labour courts and in practice, a number of criteria were developed for determining

[16] Berthelot, *Works Councils in Germany*, pp. 83–7; Hermann Dersch, "The Legal Nature and Economic Significance of the German Works Councils", *International Labour Review*, vol. 11, 1925, pp. 176–7; Georg Flatlow and Otto Kahn-Freund, *Betriebsrätegesetz vom 4 Februar 1920*, 13th ed., J. Springer, Berlin, 1931, pp. 673–86; Guillebaud, *The Works Council*, pp. 188–96; McPherson, *Works Councils*, p. 12; McPherson, "Collaboration between Management and Employees", pp. 115–16, 121.

[17] Guillebaud, *The Works Council*, pp. 160–1; McPherson, *Works Councils*, p. 12.

dismissals, including the worker's "usefulness" to the employer, the number of dependants, seniority and the worker's economic security. In the case of individual dismissals, some employers consulted with works councils prior to their decision, even though such consultation was not required by the legislation. The protection against unfair dismissal was a very effective part of the works council system – 44,560 or 90.7 per cent of cases heard by German labour tribunals in 1924 related to unfair dismissals – and provided an incentive for workers to establish and maintain works councils.[18]

The legislation also protected works councillors from dismissal. An employer had to obtain the works council's approval to dismiss or transfer a works councillor. The employer could appeal to a labour tribunal, whose decision was final, but was required to retain the employee until a decision was made. The dismissal of works councillors provoked labour unrest. At one Siemens plant in Berlin, the company locked out employees for one week in October 1922 after workers entered management offices in protest against the dismissal of the Chair of the works council. They accused management of dismissing him after he sought leave to attend a DMV negotiation session, and claimed that management had recently removed ten works councillors on trivial charges. While the German labour tribunals did protect thousands of works councillors, employers could get rid of troublesome works councillors during firm shutdowns or even by offering them inducements to leave for another firm. Though workers were successful in taking advantage of the legislation in favourable economic circumstances, they faced difficulties during periods of economic uncertainty, as in 1924 and 1925, when employers took advantage of a weakened labour movement and higher levels of unemployment to victimise works councillors.[19] The protection of works councillors provoked complaints from employers to the Ministry of Labour, and G. Linder, a machine tool manufacturer in Crimmitschau in eastern Germany, threatened to shut down its plant in February 1924 because the "radical left members" of its works council were encouraging their workers to engage in "passive resistance" against management.[20]

While works councils could not negotiate collective agreements, they could have an impact on their implementation and also influence workplace conditions through the regulations governing their particular workplace.

---

[18] Berthelot, *Works Councils in Germany*, pp. 108–9; Guillebaud, *The Works Council*, pp. 165–9; McPherson, "Collaboration between Management and Employees", p. 177; McPherson, *Works Councils*, pp. 13–14.

[19] Berthelot, *Works Councils in Germany*, pp. 75–6; Guillebaud, *The Works Council*, pp. 169–76; Letter, A.F.L. Gordon to Dr Steinmann, 10 Jun. 1927. BB, R/3901/504.

[20] Letter from G. Linder to the Minister of Labour, 8 Feb. 1924. BB, R/3901/500.

Works councils were responsible for supervising the observance of collective agreements and investigating grievances about non-observance. They could improve workers' earnings under the collective agreement in several ways. They could, for example, obtain a better classification for particular individuals or groups of workers. Collective agreements also provided for loadings to the regular wage rates under certain circumstances. In the Ruhr steel industry, for example, there was a higher rate for work that was hot or dirty and performed at a certain height above the floor. Works councils could persuade management that workers were working under such conditions and gain further increases in wages. As the wages outlined in collective agreements were minimum rates, works councils could negotiate contracts with management on behalf of individual workers that provided above minimum wages, except during periods of economic downturn. The works council had greater bargaining power than individuals acting alone. Finally, there was the setting of piece rates, which could not be covered precisely in collective agreements because of variation between workplace conditions. Depending upon the provisions for the local setting of piece rates, works councils could increase workers' earnings by obtaining a higher piece rate and by increasing the number of workers on piece rate.[21]

In intervals between the expiration of an old collective agreement and the signing of a new agreement, works councils could draw up temporary agreements with employers and stabilise the employment situation. This role was highlighted during the period of hyperinflation in 1923, when works councils and employers revised wage rates to keep pace with the rapidly rising cost of living.[22]

Collective agreements were not very detailed, however, and the factory regulations filled the gaps in the workplace. Employers had been legally required to provide these regulations since 1891, but the works council legislation gave works councils equal rights to the employers in developing the regulations, which included general rules of behaviour, methods of calculating wages, the duties of supervisors, safety, fines and the particular conditions of recruitment and dismissal. If an agreement could not be reached then the matter could be referred to a conciliation board, which could issue a final binding award if mediation failed. These rules could not be inconsistent with the collective agreement and trade unions and employers associations often joined forces to try and control local negoti-ations by drawing up a *Musterarbeitsordnung* or model code of rules, which they asked members to apply locally. The model code did play an important

[21] Letter, A.F.L. Gordon to Dr Steinmann, 10 Jun. 1927. BB, R/3901/504; McPherson, "Collaboration between Management and Employees", pp. 195–9.

[22] McPherson, "Collaboration between Management and Employees", pp. 198–200.

role in ensuring the uniformity of shop regulations as the conciliation boards were reluctant to endorse a provision that differed from the model code. One particular area of dispute between management and the works councils was the imposition of fines; the Federal Labour Court ruled in October 1927 that management could not impose individual fines without the consent of the works councils.[23]

Like other forms of workplace employee representation, works councils had a responsibility for safety and welfare. Since 1878, German industrial inspectors supervised health and safety conditions in factories and ensured that labour protection laws were enforced. Works councils could now assist them to ensure that safety regulations were complied with and that works councillors, with employer representatives or, in the case of a serious accident, the industrial inspector or workers compensation insurance official, formed special safety commissions to conduct accident investigations and promote safety. Works councils in larger plants played a crucial role in encouraging workers to follow safety protocols and ensuring the upkeep and maintenance of washrooms, bathing facilities and toilets, despite resistance from employers on the grounds of practicality and cost. Works councillors in these plants would focus on specific departments to gain expertise on local safety issues and some works councils formed safety subcommittees. At the Zeiss Optics factory at Jena in eastern Germany, which employed 6,000 workers in April 1930, the works council had an accident subcommittee that was assisted by a trained safety engineer. Where employers formed their own joint safety committees, works councillors had representation. At one Mannheim chemical factory, management established a committee in 1927 that consisted of two supervisors, two workers and a works council representative, which, in addition to its safety and accident investigation functions, tested workers for physical and psychological fitness. It was claimed that as a result of its efforts the number of accidents fell from 384 in 1926 to 271 in 1929. Despite the role in safety issues played by works councils in larger firms, works councils were generally uninterested in these issues due to a lack of specialist expertise or worker apathy.[24]

While the legislation encouraged works councils to participate in plant welfare activities, there were barriers to full participation. There was a

[23] Letter, A.F.L. Gordon to Dr Steinmann, 10 Jun. 1927. BB, R/3901/504; McPherson, "Collaboration between Management and Employees", pp. 200–8.

[24] K. Felgentree, "Praktische Arbeit der Betriebsräte im Wirtschafts-Gebiet Mannheim", *Gewerkschafts-Zeitung*, vol. 40, no. 18, 1930, p. 278; Geist, "Employees' Councils in Germany", p. 21. HD 5655 G3U5, DLL; Guillebaud, *The Works Council*, pp. 143–9; McPherson, "Collaboration between Management and Employees", pp. 217–22; Thomas Spates, "Industrial Relations in the Zeiss Factory", *International Labour Review*, vol. 22, no. 2, 1930, pp. 181, 196; Stern, *Works Council Movement*, pp. 39–40.

long-standing hostility in the German trade union movement towards corporate welfarism, which was viewed as a means of weakening unions' influence in the workplace; unionists believed that welfare should be administered by the state. The legislation was also vague and gave considerable authority to the employer, who could contract out the administration of company housing and pension schemes to another corporation and thus avoid works council involvement in welfare schemes. Where existing welfare institutions provided for employee representation, some employers allowed the inclusion of a works councillor. Some employers also gave their works councillors the opportunity to investigate welfare concerns such as the quality of food in canteens.[25]

The works council legislation implied a community of interest between management and labour regarding the reorganisation of production and promotion of efficiency with the works council performing an advisory role to management. But works councils were strongly opposed to changes involving the introduction of scientific management and increased division of labour. As noted previously, management was reluctant to provide workers sufficient information on the operation of the workplace, both in the interests of defending managerial prerogative and preventing information being leaked to the unions. Employers also believed that works councillors had neither the time nor education to deal with the ideas put forward by university-trained company managers and their experts. The ideology of the German labour movement, on the other hand, questioned the need to collaborate with employers given their concerns about the private ownership of capital and profits.[26]

While McPherson argues that the accomplishments of works councils were generally "relatively meagre"[27] in terms of collaboration with management in production, there were firms where the works councils played an active role in improving efficiency. At the Berlin plant of the US car company Chrysler, management wanted to speed up the assembly line. The works council took the initiative and approached the General Manager directly with suggestions for the use of additional tools that could increase efficiency. Management claimed that these new tools allowed workers to increase output by ten per cent in three days. In the machine shop of the heavy engineering company Demag in Duisburg, the works council saved labour time with its suggestion to simplify wages administration so that workers would no longer have to stop work to fill out wage sheets. The

---

[25] McPherson, "Collaboration between Management and Employees", pp. 209–17.

[26] Guillebaud, *The Works Council*, pp. 240–5; McPherson, "Collaboration between Management and Employees", p. 267.

[27] McPherson, "Collaboration between Management and Employees", p. 230.

works council at the Bolle dairy in Berlin minimised the waste of surplus milk by convincing management to expand the dairy's range of products to include lactose or milk sugar.[28]

The works councils took up broader political and economic issues. Works councils in Chemnitz and Greiz in eastern Germany petitioned the government for unemployment relief in their district in February 1921.[29] In May 1931, against the background of a deepening Great Depression, the works council at the United Steelworks Company in Bochum petitioned Chancellor Brüning against the mass layoffs of miners in the Ruhr, reminding him of the generous subsidies the government paid to Ruhr industrialists. They demanded that the government take legislative action to allow the miners a "tolerable existence."[30] From 1929, however, growing restrictions had been imposed by the Reich Labour Court on the ability of works councillors to engage in trade union and political activities. The court took the view that the works councillors' priority was not the employees but the interest of the works as a whole. In December 1929, for example, it approved the dismissal of a communist works councillor for distributing pamphlets calling for a strike outside the factory gate, even though the pamphlet did not specifically refer to the factory in question.[31]

The Impact on Unions, Women and Employers

According to one contemporary researcher on the German works councils, the fears expressed by the German unions that their leadership of workers would be undermined despite the legislation proclaiming that it was the duty of works councils to safeguard the employee's right of representation, proved "to be exaggerated."[32] Writing on the tenth anniversary of the works council legislation in 1930, Clemens Nörpel, an ADGB official, went further, claiming that the rivalry between the works council movement and the trade unions no longer existed and that the works councils, quoting leading German labour jurist, Georg Flatlow, had "become the elongated arm of trade unionism reaching into the workshop."[33]

The ADGB generally dominated the works councils. With a vast bureaucracy and newspaper network, the ADGB unions could organise and

---

[28] McPherson, "Collaboration between Management and Employees", pp. 231–9.

[29] Vorläufiger Reichswirtschaftsrat (Provisional National Economic Council), Press Release, 2 Mar. 1921. BB, R/401/661.

[30] Petition to Chancellor Heinrich Brüning, 3 May 1930. BB, R/3901/502.

[31] Kahn-Freund, *Labour Law and Politics*, pp. 113–14.

[32] Guillebaud, *The Works Council*, p. 52.

[33] Clemens Nörpel, "Zehn Jahre Betriebsrätegesetz", Gewerkschafts-Zeitung, vol. 40, no. 8, 1930, p. 121.

publicise trade union lists of candidates in each factory. They established a Works Council Bureau at their headquarters in Berlin in June 1920, which organised the first National Congress of Works Councils in October 1920, which was attended by 953 delegates. The Congress endorsed the idea that works councils were to be organised within the trade union movement and there was to be no separate organisation for works councils. There were to be local groupings of works councils overseen by the local committees of the ADGB and Allgemeiner freier Angestelltenbund (AfA) or General Free Federation of Employees, its white collar counterpart. While the Works Council Bureau of the ADGB planned and directed the first annual works council elections in 1921 and continued to do so in subsequent years, it did not organise any further congresses, the first one being a "tactical manoeuvre" by the ADGB to ensure control. As the works council legislation did not provide for any central administration of works councils, the ADGB performed this role. While the communists continued to hold their own congresses of works councils, the ADGB did not recognise them.[34]

The ADGB did not completely dominate the German works councils. In some regions, such the Ruhr mining district, syndicalists and communists were able to establish their own unions through local works councils. The main challenge to ADGB came during the great inflation crisis of 1924, when workers joined communist or syndicalist groups and it lost control of numerous works councils. Employers took a hard line against these independent unions and refused to negotiate with their works councillors. This employer attitude, combined with an improving economic situation, helped the ADGB regain a lot of lost ground on the works councils.[35]

Works councils reinforced trade union membership by refusing to take up the grievances of workers who were non-unionists or did not belong to an appropriate labour organisation. While the works councils could not influence the recruitment of employees directly, their chairs could ensure that only union members were hired through their links with the local gatekeeper or members of a local Labour Exchange Committee. When dismissals on economic grounds arose and employers consulted with the works councils over the list of workers to be dismissed, this provided an opportunity for the works councils to promote the benefits of union membership. Workers also found that, despite statutory protection, works councils with trade union support were more likely to be effective in raising their grievances with employers.[36]

---

[34] *Correspondenzblatt Der GeneralKomission der Gewerkschaften Deutschlands*, 16 Oct. 1920, pp. 559–61; Moses, *Trade Unionism in Germany*, pp. 315–18.

[35] Moses, *Trade Unionism in Germany*, pp. 318–19.

[36] Guillebaud, *The Works Council*, pp. 54–5.

The German unions placed an emphasis on the education of works councillors to increase their effectiveness in dealing with managers and the Supervisory Board. Unions periodically conducted national and district congresses for works councillors to keep them informed of the latest developments. They funded courses for works councillors that were held at venues ranging from adult education colleges to universities and covered the expenses of works councillors who went to government-supported workers' schools in Berlin, Frankfurt and Düsseldorf, which offered one- and two-year courses. Some employers helped their employees meet the expenses of these schools. The courses covered the practical and theoretical aspects of labour law and business economics. There were difficulties in running such courses, such as the turnover of works councillors and the strain of attending classes outside normal working hours. Labour organisations also published special papers for works councillors to keep them informed of the latest developments. The ADGB had the *Betriebsrätezeitung* from 1920 to 1923, while the DMV produced the *Betriebsrätezeitschrift*, which by 1928 was fortnightly and ran to 30 or more pages. The Christian unions published the *Betriebsrätepost* and the liberal Hirsch-Duncker unions published the *Wirtschaftliche Selbstverwaltung*. These publications and courses challenged syndicalism and communism by emphasising that the unions controlled the broad strategies for workers and the works councils were "outposts" of the unions.[37]

However, while unions dominated the German works councils, non-unionists did gain varying representation. As Table 6.1 indicates, in the case of Siemens, the electrical engineering company, the percentage of non-unionists on the works councils rose from 1.3 in 1921 to 17.3 in 1925. There were also a small number of representatives elected from the "yellow unions." While Siemens's management supported the idea of social partnership with unions in the wake of the upheavals of 1918–19 and observed collective agreements, it did not refrain from attempting "to reduce the impact of the collective agreements and to curtail the trade union's influence at the work-place."[38] The growth of non-unionist representation on the Siemens works councils reflected the weakening of the company's commitment to social partnership that culminated in its silent acceptance of the dissolution of trade unions after Hitler came to power.[39]

---

[37] Berthelot, *Works Councils in Germany*, pp. 61–5; *Correspondenzblatt Der GeneralKomission der Gewerkschaften Deutschlands*, 4 Sept. 1920, p. 485; Dersch, "The Legal Nature and Economic Significance", p. 177; Guillebaud, *The Works Council*, pp. 75–82; McPherson, "Collaboration between Management and Employees", pp. 75–6.

[38] Homburg, "Scientific Management and Personnel Policy", p. 143.

[39] Homburg, "Scientific management and Personnel Policy", p. 143.

Table 6.1 Works Councillors and Trade Union Membership – Siemens 1920–25 (%)

	1920	1921	1922	1923	1924	1925
Socialist (includes communist)	85.6	85.1	84.3	77.4	70.2	71.1
Hirsch-Duncker	3.7	5.5	6.7	2.4	5.8	4.5
Christian	3.7	5.9	5.8	7.9	7.0	5.0
Yellow	1.7	2.0	0.6	0.5	3.9	2.1
Unorganised	5.3	1.3	2.6	11.8	13.1	17.3
Total	100.0	100.0	100.0	100.0	100.0	100.0

Source: Letter from A.F.L. Gordon to Dr Steinmann, 10 Jun. 1927. BB, R/3901/504.

Table 6.2 Works Councillors and Trade Union Membership – Ruhr Coal Mining Wage Earners 1920–26 (%)

	1920	1921	1922	1923	1924	1925	1926
ADGB	45.66	45.67	41.70	*	33.04	42.65	69.02
Christian	18.87	17.14	20.58	*	20.87	23.94	24.89
Hirsch-Duncker	0.71	0.67	1.33	*	1.10	0.70	0.99
Syndicalist (communist)	26.95	31.74	32.87	*	42.17	31.06	2.74
Yellow	0.07	0.00	0.03	*	0.23	0.04	0.22
Unorganised	0.07	0.11	0.01	*	0.63	0.54	0.67
Various unions	7.67	4.67	3.18	*	1.98	1.07	1.47
Total	100.00	100.00	100.00	*	100.00	100.00	100.00

* Figures not available due to the French occupation of the Ruhr
Source: Letter from A.F.L. Gordon to Dr Steinmann, 10 Jun. 1927. BB, R/3901/504.

In the well-organised Ruhr coal mining region, as Table 6.2 indicates, the number of non-unionists and "yellow union" representatives for wage earners never exceeded one per cent between 1920 and 1926. The dramatic rise in ABGB representation and fall in communist representation in 1926 was due to the decision of the Union der Hand and Kopf Arbeiter in early

1926 to renounce communism and switch affiliation from the communists to the ADGB.[40]

The revolution of 1919 and the new Weimar Republic promised much for women with the granting of suffrage and protection against dismissal on the basis of gender. The works council legislation had direct benefits for women in cases of unfair dismissal and various conciliation boards and courts overruled dismissals of women on the grounds that they worked in sole support of their husband or were pregnant, irrespective of marital status. Despite their right to vote and participate in works councils, women did not have proportional representation. In 1923–24, factory inspector reports on 374 businesses in Berlin found that while women formed 41 per cent of the workforce, they represented only 22 per cent of the works councillors and works stewards. Elisabeth Ridder, a sales assistant, was the only woman on the 23-member salaried staff works council of the cast steel factory at the Krupp steelworks in Essen in 1921–22. The major reasons put forward for the low level of female representation included their age, which was generally lower than the minimum voting and candidate age for works council election, and the social convention that women left employment upon marriage. It is also true that some men refused to cooperate with women on the works councils.[41]

Employers took a range of approaches to works councils and there were initial fears that they were the first step towards the socialisation of industry. As noted, some managers were able to prevent the establishment of works councils despite the legislative requirements. Edmund Heine, manager of the assembly plant of the Ford Motor Company in the Westhafen district of Berlin, told workers wishing to set up a works council in 1926 that he was opposed to the idea as it would interfere with the efficient operation of the business and end his policy of paying relatively high wages to Ford employees, that he would reduce them to the minimum required by the collective agreement. This effectively ended the Ford employees' push for the establishment of a works council. A different approach was taken by one large insurance company, which offered to increase salaries if no works council was established.[42]

Some employers used a range of other tactics to undermine and weaken

---

[40] Letter from A.F.L. Gordon to Dr Steinmann, 10 Jun. 1927. BB, R/3901/504.

[41] Guillebaud, *The Works Council*, pp. 130–1, 166; Krupp, *1921. Betriebsrat für die Gußstahl-fabrik*, Essen, 1921; Krupp, *1922. Betriebsrat für die Gußstahlfabrik*, Essen, 1922. FAH21/659, HAK.

[42] Letters, Prussian Minister for Commerce and Trade to the Minister for Labour, 30 Sept. 1926, 5 Feb. 1927. BB, R/3901/363; McPherson, "Collaboration between Management and Employees", pp. 48–9; Scott Nehmer, *Ford, General Motors and the Nazis*, Author House, Bloomington, 2013, p. 14.

works councils. There were threats of discharge or discrimination for works councillors had little legal protection once they completed their term of office. Similarly, candidates for works council elections faced the threat of dismissal before election, leading to calls for an amendment of the legislation, which never materialised. These fears particularly affected salaried workers, who had more direct contact with employers than wage earners, and are an important explanation for the smaller number of salaried employee wage councils compared to wage earner councils.[43]

While there were employers who actively opposed works councils, McPherson has argued that "probably the majority accepted the presence of councils in their shops."[44] Even among such employers there was a reluctance to concede to works councils anything beyond the minimum that was legally required, and the VDA took this position as soon as the legislation was passed. The works council legislation increased the trend among large employers to create personnel departments with a focus on legal oversight to ensure that the employer complied with the law and that the works councils did not infringe upon managerial prerogatives. The lawyers in these personnel departments strengthened employers' bargaining power with works councils and increased employer effectiveness in dealing with conciliation boards and labour courts. The personnel departments became the intermediary between the works councils and senior management, who had the final authority on labour issues, and preferred to deal with the works councils through the exchange of memoranda rather than direct personal contact. Employers also limited the activity of works councils by distracting their attention with less important issues, such as the administration of welfare funds and the tax deductions from workers' wages. They tried to influence works councillors through flattery, hints of promotion, liberal amounts of time off work to perform their duties, offering them the use company cars and providing them with relatively lavish office facilities including coffee warmers. Employers could also make themselves appear amenable to works councillors by adopting a policy of frequent concessions in matters of minor importance. Employers also weakened the works councils by taking advantage of divisions within the German trade union movement and playing off ADGB unionists against Christian unionists, for example, and encouraging inter-union rivalry on the works councils. Overall, as time passed, employers' attitudes to works councils softened as they recognised that they were there to stay and did not pose a radical threat to their control of industry. By 1926 the VDA even took the view that the works councils

[43] McPherson, "Collaboration between Management and Employees", pp. 49–51.
[44] McPherson, "Collaboration between Management and Employees", p. 51.

had the potential to provide a form of employee representation that could ultimately challenge trade unionism and collective agreements.[45]

One issue of concern for employers was the cost of works councils, which were generally borne by employers except where a collective agreement provided an alternative arrangement. This was a particular question at larger plants where time for payment lost by works councillors was the major liability. Employers also complained that works councils were costly in that they wasted time because of the inexperience of works councillors, and that they could make decisions without them were it not for the legislation. At Siemens's Greater Berlin works, the regular monthly meetings between senior management and the United Works Council lasted two hours and 18 minutes on average with four to eight senior managers present. At the same works it has been estimated that by 1930 works councillors devoted over 2,000 hours per week to meetings and interviews with workers, with the firm paying the lost wages. There was also the cost to Siemens of providing up to two offices for each plant works council, and the personal expenses of works councillors and four typists. At the Krupp Steel Casting Works in Essen, in March 1924 management allowed the Chair of the Works Council three days a week on full pay to carry out his duties. The German Federal Railways, which had 50,798 representatives, had an estimated loss of 200,000 working hours a month by 1922 at a cost of 850,000 marks. Employers also had to bear the cost of the works council elections, which were estimated to cost 417.53 marks for a large plant of approximately 3,000 employees in 1927.[46] Though employers complained about the costs of works councils, as the Berlin-based US Consul noted in 1933, there was no widespread belief in Germany that this was "a material reason for abolishing" works councils.[47]

---

[45] Guillebaud, *The Works Council*, pp. 99–106; McPherson, "Collaboration between Management and Employees", pp. 51–9.

[46] Bernstein, "The German Works Council", p. 178; Berthelot, *Works Councils in Germany*, pp. 79–80; Guillebaud, *The Works Council*, p. 91; ILO, *Studies on Industrial Relations I*, pp. 16–17; Memo, "An die Betriebe", typescript, 11 Mar. 1924, FAH21/659, HAK; Minutes, Meetings between Management and the Works Council, Greater Berlin Works, Siemens, 3 May 1921, 20 Dec. 1921, 21 Jul. 1922, 20 Oct. 1922, 11 Apr. 1923, 6 Dec. 1923. Box 3, ELC, FSA; Stern, *Works Council Movement*, p. 83; Walter von Bonin, *Die volkswirtschaftliche Bedeutung und die praktische Auswirkung des deutschen Betriebsrätegesetzes*, Verlag Ratsbuchhandlung L. Bamberg, Greifswald, 1927, p. 125.

[47] Geist, "Employees' Councils in Germany", p. 30. HD 5655 G3U5, DLL.

The Demise of German Works Councils

The demise of the works councils highlights their close relationship to the German trade union movement and the Weimar Republic. The Nazis had run candidates in the works council elections but they did poorly in 1931 and 1933. The government suspended the 1932 elections due to concerns about possible violent confrontations between Nazis and communists. Preliminary results in the 1933 elections indicated that the Nazis won only 11.7 per cent of the seats in the 1933 works council elections compared to the ADGB's 73.4 per cent. Despite the ADGB's insistence on party political neutrality in the elections and an appeal to Franz Seldte, the Minister for Labour in Hitler's Cabinet, to protect its members, the Nazi authorities allowed the SA and SS to harass and arrest works council members. They were not freed until the elections were cancelled. Following their poor early results in the 1933 works council elections, the Nazis abruptly cancelled the elections. Nazi politicians were concerned that the works councils could become centres of resistance due to the influence of communists and Social Democrats, and undermine Hitler's claims of universal acclaim by the German people.[48] They were also concerned with specific sections of the legislation such as Section 84, which prohibited discrimination in dismissal on the basis of politics and religion and conflicted with their strategies to persecute political opponents and Jews.[49]

While the new Nazi-led government declared May Day a public holiday in 1933, it moved on the following day to destroy the German trade union movement: the SA and SS occupied all ADGB offices and placed all leading union officials in "protective custody."[50] The Nazis replaced the unions with the Labour Front and repealed the works council legislation on 1 May 1934.[51] They introduced a new system of workplace labour relations, which gave enormous power to the "plant leader" or employer. There were elections of

---

[48] Gerhard Beier, *Willi Richter. Ein Leben für die soziale Neuordnung*, Bund-Verlag, Köln, 1978, pp. 98, 426; Willi Derkow, *The "Other Germany": Facts and Figures*, Trade Union Centre for German Workers in Great Britain, London, 1943, p. 22; Vol. 25, Kurt Heinig Collection, The Labour Movement Archives and Library, Stockholm, Sweden; Geist, "Employees' Councils in Germany", p. 9. HD 5655 G3U5, DLL; Letter from O. Friedrich to Minister of Labour, 4 Apr. 1933; Memorandum, Minister for Transport, 18 Apr. 1933; Memorandum, Minister for Post, 22 Apr. 1933. BB, R/3901/505; Moses, *Trade Unionism in Germany*, pp. 426–7; Dirk Schumann, *Political Violence in the Weimar Republic 1918–1933: The Fight for the Streets and Fear of Civil War*, Berghahn Books, New York, 2009, p. 229.

[49] Letter from National Socialist Organisation (DAP) to the Minister of Labour, 14 Jul. 1933. BB, R/3901/505.

[50] Moses, *Trade Unionism in Germany*, 518.

[51] McPherson, "Collaboration between Management and Employees", p. iv.

"confidential men" to advisory "business councils" in 1934 and 1935 in which workers were able to vote for one list approved by the Nazis. Workers either left ballot papers blank or crossed out particular names on the voting list, favouring candidates who were willing to make complaints on their behalf. At employers' suggestion, the Labor Front ended the experiment, fearing that the "business councils" could lead to a new kind of trade unionism. From then on, works managers nominated the workers they wanted to serve for virtually unlimited terms.[52]

The relationship between German works councils with the Nazi government highlights a broader point that goes beyond whether employee representation protects freedom of association. While Robin Archer reminds us that the basic ethical commitments that lead to political democracy should also promote economic democracy,[53] the reverse is also true. Note only did German works councils assist union organisation, but the democratic principles underlying them became a barrier for the forces in Germany that were attempting to destroy the Weimar Republic, eliminate free trade unions and promote totalitarianism in the political arena in 1933.[54]

Conclusion

The German experience reinforces the historical cycle approach to industrial democracy. While the idea of works councils in Germany predated the Weimar Republic, the passage of the works council legislation in 1920 was linked to the economic and political upheavals that accompanied Germany's defeat in the First World War. The mandatory status of the German works councils helped them survive the economic turmoil of the 1920s. Ultimately, the formation of a hostile Nazi government in 1933 ended state support for the Weimar works councils.

The German works councils' experience supports the argument that is possible for unions to coexist and thrive alongside NUER. Where these schemes are voluntary, unions may see little need for them when there is a strongly established system of collective bargaining and management recognition of unions. When the schemes are based on a legislative framework, however, which recognises unions and provides the NUER

[52] Pierre Ayçoberry, *The Social History of the Third Reich, 1933–1945*, The New Press, New York, 1999, pp. 160–1; Evans, *The Third Reich in Power*, pp. 460–2.

[53] Robin Archer, "Freedom, Democracy and Capitalism: Ethics and Employee Participation", Adrian Wilkinson, Paul Gollan, Mick Marchington and David Lewin (eds.), *The Oxford Handbook of Participation in Organizations*, Oxford University Press, Oxford, 2010, p. 590.

[54] Beier, *Willi Richter*, p. 98; Moses, *Trade Unionism in Germany*, p. 426.

with a meaningful role, as was the case with the German works councils in regard to dismissals, unions generally appear willing to live alongside these forms of employee representation.

There was another important message for unions where NUER existed. The fears that NUER could be captured by workers hostile to unions or manipulated by employers with an anti-union agenda could be realised if unions did not play an active role in ensuring that union candidates contest elections and win positions on these bodies. The support of German unions for their respective forms of NUER was built on them taking an active role in these bodies and ensuring through participation in the NUER elections that they did not undermine their interests. They also emphasised education to ensure that their works councillors could carry out their duties in dealing with management.

While there were positive aspects of the German works councils, they posed problems for the system. A significant number of eligible workplaces did not have works councils. While most employers tolerated the presence of works councils, they undertook the minimum required by the law. There was a lack of trust in works councils' role to improve productivity and production methods. Management, despite the legislative requirements, was reluctant to share information with unions that may have highlighted the need to reform production. Trade unions were unwilling to assist management for ideological reasons. Women, despite the reforms of the Weimar Republic, were underrepresented on the works councils and indeed in some cases faced hostility from their male counterparts.

7

Canada

This chapter explores Canadian experience with the prevailing ideas on forms of employee representation. Given the importance of US capital and the coverage of US international unions, Canada saw the extension of ERPs and union-management cooperation into its industrial relations system, the former dominating. The chapter will focus particularly on the experiences of the steel plants at Sydney, Nova Scotia and the CNR.

ERPs – The Extent and Impact

The Rockefeller Plan directly affected Canadian industrial relations in two ways. MacKenzie King, who helped John D. Rockefeller Junior (JDR Jr.) frame the Rockefeller Plan, was Canadian Prime Minister from 1921 to 1930 and from 1935 to 1948. As Prime Minister he delayed the introduction of legislation similar to the NLRA that favoured collective bargaining between employers and unions. The Wartime Labour Regulations Act of 1944, which was modelled on the NLRA, did not explicitly ban non-union forms of representation. The Rockefeller family also had the controlling interest in the Imperial Oil Company (IOC), which adopted the Rockefeller Plan in 1919 to reduce labour unrest and prevent unionisation. As with the CF&I plan, while the IOC claimed its plan did not discriminate against individuals who were union members, the plan aimed to maintain an "open shop." It was part of a package that included pension benefits and a share purchase plan. By February 1921 there were 14 IOC plant councils and the company claimed that 235 issues had been settled satisfactorily, including 35 relating to wages and 58 relating to questions of sanitation, housing and social matters.[1]

---

[1] Canada. Department of Labour, *National Industrial Conference, Ottawa, September 15–20, 1919: Official Report of Proceedings and Discussions*, Ottawa, 1919, p. 153; Canada. Department of Labour, *Report of a Conference on Industrial Relations held at Ottawa. February*

Wartime labour shortages enhanced the power of Canadian unions and their membership grew from 160,000 in 1916 to 378,000 in 1919. There was a surge of industrial unrest in 1917 with 1,123,916 striker days lost. The reasons for the discontent included inflation and demands for shorter hours. The popularity of the appeals for labour solidarity and mutual support encouraged employers to seek forms of workplace organisation that would insulate workers in each establishment from those in others, such as ERPs.[2]

The Canadian federal government responded to the growth of labour power by appointing the Mathers Royal Commission, whose inquiries from 26 April to 13 June 1919 coincided with the greatest period of industrial unrest in Canadian history, including the Winnipeg General Strike, with 3,401,843 striker days lost in 1919. As in the UK, the Canadian Cabinet led by Prime Minister Robert Borden was concerned about the impact of the end of the First World War on the economy and society. It established a Reconstruction and Development Committee and in December 1917 announced the formation of a tripartite "Sub-committee on Labour Problems."[3]

The Cabinet accepted the Subcommittee's recommendation to establish a Royal Commission led by Chief Justice T.C. Mathers of Manitoba. Representatives from labour, capital and the "public" assisted Chief Justice Mathers, including unionist Tom Moore, the moderate President of the TLCC, and socialist electrical workers organiser John Bruce. One of the commissioners' tasks was to investigate progress made by "joint industrial councils" in Canada, the UK and the US. The Commission's report, completed in late June 1919, also made reference to Whitleyism in Great Britain and to the Rockefeller and the Leitch plans in the US. The Commission praised both the Rockefeller and Whitley schemes as a means of reducing unrest and recognising the "human factor" in industry, recommending that a "bureau for promoting Industrial Councils" be set up and that steps be taken to establish joint plant and industrial councils. It

---

21st and 22nd, 1921, Bulletin No. 2, Industrial Relations Series, Ottawa, 1921, pp. 24–5; H.M. Grant, "Solving the Labour Problem at Imperial Oil: Welfare Capitalism in the Canadian Petroleum Industry, 1919–1929", *Labour/Le Travail*, no. 41, 1998, pp. 69–73; Laurel Sefton MacDowell, "Company Unionism in Canada, 1915–1948", in Bruce Kaufman and Daphne Taras (eds.), *Non-Union Employee Representation: History, Contemporary Practice and Policy*, M.E. Sharpe, Armonk, 2000, pp. 97–8; Daphne Taras, "Portrait of Non-Union Employee Representation in Canada: History, Law, and Contemporary Plans", in Bruce Kaufman and Daphne Taras (eds.), *Non-Union Employee Representation: History, Contemporary Practice and Policy*, M.E. Sharpe, Armonk, 2000, pp. 126–7.

[2] Gregory Kealey, *Workers and Canadian History*, McGill-Queens University Press, Montreal, 1995, p. 295; Patmore, "Employee Representation Plans in the United States", p. 51.

[3] Kealey, *Workers and Canadian History*, p. 289; Naylor, *The New Democracy*, pp. 160–2.

saw workplace plant councils as the first step towards district and national industry councils given the sparse population and huge geographical area of Canada. The report emphasised that these councils were not intended to be anti-union devices or to interfere with workers' freedom of association or current industrial relations arrangements. Where unions existed then unions should choose representatives, but in non-unionised plants employees should choose their representatives in whatever manner they saw fit. While it was not clear at what level these issues would be dealt with, the industrial councils were to cover a wide range of questions including wages, workplace conditions, welfarism and production improvements. Two commissioners, Frank Pauzé, a representative of capital from Montreal, and Smeaton White, a representative of the "public" and managing editor of the *Montreal Gazette*, in their minority report favoured the Rockefeller scheme because of the lack of organisation among Canadian employers and workers relative to Great Britain, the ethnic diversity of the Canadian workforce and the wider geographical dispersion of industry in Canada.[4] As Naylor argues, however, the "Canadian government, unlike the British, lacked either the will or the power (or both) to initiate such schemes on a large scale."[5]

The federal government called together a National Industrial Conference in Ottawa in December 1919 to discuss the Mathers Report. There were 176 employer and labour delegates from among whom the Canadian Manufacturers Association (CMA) chose 72 employer delegates and the TLCC chose 79 labour delegates, who were drawn from the conservative side of the Canadian labour movement. Gideon Robertson, the Minister for Labour from 1918 to 1921 and a former telegraphist with a conservative trade union background, chose the third group of 34 delegates, which included members of the Mathers Commission and "interested" individuals such as Mackenzie King, then the leader of the Liberal Party. Employers were not convinced there was any need for change, particularly if organised labour was the involved and the CMA drew advice from the anti-union NAM in the US. While Colonel D. Carnegie from England gave a favourable presentation on Whitleyism, including the works committees, Canadian employers, with the exception of the building employers, dismissed the idea because it recognised unions and would stop the rollback of union gains during an anticipated post-war depression. The CMA refused to recognise labour interests beyond the individual firm. Unionists were disappointed with the conference because employers refused to accept either the eight-hour

---

[4] Canada, Department of Labour, *Report of the Royal Commission*, Supplement to *LGC*, Dec. 1919, pp. 14–19, 24; Kealey, *Workers and Canadian History*, p. 289; Naylor, *The New Democracy*, pp. 162–4, 188.

[5] Naylor, *The New Democracy*, p. 164.

day or union recognition. From a union perspective, Moore attacked the Rockefeller Plan for having it origins in the peculiar circumstances of a "civil war" in Colorado industrial relations and for aiming to prevent unionisation. Despite these differences, there was support for the establishment of JICs, because of the "urgent necessity" for greater cooperation between employer and employee. There was also a call for the Department of Labour to establish a bureau to gather data and furnish information on JICs.[6] However, employers were unwilling to endorse either Whitleyism or the Rockefeller Plan, considering it "not wise or expedient to recommend any set plan for such councils."[7]

There are some examples of JICs based on the Whitley Scheme. Robertson preferred the Whitley Scheme's focus on sector rather than enterprise bargaining. His political influence, however, was limited and his approach fickle for he urged striking militant Toronto metalworkers to bargain on an enterprise rather than a sector basis. The Canadian federal government also refused a Whitley Council for civil servants, unlike its British counterpart. There was also criticism on the left of the labour movement; the socialist Fred Flatman reproduced G.D.H. Coles's British criticism of Whitleyism. In July 1918, faced with industrial unrest on railways, where unions had sufficient power to tie up wartime railway traffic, Robertson established a Railway Board of Adjustment No. 1. The Board was modelled on a similar body in the US and was made up of equal numbers of management and union representatives. It handled 87 disputes in its first two years of operation and granted an eight-hour day to Canadian Express workers after a similar IDIA ruling had been overturned on appeal. The Canadian building and construction industries also had a National Joint Council Board with equal representation from the employer association and the international building trade unions, and a chair appointed by the Department of Labour. This council was short lived for the employers' association voted to discontinue the Board in January 1922 until union representatives recognised a number of principles including the open shop, the prohibition of sympathy strikes and the right of employers to deal directly with employees rather than union business agents. While these boards operated at the national level, there were more localised Whitley-type councils. In the Toronto building industry there was a union presence and the Whitley Council reinforced a move by building unions towards industrial unionism. Toronto builders found the Whitley Council a useful instrument for cutting wages during the post-war

[6] Canada. Department of Labour, *National Industrial Conference*, pp. 18–23, 164–5; McCallum, "Corporate Welfarism in Canada, 1919–1939", p. 59; Naylor, *The New Democracy*, pp. 192–6.

[7] Canada. Department of Labour, *National Industrial Conference*, p. vii.

economic recession, but the Council was disbanded in early 1923 as it had
served its purpose for employers and offered little protection for unions. In
contrast to the federal government, the Liberal Saskatchewan provincial
government did establish a Civil Service Joint Council in 1920, which
consisted of three deputy ministers and three members of the Saskatchewan
Civil Service Association.[8]

Despite the interest in Whitleyism, it was ERPs that flourished in
Canada during 1919–20. Large employers, particularly Canadian branches of
US firms, primarily adopted the Rockefeller schemes as part of their welfare
programmes. Besides the IOC, these firms included International Harvester,
Proctor and Gamble, and Bell Telephone. The plans also tended to be found
in mass-production or continuous process industries with large numbers of
semi-skilled workers. While the traditions of craft unionism were weak in
these industries, management had to communicate with workers because
a small group of them could halt production at strategic bottlenecks.
These plans generally played a limited role in grievance handling and
were largely concerned with working conditions and welfare programmes.
While the Toronto Industrial Council at Massey-Harris, the agricultural
machinery manufacturer, became an important forum for discussing work
safety issues, it was not successful in soliciting workers' suggestions on how
to improve productivity. There were ERPs in smaller plants, such as the
Robb Engineering Works in Amherst, Nova Scotia (NS), which had 550
employees. The Department of Labour estimated that 145,000 employees
were covered by joint councils and committees by July 1920. According to
Grant, ERPs in Canada covered half as many employees as unions by 1920.
While Taras claims that Canada had twice the penetration of non-union
ERPs compared to the US on a per capita basis by 1920, the Canadian data
cover both the Whitley and ERP schemes.[9]

Some unionists attempted to use the plans to organise and raise grievances,
but the plans diminished militancy and forestalled unionism. Massey-Harris
set up its Toronto Industrial Council and held its first elections during a
strike by the Toronto Metal Trades Council in May 1919, "effectively filtering
out any union activists in the metal trades that might have been elected."[10]

---

[8] Canada. Department of Labour, *Joint Councils in Industry*, Bulletin No. 1, Industrial
Relations Series, Ottawa, 1921, p. 8; McCallum, "Corporate Welfarism in Canada, 1919–1939",
p. 60; Naylor, *The New Democracy*, pp. 164–5, 185–7, 201–5.

[9] Canada. Department of Labour, *Joint Councils in Industry*, p. 6; Grant, "Solving the
Labour Problem at Imperial Oil", p. 125; Naylor, *The New Democracy*, pp. 175–88; Bruce Scott,
"A Place in the Sun: The Industrial Council at Massey-Harris, 1919–1929", *Labour/Le Travail*,
no. 1, 1976, pp. 160, 168–71; Taras, "Portrait of Non-Union Employee Representation", p. 125;
LGC, Apr. 1919, pp. 437–8, Aug. 1919, p. 865.

[10] Scott, "A Place in the Sun", p. 163.

At the Sarnia, Ontario plant of the IOC, the Employees' Federation, a coalition of trade union activists, elected a union member to the joint council. The activist raised union wage demands and management subsequently dismissed him. Management only reinstated him after the threat of a walkout and union membership grew at the plant. The company ultimately pre-empted union organisation by granting an eight-hour day and significant wage increases. When workers at the Armour Packing Company in Hamilton, Ontario struck for higher wages, management signed an agreement with the worker representatives of the plant "Conference Board." The agreement gave an increase in wages below what was being demanded. The strike collapsed and the company did not re-employ union members.[11]

During the 1920s and 1930s, the fortunes of Canadian ERPs varied. During the 1920s, the Canadian Department of Labour promoted the plans through its *Labour Gazette*. The department invited representatives from large companies with ERPs, half of whom were subsidiaries of US corporations, to discuss this form of employee voice at Ottawa in February 1921. Arthur Young from International Harvester in the US was one of the speakers. Robertson reminded the audience that better cooperation between management and labour was an important weapon in fighting the threat of international communism. Young reinforced Robertson's words, arguing that works councils provided protection from class struggle and revolution. No representatives from the labour movement were present and managers spoke freely about their success in getting ERP worker representatives to withdraw demands for wage increases and accept wage cuts. The ERPs were also useful in communicating management's "facts" to employees. Management's enthusiasm for the schemes fluctuated, however, according to the economic climate. The Massey-Harris Industrial Council ceased to exist when the company shut down in the 1921–22 recession. The company revived the Council when the economic climate improved in 1923. The Council then collapsed in 1931 in the depths of the Great Depression.[12]

As the Canadian economy recovered from the Great Depression there was also an upsurge in labour militancy and trade unionism. While there was no national Wagner Act and no ban on ERPs, with ERPs such as that of OIC remaining active, workers rushed to join new industrial unions, which were organised initially by the communist-led Workers' Unity League and

[11] Grant, "Solving the Labour Problem at Imperial Oil", pp. 82–3; Naylor, *The New Democracy*, pp. 175–88.

[12] Canada. Department of Labour, *Report of a Conference on Industrial Relations held at Ottawa. February 21st and 22nd, 1921*, pp. 5, 9; McCallum, "Corporate Welfarism in Canada, 1919–1939", pp. 59–60; Patmore, "Employee Representation Plans in the United States", pp. 58–9; Scott, "A Place in the Sun", pp. 160–1.

later by the CIO. Some employers again established ERPs to try to stop unionisation. Steelco, a large steel plant in Hamilton, Ontario, established an ERP at the first sign of a union. This was accompanied by the dismissal of union organisers and activists and the introduction of a profit-sharing scheme and extensive welfare benefits.[13]

An ERP – The Experience at the Sydney Steelworks, Nova Scotia

Canadian steel was an important industry for the extension of ERPs in Canada, and the Sydney, Nova Scotia steel plant is a notable example. Sydney was founded in 1785 as the capital of the new colony of Cape Breton, a refuge for British loyalists following the American Revolutionary War. Its economy grew dependent on fishing, agriculture, shipping and a coal port, which froze during the bitterly cold winters. There was no tradition of iron or steel working in the town prior to the arrival of the Dominion Iron and Steel Co. (DISCO) in 1899. DISCO was a modern corporation with a board of directors that included some of Toronto's and Montreal's leading capitalists. In 1920, DISCO merged with Nova Scotia Steel (NSS) another provincial steel company, to form British Empire Steel Corporation, which also covered extensive coal holdings and the Halifax shipyards. But this consolidation did not prevent further economic problems. BESCO was unable to adjust to the shift in demand for steel away from railways to mass-produced consumer goods, faced import competition and dealt with excessive transportation costs. With the closure of NSS's mines steel plan, Sydney became the focus of BESCO's operations from 1921. Throughout its short history, BESCO remained in a state of financial crisis and accumulated a deficit of $5.7 million by the end of 1925. It went into receivership in 1926 and was reorganised by Canadian capitalists two years later as the Dominion Steel and Coal Corporation (DOSCO), with BESCO formally ceasing to exist in May 1930. There was further reorganisation during the 1930s depression, when the blast furnaces were idle for a period of 18 months and steel was made in the open-hearth furnace from cold stock.[14]

---

[13] Patmore, "Employee Representation Plans in the United States", pp. 59–60; Storey, "Unionization Versus Corporate Welfare", pp. 15–25; Daphne Taras, "Contemporary Experience with the Rockefeller Plan: Imperial Oil's Joint Industrial Council", in Bruce Kaufman and Daphne Taras (eds.), *Non-Union Employee Representation: History, Contemporary Practice and Policy*, M.E. Sharpe, Armonk, 2000, pp. 231–58.

[14] David Frank, "The Cape Breton Coal Industry and the Rise and Fall of the British Empire Steel Corporation", *Acadiensis*, vol. 7, no. 1, 1977, pp. 3–34; Heron, *Working in Steel*, pp. 24–9, 75; Greg Patmore, "A Tale of Two Employee Representation Plans in the Steel Industry: Pueblo, Colorado, and Sydney, Nova Scotia", in Fawn-Amber Montoya (ed.),

The Sydney plant was isolated from the main centres of steel production in North America, which limited nearby employment opportunities in the steel industry and made workers more willing to accept an ERP rather than move. On 28 June 1923 there were 2,774 men on the day and 1,097 men on the night shift, but the average daily workforce fell to 790 in 1932 in the midst of the Great Depression, when the steel plant was operating at 17 per cent capacity. From this point, production increased and by 1936 the steel plant was operating at 93 per cent capacity. The workforce was overwhelmingly Canadian-born by 1923, with "rather more than" 10 per cent from "non-English speaking races" and approximately 8 per cent "coloured men" from Barbados.[15]

Prior to the introduction of the ERP at Sydney, management was generally hostile to trade unions. An organising campaign by the Provincial Workmen's Association (PWA), which commenced in 1902, culminated in June–July 1904 in a major strike, which was a union defeat. The demise of the PWA in the wake of the strike did not mean the end of labour activity at the Sydney plant. There were members of craft unions working in the plant and unions continued to organise the plant including the AAISTW, which in June 1911 established a lodge in Sydney with at least 60 members. The lodge failed to gain recognition from a hostile management and the AAISTW ran a further enrolment campaign during the First World War, organising a Sydney lodge on 13 December 1917. Despite management's refusal to recognise the union and supervisors discouraging union membership, the union formed another lodge for Sydney employees in October 1922 and claimed that it had organised 75 per cent of steelworkers by February 1923. The AAISTW was able to raise grievances through representation as a committee of employees. There were allegations that DISCO operated a system of labour espionage: "spotters" or spies were responsible for the dismissal of five union activists during the AAISTW's organising campaign in 1911; they also followed union organisers when the latter interviewed workers in their homes and attended union meetings to

Making an American Workforce: The Rockefellers and the Legacy of Ludlow, University of Colorado Press, Boulder, 2014, pp. 131–2; Greg Patmore, "Iron and Steel Unionism in Canada and Australia, 1900–1914: The Impact of the State, Ethnicity, Management and Locality", *Labour/Le Travail*, no. 58, 2006, pp. 81–2.

[15] Canada, Department of Labour, *Report of Royal Commission*, Supplement to *LGC*, Feb. 1924, Supplement, pp. 13, 22; DOSCO, Joint Committee Minutes, 21 Dec. 1933, Beaton Institute, Cape Breton University (hereafter BI), MG19/17/D; DOSCO, General Works Committee Minutes, 15 Jan. 1934, 29 Dec. 1936; Patmore, "A Tale of Two Employee Representation Plans", p. 132. United Steel Workers of America, Sydney Lodge collection, Provincial Archives of Nova Scotia, Halifax (hereafter USWA collection, PANS), Microfilm Reel 1487C.

intimidate employees. BESCO would continue to use spies in the steelworks and encouraged loyalist employees to beat union activists with iron bars.[16]

DISCO and its successors established welfare schemes to promote identification with the company. The company provided housing to attract employees and sponsored social clubs and benefit societies for employees. BESCO launched a pension fund in January 1924 for employees with 25 years' service or more and was actively involved in promoting "safety first," which incorporated a safety committee, an ambulance service and an emergency hospital.[17] In the mid-1920s, BESCO briefly published a four-page newsletter, the *BESCO Bulletin*, which called upon workers to cooperate with management to ensure that the company was pointed "to as an example of good fellowship and loyalty and united endeavour."[18] The *BESCO Bulletin* praised the benefits of ERPs, including the CF&I Plan, and criticised organised labour, for example, for wage demands that deprived members of work and the opportunity of earning a "livelihood."[19]

The introduction of the ERP at Sydney was set against BESCO's desire to maintain an open shop. The growing strength of the AAISTW in the plant represented a major threat. BESCO rejected a proposal by union members to set up a scheme for the formation of worker committees in September 1922 on the grounds that it would not recognise the union. Henry Bischoff, the General Superintendent of the Sydney plant, tried to introduce an ERP in December 1922, but workers and the AAISTW defeated the proposal in a ballot by 1,562 votes to 1,021. Opponents linked their hostility to the ERP to their demand for union recognition. The scheme involved a general works council elected by the workers. This general works council elected a group of representatives to meet with a similar number of management representatives on a joint council. Bischoff described the scheme as a form of "co-operative bargaining" which dealt with problems of mutual interest. The major influences in shaping the "Bischoff Plan" were Whitleyism, which ironically was built on union recognition, and a similar ERP at the

---

[16] *AJ*, 27 Dec. 1917, p. 4, 6 May 1920, p. 32, 17 Feb. 1920, p. 20, 9 Nov. 1922, p. 28; Canada, Department of Labour, *Report of Royal Commission*, Supplement to *LGC*, Feb. 1924, pp. 6–8; Frank, *McLachlan*, p. 294; Heron, *Working in Steel*, p. 97; Paul MacEwan, *Miners and Steelworkers: Labor in Cape Breton*, AM Hakkert, Toronto, 1976, p. 94; Patmore, "A Tale of Two Employee Representation Plans", pp. 132–3; Patmore, "Iron and Steel Unionism in Canada and Australia", pp. 85–8, 99; *The Sydney Record*, 14 Feb. 1923, p. 1.

[17] *AJ*, 4 Mar. 1920, p. 11; *BESCO Bulletin*, 21 Feb. 1925, p. 3, 13 Jun. 1925, p. 3, 27 Feb. 1926, p. 4; Patmore, "A Tale of Two Employee Representation Plans", p. 153; *The Sydney Record*, 23 Apr. 1930, p. 5.

[18] *BESCO Bulletin*, 21 Feb. 1925, p. 1.

[19] *BESCO Bulletin*, 9 May 1925, p. 4, 16 May 1925, p. 4, 23 May 1925, pp. 1–3, 5 Dec. 1925, p. 4.

Bethlehem Steel Corporation in the US. The Bethlehem Steel Corporation ERP, unlike the Rockefeller Plan, allowed workers to meet as a group independent from management and to serve with management represent-atives on joint committees.[20]

Tensions between the AAISTW and BESCO continued. Union members walked out on 13 February 1923 following the dismissal of a unionist for disobeying orders. The AAISTW accused management of dismissing the employee because of union activities. Management faced pickets, the prospect of serious damage to the plant in sub-zero temperatures and the possibility of miners joining the dispute. While it agreed to meet a committee of employees, management refused to meet any official union delegation. Management agreed on 17 February to reconsider the case of the dismissed unionist. Union leaders considered the strike a victory and believed that the company would give them full recognition upon returning to work. However, BESCO investigated the case of the dismissed unionist and upheld it on the grounds of insubordination. The police arrested more than 30 steelworkers on various charges, including intimidation and trespassing, and BESCO increased the size of its employment blacklist. The board of directors of BESCO formally rejected the request for union recognition in June 1922. Roy Wolvin, President of BESCO, saw "Cape Breton Bolshevism" as the cause of the strike and issued a warning to the local business community that unless it was driven out, he would withdraw his capital.[21]

This conflict ultimately resulted in the demise of the AAISTW and the implementation by management of the ERP. The union continued to pursue its demands for recognition, particularly for a check-off system for union dues. Other demands included a general wage increase of 30 per cent and an eight-hour day. Management still refused to recognise the union, but granted a 10 per cent wage increase on 16 April 1923. Continuing tensions culminated in another strike on 28 June 1923, which saw military and provincial police intervene with machine guns. On "Bloody Sunday," 1 July,

---

[20] *BESCO Bulletin*, 11 Apr. 1925, p. 1; Michael Earle, "The Building of Steel Union Local 1064: Sydney, 1935–1937", in James E. Candow (ed.), *Industry and Society in Nova Scotia: An Illustrated History*, Fernwood Publishing, Halifax, 2001, p. 45; Canada, Department of Labour, *Report of Royal Commission*, Supplement to *LGC*, Feb. 1924, pp. 16–17; Patmore, "A Tale of Two Employee Representation Plans", p. 135; *The Iron Age*, 14 Jun. 1926, p. 1692; *The Sydney Record*, 18 Dec. 1922, p. 1, 1 Sept. 1923, pp. 4, 12, 1 Sept. 1924, p. 6.

[21] Frank, *J.B. McLachlan*, pp. 294–7; Canada, Department of Labour, *Report of Royal Commission*, Supplement to *LGC*, Feb. 1924, pp. 9–12; George MacEachern, *George MacEachern: An Autobiography*, University College of Cape Breton Press, Sydney, 1987, pp. 28–9; Patmore, "A Tale of Two Employee Representation Plans", p. 135; *The Sydney Record*, 14 Feb. 1923, pp. 1–2.

strikers and bystanders outside the Sydney steelworks, including women and children, faced charges by mounted police and soldiers. This further undermined the strikers' collective action, but gained the steelworkers the support of 8,500 Cape Breton miners, who left work on 3 July in protest against the state's use of force. However, John L. Lewis, the President of the UMWA, moved against the Cape Breton militants following their refusal to end the sympathy strike and revoked the charter of the UMWA local on 17 July. Lewis was in direct contact with Wolvin and was concerned that the action of the miners in Cape Breton would jeopardise UMWA negotiations with anthracite coal operators in the US. Lewis alleged political intrigue between the local's leaders and their "revolutionary leaders in Moscow." The strike continued until 2 August but the AAISTW was defeated.[22]

Management introduced an ERP in August 1923 without a vote by employees. This followed a deputation of a committee of employees to Bischoff on 14 August, calling for the Plan to be put into effect and claiming that employees "whole heartily favoured" it.[23] The local newspaper, *The Sydney Record*, which supported the ERP, noted that the "level-headed section" of the steelworkers, "who have never been stamped by songs in Russian and flags of red," were in control of the plant. With the defeat of the AAISTW, some workers took the view that the Bischoff Plan was "better than nothing." Management hoped in vain that the scheme would make a proposed federal commission to inquire into labour relations at the plant "inopportune." The commission did make favourable recommendations concerning the ERP, however, and did not force the issue of union recognition.[24]

The Plan was identical to that proposed the previous December, with a general works committee of 38 employee representatives elected by workers and representatives elected to a joint committee with management representatives. The worker representatives on the joint committee also constituted a central works committee. This explicit provision for independent worker meetings was to lead to greater autonomy for employee representatives under the Bischoff Plan, though managerial prerogative remained paramount. Employee representatives could raise grievances on behalf of constituents if they were not satisfied with the response of their supervisor. If the employee representative failed to get satisfaction, then the representative could take

<hr />

[22] *AJ*, 14 Jun. 1923, p. 15; Frank, *J.B. McLachlan*, pp. 300–15; Canada, Department of Labour, *Report of Royal Commission*, Supplement to *LGC*, Feb. 1924, pp. 12–16; Macgillivray, "Military Aid to the Civil Power: The Cape Breton Experience in the 1920s", pp. 55–8; Patmore, "A Tale of Two Employee Representation Plans", p. 136.

[23] *The Sydney Record*, 15 Aug. 1923, p. i.

[24] *The Sydney Record*, 15 Aug. 1923, p. ii.

Sydney Steelworks, Nova Scotia. Steelworks during the 1923 strike
(Courtesy Beaton Institute).

the matter to the joint committee. The Bischoff Plan dealt with suggestions for safety and improvements in a similar manner. There was a secret ballot for the employee representatives, but employees elected two fellow workers in each department to assist employees in filling out the ballots as requested. All employees over 18 could vote but there were restrictions on supervisors and managers voting. Candidates had to be 21 years of age and have a minimum of one year's service at the plant. The first ballot was held on 29 and 30 August 1923 with 68 employees nominated for 36 positions and 2,729 employees or about 93 per cent of the workers in the plant voting.

In the wake of the strike, the blacklisting of union activists by BESCO and the establishment of the ERP, the Sydney lodges of the AAISTW eventually became moribund. While management publicly justified the Plan with the need to maintain the "personal touch and human touch with the men" that was being lost as the business grew and to counter the "absentee management" of the BECSO directors, the Sydney experience highlights the importance of the ERP as an anti-union strategy.[25]

What did the ERP at the Sydney steel plant do? The surviving records are limited, but sufficient to note trends. The Sydney meetings were held on

[25] *AJ*, 17 Nov. 1924, pp. 2–3; Canada, Department of Labour, *Report of Royal Commission*, Supplement to *LGC*, Feb. 1924, pp. 12–16; MacEachern, *George MacEachern*, p. 36; Patmore, "Employee Representation Plans in the United States", p. 58; Patmore, "A Tale of Two Employee Representation Plans", pp. 136–7; *The Sydney Record*, 15 Aug. 1923, p. 1, 22 Aug. 1923, p. 1, 25 Aug. 1923, pp. 4, 12.

company premises and the representatives received payment for meetings but not for other representative duties such as raising grievances. By 1925, the workload was such that the general works committee found it necessary to set up subcommittees to deal with wages, safety and personnel matters, such as promotion, discipline and dismissal. Meetings could be lengthy: one general works committee meeting in January 1934 lasted two hours and 20 minutes. Critics recognised that the Bischoff Plan provided protection to representatives taking up worker grievances and overcame some injustices. Two of the activists associated with the 1923 strike remained on the general works committee for most of its existence. The general works committee provided a forum to discuss issues of general concern and assisted management in rationing work during periods of economic downturn. Management also discussed the financial position of the company with the representatives and allowed the latter to distribute company charity to needy families at Christmas. Campaigning could be lively and turnout large in the elections for employee representatives. In May 1935, workers in the Electrical Department successfully petitioned management for the recall of their representative on the grounds of "misrepresentation." The elected representatives tended to have worked at the plant for long periods; the average service of the 36 representatives in 1925 was 11 years and the longest 20 years. During the mid-1930s there were complaints about workers' names being placed on nomination forms without their consent by management and supervisors voting despite the prohibition.[26]

The explicit provision for a worker-only forum at Sydney gave employee representatives a great deal of autonomy to pursue issues outside the company and to gain support from politicians and other outside groups. Former union activists, elected on the general works committee, pushed for the same demands they had pursued through the unions. The general works committee in 1925 called for improved tariff protection for the Canadian steel industry and in May 1930 even rejected linking a government bonus on steel to the eight-hour day. Secretary P.W. McDougall noted that the employees were confident that management would reduce working hours as soon as conditions warranted. In 1929, the workers' representatives embarrassed BESCO by persuading the Social Service Council of Canada, a Protestant reformist body, to investigate the 12-hour day at the Sydney plant. Sydney workers employed on continuous production such as the blast furnaces and open-hearth furnaces won the eight-hour day in 1930. Workers

[26] *Besco Bulletin*, 11 Apr. 1925, pp. 1–3; MacEachern, *George MacEachern*, p. 36; DOSCO, General Works Committee Minutes, 15 Jan. 1934, Joint Meeting Minutes, 21 Dec. 1933, 20 Dec. 1934, Joint Committee, 3 Jan. 1934, 9 May 1935, BI, MG19/17/D; Patmore, "A Tale of Two Employee Representation Plans", p. 142.

in other parts of the plant had their hours reduced from 12 to ten. There were compensating wage increases for workers on hourly rates.[27]

A good run of minutes for the Sydney plant ERP have survived for 1934. There were 108 issues raised at the general works committee during that year. The most frequent issue raised at the general works committee (approximately 38 per cent) related to recruitment and selection, particularly of former employees who had lost their jobs due to the economic depression. Production was reviving at the plant and the representatives wanted to ensure that management gave preference to former workers over newcomers. The second largest group of items (approximately 26 per cent) related to industrial relations issues, particularly wages, hours and conditions. In May 1934, the general works committee forwarded a petition with 1,700 signatures supporting eight-hour day legislation to the NS government. When management refused to increase wages the same month, previously cut due to the depression, because they were making losses on exports, the representatives requested that an external board of conciliation check management's claims concerning the losses. Management rejected the request, but was prepared to allow two or three representatives to check the relevant financial records. The representatives rejected this offer on the grounds that they were not experts and it was a job for "Price Waterhouse." Welfare issues (approximately 16 per cent) included pensions and company housing. Safety issues (approximately 10 per cent) included the response time in transporting accident victims to hospital and the dangers associated with railway operations around the plant. The general works committee was able to persuade management in November 1934 to institute monthly safety inspections of departments by the departmental superintendent, the safety engineer and an employee representative. The representatives also showed concern for other issues beyond the steelworks. In May 1934, they sent a letter to the local municipal authority condemning the low wages being paid to highway workers. The general works committee referred matters to the joint committee, which did not generally make decisions, but referred matters to management for further consideration. Frustrations arose over the failure of management to follow through with issues and on occasion to ignore recommendations by the joint committee. In December 1934, one representative even suggested a strike over issues such as the restoration of wage reductions and old-age pensions. Management later claimed that it had granted 69 per cent of

---

[27] *Besco Bulletin*, 24 Oct. 1925, p. 1; Heron, *Working in Steel*, p. 109; Patmore, "A Tale of Two Employee Representation Plans", pp. 142–3; Terence Power, "Steel Unionism in Eastern Canada", BA dissertation, Saint Francis Xavier University, 1942, pp. 17–18; *The Sydney Record*, 23 May 1930, p. 1.

the claims submitted by general works committee, less than the plans at CF&I and Bethlehem Steel.[28]

There was discontent among employees over the usefulness of the ERP for them. Critics noted that the ERP's success for employees depended on how "management felt" and how it responded to external pressure.[29] One former steelworker remembered that the Plan was not beneficial because "you had no strength."[30] Some former members of the AAISTW flirted with the idea of OBU during the mid-1920s. In 1930, Rannie McDonald, a former representative and critic of the managerial right of veto under the Plan, organised a lodge of the IAM. Management, however, laid him off along with approximately 50 other employees in the machine shop on the day they received their charter from the union. One exception was the financial secretary of the lodge, who was an employee representative. Nevertheless, in 1932, management did dismiss Dan Mackay, who was a former OBU organiser and the chair of the general works committee, after he began advocating for a union.[31]

Steelworkers in Sydney used their ERP as a platform for organising unions in the late 1930s. Several activists believed that they could use the council to build a "real union." Some of them successfully stood for the plant council, which gave them some freedom to move around the plant. When management rejected a request for a wage increase, four employee representatives formed a workers' committee. The committee became the basis for the independent Steelworkers' Union of Nova Scotia, which became a SWOC affiliate in December 1936. The union soon organised the majority of workers at the Sydney plant. With other workers, it successfully lobbied the Nova Scotia provincial legislature to pass a Trade Union Act in April 1937. This legislation forced employers to recognise and bargain with the trade union representing the majority of workers and fined companies for discriminating against trade unionists. This was the first Wagner-influenced legislation in Canada and contained provisions for a vote on a union check-off if employers already had a system of checking-off deductions for any other purpose. Management at the Sydney plant tried to undercut the SWOC drive for union members by offering wage increases and retrenching workers. They also tried to mobilise workers to fight the menace of "foreign controlled"

[28] DOSCO, General Works Committee Minutes, 15 Jan. 1934, 29 Dec. 1936, USWA Collection, PANS, Microfilm Reel 14877, 1 May 1934, 12 May 1934, 20 Nov. 1934, 4 Dec. 1934, BI, MG19/17/D; Patmore, "A Tale of Two Employee Representation Plans", pp. 143–5.

[29] MacEachern, *George MacEachern*, p. 36.

[30] Interview with Emmerson Campbell in *Cape Breton's Magazine*, no. 22, 1979.

[31] MacEachern, *George MacEachern*, pp. 36–7, 62; MacEwan, *Miners and Steelworkers*, pp. 207–8; Patmore, "A Tale of Two Employee Representation Plans", p. 144.

international unions. Within a week of the passage of this legislation, however, the employee representatives on the plant council, who were all union members, resigned en masse. The plant council held its last meeting on 22 April 1937 and the steelworkers' union subsequently won a ballot for a check-off system for union subscriptions.[32] Ron Crawley notes that "As with many SWOC locals in the United States, SWOC steelworkers at Sydney had essentially occupied and subverted the plant council."[33]

Union-Management Cooperation

As in the US, union-management cooperation was less successful than ERPs. One major success was the state-owned CNR, which also operated in the US. The CNR was organised in October 1922 by the Canadian federal government to administer and merge a number of former bankrupt private railways and government railways. The railway system had 22,192 miles of track across Canada by 30 December 1925. It was a larger employer than the B&O with an average of 111,383 employees in 1929. CNR management adopted the B&O scheme, which commenced operation on 1 January 1925, for employees in its major workshops and roundhouses where there was a strong union presence. There were local committees and one central committee of employee and management representatives. The plan was extended to track maintenance workers in 1929. The AFL, whose international affiliates also covered Canada, praised the CNR scheme.[34]

The CNR plan, however, was marked by the management style of Henry Thornton, the President of the CNR. He was an admirer of Willard and corresponded with him about the B&O scheme. Thornton had commenced employment as a draftsman on the Pennsylvania Railroad in 1896 and eventually became a general manager of the Great Eastern Railway in the UK. He had a good relationship with union officials both in the UK and Canada.[35] Cramp, the NUR official, noted on Thornton's departure from

[32] Patmore, "Employee Representation Plans in the United States", pp. 59–60.

[33] Ron Crawley, "What Kind of Unionism: Struggles among Sydney Steel Workers in the SWOC Years, 1936–1942", *Labor/Le Travail*, no. 39, 1996, p. 104.

[34] CNR, *Annual Report of the Canadian National Railway System for the Year Ended December 31, 1925*, p. 5, *Annual Report of the Canadian National Railway System for the Year Ended December 31, 1933*, p. 4; Patmore, "Employee Representation Plans in the United States", p. 59.

[35] *Chicago Tribune*, 15 Mar. 1933, p. 19; Letter, Daniel Willard to Henry Thornton, 6 Mar. 1924. File – "Co-operative Plan, Development. ca. 1924", Container 96, B.P.; Letter, Henry Thornton to Otto Beyer, 3 Dec. 1924. File – "Correspondence 1923–24", Container 75, B.P.; J. Plomer, "Sir Henry. Some Notes on the Life of Sir Henry Thornton", *The Railway and Locomotive Historical Society Bulletin*, no. 103, 1960, p. 8.

Henry Thornton
(Courtesy of
Library and
Archives of Canada)

the UK in 1922 that "both railway workers and their unions are losing a
very sincere and valued friend."[36] The AFL invited Thornton to be a guest
speaker at its 1929 Toronto convention. Like Willard, Thornton became a
public advocate for union-management cooperation and business leaders
viewed him as a radical.[37] He argued that "Labour unions are here to stay"
and that management should become "allies of existing unions" through
union-management cooperation.[38]

As in the US, workers resented the top-down approach of union-
management cooperation and the lack of direct rank-and-file representation
on the committees. The CNR management found that it was necessary
to allow direct representation by rank-and-file union members in some
workshops to win employee support for cooperative management. In July
1928 only two out of six representatives at its London workshop and two

---

[36] *The Railway Review*, 27 Oct. 1922, p. 3.
[37] *Chicago Tribune*, 15 Mar. 1933, p. 19.
[38] *Factory and Industrial Management*, Dec. 1929, p. 1320.

out of nine representatives at its Leaside, Ontario, workshop near Toronto were on the union shop committees.[39] The CBRE, a Canadian union not affiliated to the AFL, was critical of union-management cooperation.[40] A.W. Atwater, General Chair of the Maintenance of Way Division of the CBRE, was reported as describing the scheme in April 1930 as "a system to enslave" workers and "put lots of men out of work."[41]

Like US unions, the CNR unions highlighted the benefits of the cooperative committees for reductions in working expenses and increasing dividends. While good runs of surviving minutes are hard to find for the CNR cooperative committees, a virtually complete set can be found for the Allandale Division of the Maintenance of Way Department of the CNR in Ontario. The division gathered 45 times between the first regular committee meeting in June 1930 and December 1940. The meetings were generally held quarterly and lasted three hours and 20 minutes on average. They were chaired by the Division Engineer and the employee representatives were generally drawn from among the foremen, who were union members. Senior union officials from the Brotherhood of Maintenance Way Employees (BMWE), which covered these employees, would occasionally attend as observers. The number of management representatives involved ranged from two to nine, while the number of employee representatives ranged from three to six. There was no requirement for equal numbers of employer and employee representatives to be present for a meeting to proceed. Employee representatives were allowed to travel across a section of the division by car for two days each month to hear suggestions from their fellow employees.[42]

The union and management encouraged workers to submit their ideas to the committee; 403 issues were raised, of which 236 were adopted and 155 dropped over this period, 1930–40, and issues remained pending. The issues discussed included suggestions to improve efficiency and promote the welfare of employees. For example, at a meeting on 2 February 1931 the committee adopted suggestions to construct a protector to prevent damage to track switches in railway yards and to provide first aid kits to maintenance gangs. The committee also acted upon complaints concerning defective equipment, such as shovels, and building maintenance. The committee was also given the task of fire prevention and safety, dealing with, for example, the correct

---

[39] Wood, *Union-Management Co-operation on the Railroads*, pp. 106–7.

[40] *The Canadian Railway Employees' Monthly*, Apr. 1930, p. 87.

[41] Letter, George Brown to W. Aspinell, 7 Apr. 1930. "File – Correspondence, 1930 1", Container 71, B.P.

[42] File – "Maintenance of Way. Co-operative Meetings – Minutes. Allandale Division. ca. 1930–1943", Container 75, B.P.

procedures for handling and loading heavy items. If certain issues had broader implications, the committee would refer it to a regional committee and then to a national committee for the whole CNR Maintenance of Way Department.[43]

Union-management cooperation delivered a number of benefits for CNR management, including useful suggestions from unions to improve work practices and improve productivity. Between 1925 and 1938, 23,769 suggestions were discussed at cooperative committees of the CNR and its subsidiary, the Central Vermont Railway, of which 83.6 per cent were accepted.[44] A.J. Thomas, Assistant to the General Supervisor of Shop Methods on the CNR, claimed that one of the most "interesting" developments in connection to the plan from management's viewpoint "has been the discussion in trade union meetings of methods of getting new business."[45]

Did these schemes deliver benefits for CNR employees in terms of increased wages and employment stabilisation? Thornton claimed that cooperative management had increased the stability of employment on the CNR by 10 per cent in the period 1924–27, measured in terms of actual hours as opposed to potential hours of work. According to Thornton, the increased hours led to a 13.3 per cent growth in employee yearly earnings in the CNR workshops over the same period.[46]

The benefits of cooperative management for the stabilisation of CNR employment, however, came under challenge with the onset of the Great Depression. The CNR tried to preserve jobs through cooperative management in the Maintenance of Way Division by searching for additional maintenance work such as fencing, but at the expense of casual employees, and by finding outside work, such as harvesting, for workers temporarily retrenched. CNR management claimed in March 1931 that 93,673 extra days of employment had been provided for permanent employees over the previous year in track maintenance work due to cooperative management.[47]

---

[43] *Canadian National Railways Magazine*, 6 Jun. 1935, pp. 6, 29; File – "Maintenance of Way. Co-operative Meetings – Minutes. Allandale Division. Ca 1930–1943", Container 75, BP.

[44] Aultz, "Union-Management Co-operation", p. 58.

[45] A.J. Thomas, "The Union Management Co-operative Plan on the Canadian National Railways", *Personnel*, vol. 5, no. 3, 1928, p. 224.

[46] *Canadian National Railways Magazine*, Apr. 1928, p. 11.

[47] CNR, *Annual Report of the Canadian National Railway System for the Year Ended December 31, 1933*, p. 4; CNR Circular, A.A. Tisdale, Winnipeg, 7 Aug. 1929. Box 89, FF 3, Code # 36-6-A-2. RED KA; CNR Maintenance of Way Union Management Co-operative Movement Executive Minutes, 10 Jul. 1930. File – "Correspondence, 1930 2", Container 71, BP; Letter, Fred Flojzdal to Otto Beyer, 31 Mar. 1931. File – "Correspondence – 1931 2". Container 71, BP.

What impact did this scheme have on union membership? There were union claims that union-management cooperation on the CNR increased union membership. The BMWE claimed that the scheme helped to increase its membership during the early years of the 1930s depression by directly improving conditions and attracting non-unionists and members of rival unions that did not support the scheme. It also claimed that management was more willing to retain rather than retrench workers to maintain a good relationship with the union. The union's average yearly membership increased from 8,826 in 1929 to 10,160 in 1931.[48]

Sir Henry Thornton was forced to resign as President of the CNR by political opponents in July 1932 and died in March 1933. His memory kept the strong support of organised labour and 17 labour organisations contributed to the placement of bronze memorial plaques in his honour in 11 of the largest CNR depots. Despite McDowell's claims that the plan "lapsed" in the CNR with Thornton's departure in 1932, it persisted. Samuel Hungerford, who succeeded Thornton as President, continued the scheme. As late as 1958, 40 cooperative committees were still in operation in the CNR's rail maintenance department.[49]

Conclusion

As in the other countries examined so far in this book, the Canadian experience reinforces the historical cycle approach to industrial democracy as can be seen in the general wave of interest in NUER that accompanied the upsurge in labour unrest at the end of the First World War and during the immediate post-war period. As the Mathers Commission and various industrial relations forums highlighted, employers were very interested in looking for ways to increase the loyalty of employees and shared a common interest with some union officials in fending off challenges from worker militancy and Bolshevism. While both Whitleyism and ERPs were looked at in Canada, employers preferred the ERP as it provided an alternative to unions. The influence of Mackenzie King and US firms operating in Canada reinforced this trend.

The major motivation for most Canadian employers in introducing ERPs,

[48] BMWE Circular, 27 Jul. 1932, File – "Maintenance of Way. Co-op Program. Ca 1930–1939", Container 91, B.P.

[49] *Canadian National Railways Magazine*, 6 Jun. 1935, pp. 6, 29, 1 Jan. 1937, pp. 7, 15; Canadian National Railways, Union-Management Co-operative Movement – Maintenance of Way Department. 28th Annual Report 1958. NLAC, RG 30 Volume 11839, C.406.3; D'arcy Marsh, *The Tragedy of Henry Thornton*, Macmillan, Toronto, 1935; MacDowell, "Company Unionism in Canada", p. 104; Plomer, "Sir Henry", pp. 14–16.

as highlighted by the case of the Sydney steel plant, was the avoidance of unions and state intervention in the internal affairs of their companies. As in the US, the plans also tended to be found in large-scale industries with continuous or mass production, where communication problems were intensified and strategic groups of workers could create bottlenecks in the production process if alienated. The example of the Sydney plant highlights the variety of forms that an ERP could take, both in Canada and the US. Unlike the CF&I plan, there was a provision for worker represent-atives at Sydney to hold their own meetings, which gave them greater autonomy from management. Workers became involved in the Sydney ERP because they had no viable alternative given the success of management's anti-unionism. As the Sydney case study highlights, employee represent-atives could use the ERP to make some gains.

Could an ERP be a platform for trade union organising? As in the US, it was very difficult except in exceptional circumstances. The union required both a well-resourced organising campaign and a favourable political and legal climate. As in the US, steelworkers at Sydney Nova Scotia used their ERP as a springboard for unionisation. SWOC ran a determined organising campaign. The Nova Scotia Trade Union Act, like the NLRA, provided a favourable legal climate for Sydney steelworkers to push for unionisation and reject the ERP.

As in the US, union-management cooperation had a limited impact compared to ERPs. The CNR, however, was the largest organisation to adopt the union-management cooperation. As Willard championed union-management cooperation on the B&O, Thornton again highlighted the significant role that a progressive CEO could play in shaping the form of employee representation. As in the US, the top-down approach of union-management cooperation provoked worker opposition, and the scheme was modified to allow the direct election of worker representatives in some railway workshops. The plan was of great assistance to CNR management in obtaining suggestions for improvements. While there were management claims that there were benefits for CNR employees in terms of increased earnings and employment stabilisation, at least one union found that union-management cooperation had positive benefits in terms of increasing union membership.

8

Australia

This chapter explores the Australian experience with the various ideas of workplace employee representation during the interwar period. As in the other four countries, there was interest in exploring ideas of employee participation in the Australian workplace against a background of industrial and political unrest at the end of the First World War and during its aftermath. While Australians were interested in German works councils, Whitleyism, union-management cooperation and ERPs, they had very little impact in practice. The union movement was particularly hostile to the concept of ERPs and there were doubts about the relevance of the various forms of employee representation in an industrial relations system of state tribunals.

Influences

As in the other countries examined in this book, the industrial and political turmoil during the last years of the First World War and the immediate post-war period heightened Australian interest in ERPs and other management labour strategies. A major strike in NSW in 1917 centred on the state railways and tramways. In 1919–20, there was an unprecedented wave of strikes that included maritime workers and Broken Hill miners. The Russian Revolution and the movement towards the OBU led to conservative hysteria over a possible Bolshevik challenge to Australian capitalism. Some conservatives argued that the Bolshevik threat could be neutralised by raising workers' living standards through increasing productivity and allowing employees to participate in management decisions. Fears also arose that Australian industry would not survive international competition in the post-war world unless reforms were introduced. While the Bolshevik threat declined in the 1920s, international competition remained an issue.[1]

---

[1] Patmore, *Australian Labour History*, pp. 146–7.

The Australian state played an important role in promoting new ideas to deal with these issues. The British government communicated directly with the Australian government highlighting the benefits of Whitleyism. In 1919–20, the Commonwealth Advisory Council of Science and Industry published reports on industrial cooperation and welfarism, which included a discussion of Whitleyism and examined case studies of employee representation such as that at Rowntree in Great Britain and Filene's Sons & Co. in the US. Following an overseas trip to the US and the UK in 1918, barrister George Beeby, former Labor Party parliamentarian and by then Minister for Labour and Industry in the Nationalist NSW government, issued a report that recommended the introduction of Whitleyism rather than ERPs to defeat worker militancy and increase productivity. JDR Jr. sent Beeby material concerning his plan. When Beeby visited New York in January 1919, JDR Jr. suggested that Beeby meet Clarence Hicks and McKenzie King. While Beeby did review the Rockefeller Plan, he noted that there was "smouldering resentment" among US labour over the non-recognition of trade unions. Beeby did not include the Rockefeller Plan in his proposals for legislative reform. J.B. Holme, Deputy President of the NSW Board of Trade, also published reports on Whitleyism in 1919 and 1920, which included a detailed discussion of Whitley works committees. Holme emphasised the need to recognise the "paramount" importance of the "human factor" in industry and of close cooperation between employers and employees.[2]

Beeby actively promoted Whitleyism through his role as Minister for Labour and later as a judge of the NSW Court of Industrial Arbitration. Beeby amended the NSW Industrial Arbitration Act in 1918 to empower a Board of Trade to establish "mutual welfare committees," "industrial councils" and "shop committees." Drawing directly from the British experience, it was

[2] George Beeby, "Industrial Conditions in Great Britain and the United States of America. Report of Investigations", *NSW Industrial Gazette*, Special Supplement, vol. 15, no. 2, 1919, pp. 60A, 157A–8A; Commonwealth of Australia, Advisory Council of Science and Industry, *Welfare Work*, Bulletin No. 15, Government Printer, Melbourne, 1919; Commonwealth of Australia, Advisory Council of Science and Industry, *Industrial Co-operation in Australia*, Bulletin No. 17, Government Printer, Melbourne, 1920; Dispatch Dominions no. 448, Walter Long, 8 Nov. 1917. National Archives of Australia (NAA), CP211/2, 29/70; J.B. Holme, *The British Scheme for Self-Government of Industry; and its Counterpart in New South Wales*, Government Printer, Sydney, 1918, p. 18; J.B. Holme, *The British Scheme for Self-Government of Industry; and its Counterpart in New South Wales No. 2*, Government Printer, Sydney, 1919; Letter, JDR Jr. to Walter M. McGee, 13 Jan 1919. Box 13. Folder 107. Record Group III2C. RFA RAC; Patmore, *Australian Labour History*, p. 147; Lucy Taksa, "George Stephenson Beeby 1920–1926", in Greg Patmore (ed.), *Laying the Foundations of Industrial Justice: The Presidents of the Industrial Relations Commission of NSW 1902–1998*, Federation Press, Sydney, 2003, pp. 129–41.

George Beeby
(Courtesy of
State Library of
NSW)

hoped that the legislation "would find a solution for some of the graver of the industrial problems which militate against the internal peace and the prosperity of the nation."[3] As in Great Britain, there was a clear statement that these committees were not to be used by employers to undermine trade unions. The proposed shop committees would meet fortnightly to discuss grievances. If there were no grievances then meetings would still be held to discuss suggestions "tending to the improvement of industrial conditions or the better utilisation of the practical knowledge or experience of employees ..."[4] Beeby wanted to shift industrial regulation away from state tribunals and judges towards industry and the workplace, leaving the state tribunals to dealing with wages and hours. These provisions attracted little interest from employers and unions and while they persisted in the NSW arbitration system, they were practically moribund. In 1923, Beeby changed the Boot and Shoe (State) Award in his capacity as a judge, tying the implementation of a "satisfactory system of piecework" in the industry

[3] Holme, *The British Scheme for Self-Government*, p. 15.
[4] Holme, *The British Scheme for Self-Government*, p. 17.

with the establishment of joint committees of employers and employees to discuss any scheme.[5]

Australian interest in ideas of employee representation continued during the 1920s. The Nationalist federal government led by Prime Minister Stanley Bruce had already tried to reform Australian industrial relations by unsuccessfully initiating a referendum in September 1926 that would have led to the federal government taking over state industrial jurisdictions and thereby removing concerns relating to conflicts of jurisdictions and potential industrial conflict. Bruce also hoped that the changes would allow for a more flexible approach to industrial relations, including the establishment of Whitley JICs.[6]

The Bruce government sponsored an industrial mission to the US in 1927 to examine labour practices. It hoped that the mission "would increase the efficiency and promote the development of secondary industries in Australia" by examining issues such as profit sharing, the employer-employee relationship and "methods making for greater efficiency."[7] The government met all the delegates' expenses and the mission, with the exception of one delegate, left Sydney for Vancouver on 10 February 1927. The mission consisted of four employer representatives, four union representatives, two press representatives, a civil servant representing the government and two women advisers, who were not members of the industrial mission and were not to be involved in drafting the final report, but were to draft a separate report relating to the employment of females in the US manufacturing industry.[8]

Despite the initial interest of several state trades and labour councils in sending delegates, they refused to recognise the mission unless they could nominate and elect the union delegates. The government was willing to accept the union nominations but wanted the final right to choose the union delegates. When the trades and labour councils refused to nominate delegates, the government took nominations from any labour organisation, such as the moderate Australian Workers' Union (AWU). The Queensland

---

[5] Greg Patmore, "A Voice for Whom? Employee Representation and Labour Legislation in Australia", *The University of New South Wales Law Journal*, vol. 29, no. 1, 2006, p. 14; Taksa, "George Stephenson Beeby 1920–1926", pp. 141–3.

[6] Patmore, "Industrial Conciliation and Arbitration", p. 26; Graeme Powell, "The Role of the Commonwealth Government in Industrial Relations", MA dissertation, Australian National University, 1974, p. 197; *The Sydney Morning Herald* (hereafter *SMH*), 27 May 1926, p. 10.

[7] Commonwealth of Australia, *Report of Industrial Mission. Appointed by Commonwealth Government to Investigate the Method Employed in, and the Working Conditions Associated with the Manufacturing Industries of the United States and to Report Thereon*, Government Printer, Canberra, 1927, p. 5.

[8] Commonwealth of Australia, *Report of Industrial Mission*, pp. 5–6.

Trades and Labour Council condemned John Valentine, the Queensland Secretary of the Australian Federated Union of Locomotive Enginemen (AFULE), for his participation in the mission, even though the Council had initially nominated him. Valentine ignored the AFULE Federal Executive's efforts to stop him going, but retained the support of his union state branch. A union moderate, Valentine was critical of the "red element" in the Australian labour movement.[9] The AFL was willing to recognise the industrial mission, despite the controversy in Australia as AFL President William Green, who was in communication with the Australian government, was "a very level headed man ... who also knows a good deal of the red leanings of many of the Trades Hall people in Australia who are voicing the protest against the composition of the Delegation ..."[10] The AFL Executive ignored pleas from the Melbourne Trades Hall Council to boycott the industrial mission; Eric Grayndler, a mission delegate and AWU General Secretary, addressed the AFL Executive in May 1927.[11]

The industrial mission continued its investigation in the US until 15 July. It inspected a number of workplaces, including B&O, Goodyear Rubber, Ford and General Electric. President Calvin Coolidge received the deputation in Washington, DC and there were a number of conferences with employer and employee representatives. The Federal Council of Churches of Christ of America hosted a conference in New York, which was chaired by Mary Van Kleeck, the social researcher from the Sage Foundation who had undertaken a major study of the ERP at the CF&I coalmines. Other participants included Arthur Young, formerly from International Harvester and then with Industrial Relations Counsellors, an AFL and NAM representative. The mission reported on the "striking success" of union-management cooperation in the B&O workshops, but recognised that ERPs promoted "a better spirit of co-operation and understanding." The report also contained a copy of the Union-Management Cooperation Plan and ERP rules of several

[9] AFULE, Federal Executive Minutes, 5 Feb. 1927. AFULE Deposit, T60/1/2. Noel Butlin Archives Centre, Australian National University (hereafter NBAC); AFULE Queensland Division, Circular/Memo, 15 Feb. 1927; AFULE Queensland Executive Council Minutes, 6 Feb. 1927. AFULE Deposit, E212/5. NBAC; Letters, R.J. Mulvey to Prime Minister, 4 Nov. 1926, M.D. Duffy to E. Page, 8 Dec. 1926. NAA, A458, AK502/4 PART 6; Letters, Acting Prime Minister to Secretary Labor Council of NSW, 20 Sept. 1926, J.S. Garden to G.F. Pearce, 27 Sept. 1926. NAA, A458, AK502/4 Part 7; Letter, J. Valentine to A.E. Pradillo, 13 Oct. 1927. Telegram, Drakeford to J. Valentine, 6 Feb. 1927. AFULE Deposit, E212/486. NBAC; Telegrams, Pearce to Grayndler, 11 Jan. 1927, Grayndler to Acting Prime Minister, 12 Jan. 1927. NAA, A458, AK502/4 Part 7.

[10] Letter, Hugh R. Dennison to Stanley M. Bruce, 4 Mar. 1927. NAA, A458, AK502/4 Part 12.

[11] AFL, Executive Minutes, 12 May 1927, 13 May 1927, 16 May 1927. GMMA, RG4-001.

companies, including International Harvester and Goodyear. In a minority report, union representatives Grayndler and Archibald McInnes from the Adelaide Branch of the Boilermakers criticised the mission's report for not containing "definite conclusions" and recommended union participation in any Australian scheme of workplace employee representation. They argued that ERPs had no place in Australia, where they would be regarded as "bogus" and create "dissension and disorder."[12]

Hugh Adam Grant, a journalist who accompanied the mission and subsequently published a book outlining his experiences, reinforced concerns about the adoption of ERPs in Australia, arguing that they were a "device invented by employers for the purpose of keeping trade unions out of their factories" and that there was no demand for ERPs among workers.[13] While he noted that ERPs were confined to "small matters of rather vague and general application," he did recognise that the ERP at International Harvester had the potential to engage in collective bargaining because it allowed an appeal against the decision of a CEO to outside arbitration.[14]

Two of the union delegates to the mission returned advocating union-management cooperation. Valentine visited the B&O workshops, which he claimed was a "revelation in efficiency" and believed it was "the only way to progress and prosperity."[15] Beyer corresponded with Australians, including Valentine, about union-management cooperation. Valentine advocated union-management cooperation within the AFULE and unsuccessfully placed a union-management cooperation plan before the state-owned Queensland Government Railways in the hope that union members would "share in the gains of co-operation."[16] McInnes, whose nomination was withdrawn by the Adelaide Trades and Labour Council but was endorsed by his union, publicly promoted union-management cooperation as practised by the B&O and CNR, as it was built upon trade union organisation.[17]

[12] Commonwealth of Australia, *Report of Industrial Mission*, pp. 6, 26, 28–9, 50–3, 58–9, 65–70; *The Mercury* (Hobart), 30 Mar. 1927, p. 7, 9 Apr. 1927, p. 9; Selekman and Van Kleeck, *Employees' Representation in Coal Mine*.

[13] Hugh Adam Grant, *An Australian Looks at America: Are Wages Really Higher?* Cornstalk Publishing, Sydney, 1927, p. 65.

[14] Grant, *An Australian Looks at America*, pp. 68–70.

[15] Letter, James Valentine to Otto Beyer, 14 Oct. 1927. Railway Employees' Department. AFL-CIO Records, FF 2B Code # 36-1 Pt. 2. KA.

[16] Queensland Executive Council Minutes, 5 Feb. 1928. AFULE Deposit, E212/5. NBAC; AFULE, *Report of the Seventh Annual Conference of the Australian Federated Union of Locomotive Enginemen Held at the Trades' Hall Launceston, Tasmania, Commencing on Monday, April 16th, Concluding on Friday, April 20th 1928*, Melbourne, 1928, pp. 5, 10; Letter, Otto Beyer to James Valentine, 6 Jul. 1927. AFULE Deposit, E212/486. NBAC; Letter, James Valentine to Otto Beyer, 5 Sept. 1930. File – "Correspondence V Miscellaneous, 1929–1942". Container 8, B.P.

[17] *The Advertiser* (Adelaide), 12 Jan. 1929, p. 25.

There was employer interest in Whitleyism in the private sector. The NSW Master Builders Association (MBA) examined the Whitley Scheme of Industrial Councils, while the NSW Chamber of Manufactures published a detailed analysis of the Whitley Report in its journal. Both bodies, however, were concerned that Whitleyism was incompatible with the Australian industrial arbitration system and would have to be redrafted to meet Australian needs.[18] F.M. Mitchell, assistant works manager at the BHP Newcastle steelworks,[19] visited the Orb Works Whitley committee in August 1922 to take "the opportunity of seeing a Whitley Committee actually at work."[20] BHP did not adopt this approach in its steelworks.

Australian academics were interested in overseas developments in employee representation. Frank Mauldon was a resident tutor at the University of Sydney in Hunter River Valley before being appointed to a senior lectureship in economics at the University of Melbourne in 1926. He won a Rockefeller Foundation Fellowship at Harvard University and obtained a chair in economics at the University of Tasmania in 1935. Mauldon visited the workshops of the Grand Trunk Western Railway, a US subsidiary of the CNR at Battle Creek Michigan, to research union-management cooperation in August 1931. He interviewed workers and used the material to teach economics students at the University of Melbourne. Mauldon also wrote contributions to newspapers on employee representation including German works councils.[21] His 1931 study of 78 private Australian establishments revealed that only two had works councils. Mauldon concluded "that management sharing ... has scarcely come within the imagination of Australian business leaders."[22]

---

[18] Philip Russell, "The Response of Management Policy to the Industrial Conditions of the Later World War One and Reconstruction Era, 1917–1921", BEc (hons.) dissertation, Department of Industrial Relations, The University of Sydney, 1985, pp. 15–16, 35–6.

[19] Edith Mary Johnston-Liik, George Liik and Robert Ward, *A Measure of Greatness: The Origins of the Australian Iron and Steel Industry*, Melbourne University Press, Carlton South, 1998, p. 234.

[20] Orb Works Whitley Committee Minutes, 1 Aug. 1922. MSS.36/016, ISTC Collection, MRC.

[21] Letter, Frank Mauldon to M.H. Westbrook, 29 Oct. 1931. File – "Union-Management Co-operation. General Statements ca. 1924–1931", Container 38, B.P; Ray Petridis, "Frank Richard Edward Mauldon (1891–1961)", in J.E. King (ed.), *A Biographical Dictionary of Australian and New Zealand Economists*, Edward Elgar, Cheltenham, 2007, pp. 183–5; *The Mercury* (Hobart), 26 Jun. 1929, p. 13; *SMH*, 26 Feb. 1932, p. 8.

[22] Frank Mauldon, "Co-operation and Welfare in Industry", in D.B. Copland (ed.), *An Economic Survey of Australia*, *The Annals of the American Academy of Political and Social Science*, vol. 158, Nov. 1931, pp. 186–7.

The Impact

As Mauldon's study highlights, while there was some public interest in Whitleyism, it failed to gain momentum. Beeby argued that state enterprises, such as the railways, should be the initial starting point for the introduction of Whitleyism. With Beeby's encouragement, the NSW Government Railways had tried to establish Whitley committees in 1919. They were supposed to deal with all matters relating to "staff well-being and comfort," excluding award matters dealt with by industrial tribunals. However, the bitterness between management and the railway unions following the 1917 General Strike prevented cooperation. Eveleigh workshop employees in Sydney rejected the scheme at a time when management was trying to introduce the unpopular Halsey bonus scheme. Workers saw the proposed committees and the bonus scheme as part of a "speed-up." The Labor Council of NSW condemned the committees for being an objectionable form of "labour exploitation." The Australian Socialist Party published a pamphlet entitled *The Danger of the Whitley Scheme*, which claimed that the scheme was against workers' interests. It circulated the pamphlet widely among railway workers. Eveleigh workers adopted their own scheme for shop committees and a works committee, which had no management representatives and elected worker representatives. By August 1920, the works committee had dealt with issues such as superannuation, holidays and faulty drains. Nevertheless, it was defunct by June 1921. The Railway Commissioners were more successful at the Randwick tramway workshops in Sydney, where a committee was still operating in 1924.[23]

The federal Department of Defence did not share Beeby's enthusiasm for Whitleyism. Senator George Pearce, the Nationalist Minister for Defence, requested in November 1920 that a report be made to investigate the application of the Whitley Scheme in defence factories. In November 1921, an internal memo concluded that Whitley committees were not needed in the defence factories due to the existence of industrial tribunals and the greater "power" of Australian workers through their strong trade union movement. In the factories, managers already recognised the union representatives of workers and therefore there was no need for works committees. The report also questioned the value of workers' suggestions, claiming that workers lacked knowledge of prior patents and the costs involved in implementing new ideas.[24]

---

[23] Moses Baritz, *The Danger of the Whitley Scheme*, Australian Socialist Party, Sydney, 1919; Greg Patmore, "A History of Industrial Relations in the NSW Government Railways, 1855–1929", PhD thesis, University of Sydney, 1985, pp. 355–8.

[24] Memo, B. Chomley to the Controller-General, Munitions Supply, 8 Nov. 1921. Minute,

There was some interest in employee representation in the private sector. Employers and unions agreed to introduce Whitleyism in the NSW bootmaking industry in 1919. This scheme was little more than an attempt to formalise collective bargaining and it broke down in 1920 over the issues of the 44-hour week and unemployment. Joint committees also existed at the Broken Hill Associated Smelters (BHAS) at Port Pirie, the Sydney retailer Farmers and the Melbourne shirt manufacturer Pelaco. From 1917, the BHAS at Port Pirie had several committees with elected workers' representatives, to manage welfarist programmes. Their decisions were subject to veto by the general manager.[25] As Erik Eklund has argued, the committee system at the BHAS "gave workers a sense of participation without significantly altering management authority."[26] The BHP steelworks at Newcastle and Australian Iron and Steel at Port Kembla, which the BHP acquired in 1935, established safety committees without direct union representation. At the BHP's Newcastle steelworks, workers served on the Departmental Safety Committees (DSC) on a rotational basis and management hoped that all workers would thus become familiar with safety practices. In some cases, workers nominated their representatives to the DSC. At Port Kembla, employees selected their representatives on the DSC for three-month terms.[27]

Employers also experimented with an Australian version of company unionism, which remained within the conciliation and arbitration system. Workers formed unions with management encouragement and obtained registration within the arbitration system. Company unions could minimise outside intervention in the enterprise by unions with a wider coverage and the arbitration courts. They also reduced the gap between management and workers in large-scale enterprises. These unions were significant in NSW following the 1917 General Strike, when the NSW industrial arbitration tribunal deregistered over 20 unions. Employers took advantage of the deregistrations to encourage the formation of company unions. Such unions appeared at Arnotts Biscuits, the Newcastle steelworks of BHP, Elliot Brothers Chemicals, the NSW Government Railways, Schweppes Mineral Waters, the Riverstone Meatworks and the Vacuum Oil Company. They failed to

---

George Foster Pierce to the Factories Management Committee, 11 Nov. 1920, NAA, A1952, E404/17/21.

[25] Erik Eklund, "'Intelligently Directed Welfare Work'? Labour Management Strategies in Local Context: Port Pirie, 1915–1929", *Labour History*, no. 76, 1999, pp. 131–4; Patmore, *Australian Labour History*, p. 150.

[26] Eklund, "Intelligently Directed Welfare Work", p. 133.

[27] Broken Hill Proprietary Co., *The BHP Review Jubilee Number*, Melbourne, 1935, pp. 96–7; Markey and Patmore, "Employee Participation in Health and Safety in the Australian Steel Industry", pp. 51–2.

gain worker support in the Newcastle steelworks and the NSW Government Railways, despite management's concessions to them. Arbitration generally provided the company unions with greater independence than management desired. The Newcastle steelworks' management eventually persuaded its company union to amalgamate with the moderate AWU rather than the militant Federated Ironworkers' Association. The company union secretary accused management of providing minimal support to his organisation. While BHP management was aware of labour practices at Bethlehem Steel, it saw more value in its bonus schemes than the ERP for increasing labour efficiency. The company unions in the NSW Government Railways eventually amalgamated to form the National Union of Railwaymen.[28] Ironically, at least one official of a company union saw Whitley committees as a rival. The general secretary of the workshops union in the NSW Government Railways protested that the committees were a waste of time and money as "we are already doing the work which it is claimed the Whitely [sic] Scheme would do."[29]

Though there were overseas firms operating in Australia, there is mixed evidence about the active promoters of these ideas in their home countries implementing them in Australia. H.R. Lysaght, the managing director of Lysaght (Australia), was encouraged to form a Whitley committee at its Newcastle plant on a visit to the Lysaght Orb Works Whitley committee in the UK in May 1922. R. Parry-Okeden, the manager of the Lysaght Newcastle plant, later claimed in September 1933 that the works committee there was modelled on the Orb Whitley committee. The ICI subsidiary in Australia, by contrast, did not begin experimenting with works councils at its Yarraville factory in Victoria until 1942, when it faced the wartime problems of labour turnover and training new staff.[30]

[28] Letter, F.N. Wiggin to Essington Lewis, 11 Oct. 1919. BHP Billiton Archives, Melbourne, W005/004/0001; Letter from Essington Lewis to David Baker, 16 May 1922. BHP Billiton Archives, Melbourne, W005/002/001; Patmore, *Australian Labour History*, p. 149.

[29] Minutes of general and special meetings of the NSW Railways Mechanical Branch Association of Employees, 14 Oct. 1919. National Union of Rail Workers of Australia, E/80/4/1, NBAC. NUR Australia not linked to NUR UK.

[30] Markey and Patmore, "ICI Works Councils in Australia", p. 61; Orb Works Whitley Committee Minutes, 22 May 1922, 1 May 1933, 4 Sept. 1933. MSS.36/016, ISTC Collection, MRC.

Electrolytic Zinc

One significant Australian case study of employee representation during this period is the Electrolytic Zinc (EZ) works at Risdon, Tasmania, then a wilderness area five miles from the state capital of Hobart. The plant was constructed to provide zinc for munitions during the First World War. Tasmania was attractive because of the abundance of cheap hydroelectricity, which was crucial for the processing of zinc. It produced zinc ingots through a process that involved an electric current running through cells containing a zinc sulphate solution, which led the zinc to precipitate onto cathodes. The plant was run on a continuous basis and required workers to be nearby for emergencies. This resulted in management building a workers' village for its employees. Employment at the plant grew to 800 in April 1920 and 1,094 in March 1930.[31]

Tasmania, with its weaker legislative environment for industrial relations, few strikes and little union activity, proved attractive to investors. The state had a wages board system rather than a conciliation and arbitration system, which did not rely on registered trade unions and did not allow unions to present evidence. Wages boards consisted of an equal number of employer and employee representatives, nominated by their respective constituencies and appointed by the relevant minister, with an independent chair, who voted if there was a tie. The boards fixed minimum wages, maximum hours and other industrial matters such as overtime and leave entitlements. Unions objected to the legislation as it disqualified many full-time union officials from sitting on wages boards because it required employee representatives to have been employed in the industry for 12 months over the past five years. The unions also criticised the Tasmanian wages boards for paying lower wage rates than the Commonwealth Arbitration Court. The Hobart Trades Hall Council recommended that unions boycott the nomination of wage board employee representatives.[32] As Ruth Barton notes, the Tasmanian wages board system "enabled the employer to set up a self-contained body free of formal trade union influence that could make binding decisions on the entire workforce."[33]

[31] Alison Alexander, *A Heritage of Welfare and Caring: The EZ Community Council, 1918–1991*, Pasminco Metals, Ridson, Tasmania, 1991, pp. 3–4, 8, 65; Ruth Barton, "Co-operation and Labour Management at Electrolytic Zinc and Cadbury-Fry-Pascal between 1918–1939", MA dissertation, University of Tasmania, 1989, pp. 51–2; Ruth Barton, "The State, Labour Management and Union Marginalisation at Electrolytic Zinc, Tasmania, 1920–1948", *Labour History*, no. 101, 2011, pp. 55.

[32] Alexander, *A Heritage of Welfare and Caring*, pp. 1–2; Barton, "The State, Labour Management and Union Marginalisation", pp. 54–7.

[33] Barton, "The State, Labour Management and Union Marginalisation", p. 57.

The Collins House Group, the Melbourne-based company that owned EZ, was an alliance of Australian and British lead-zinc interests. The director of Collins House, W.S. Robinson, was strongly influenced by British management strategies, while American management strategies, particularly those with a focus on efficiency, influenced Herbert Gepp, EZ's General Manager, and Gerald Mussen, the EZ industrial consultant. There was also a strong management interest in industrial welfarism and employee participation. Robinson was more interested in profitability and was increasingly concerned with Gepp's expensive welfare programmes. As previously noted, the Port Pirie smelting plant of the BHAS, which was owned by the Collins Group and where Mussen served as industrial adviser, emphasised employee participation and industrial welfarism. While EZ's management, like overseas employers, saw the need to maintain close links with employees in a large organisation and provide workers with a "fair deal," EZ management used this combination of industrial welfarism and employee participation to weaken the appeal of unions.[34]

There were two forms of employee representation at EZ – the Works Committee and the Cooperative Council, which oversaw the EZ welfare programmes. Gepp spent four months in the US from August to December 1919 investigating several matters, including "the whole question of industrial relations and of co-operation, health etc., in relation to efficiency and logical contentment."[35] The trip included a meeting with CF&I to discuss its ERP. In January 1920, after Gepp had presented a report on his trip to a meeting of Collins House managers in Melbourne, he was asked to look into the idea of developing a works council alongside a works union where this did not disrupt "an already organised union."[36]

While management did not proceed with a works union, a temporary Works Committee arose in early 1920 to discuss a management proposal to link wages to the cost of living, which later became permanent. The Works Committee consisted of employee representatives from each division, elected on an annual basis, the number of representatives determined by the number

---

[34] Alexander, *A Heritage of Welfare and Caring*, pp. 2–3; Barton, "The State, Labour Management and Union Marginalisation", pp. 54–6; University of Tasmania, *Employment Wages and the Basic Wage: Lectures and Papers Published in Connection with the Pitt Corbett Foundation*, Hobart, 1925, p. 13.

[35] Letter, Herbert Gepp to E.H. Shackell, 2 Jan. 1920. NS3753/1/19, E/872. Electrolytic Zinc Company Collection, Tasmanian Archive, Hobart (hereafter EZCCTAH).

[36] Alexander, *A Heritage of Welfare and Caring*, pp. 27–8, 53; Barton, "Co-operation and Labour Management", pp. 113–18; Barton, "The State, Labour Management and Union Marginalisation", pp. 57–8; Head Office General Staff Meeting minutes, 18 Jan. 1920. NS569/1/558. Letter, Herbert Gepp to E.H. Shackell, 2 Jan. 1920. NS3753/1/19, E/872. EZCCTAH.

of employees in each division. There were also management representatives and representatives from the EZ Cooperative Council. The ratio of employee representatives to company representatives on the Works Committee was to be at least 3:1. As President of the Works Committee, the General Manager nominated the Chair of the Works Committee. Chief Accountant George Mackay Hunter chaired the Works Committee from its inception until his death in 1936, when management replaced him with Chief Engineer Harry Warlow-Davies. Some unionists, such as George Hargreaves, President of the Hobart Branch of the Amalgamated Engineering Union (AEU), were elected to the Works Committee as employee representatives. Management allowed the employee representatives to meet separately during this period and to refer matters to the Works Committee, but the employee represent-atives complained in January 1926 that they had insufficient time to prepare for the Works Committee meetings, despite having two and half hours for their discussions. While the wages board that covered EZ dealt with wage determination, and ratified Works Committee decisions concerning wages, it could only meet at the Works Committee's request. Management used the Works Committee and wages board to justify exemptions from federal arbitration awards. As with ERPs in the US, EZ management used the Works Committee to legitimate wage reductions during the post-First World War recession. The Works Committee played an important role in handling grievances and communication between management and labour. A joint meeting of the Cooperative Council and the Works Committee, for example, was held in December 1920 for management to announce retrenchments at the plant.[37]

As with other schemes of employee representation, supervisors were concerned about challenges to their status and authority. Supervisors claimed that they would be "shot in the back" for worker representatives were bringing complaints to the Committee about which they had no knowledge. Management amended the Works Committee constitution in May 1923 to meet these concerns, requiring employees and their representatives to discuss all complaints with the relevant supervisor before taking them to the Works Committee. Despite this, management was still concerned in January 1924

---

[37] Ruth Barton, "Goose Clubs and Wages Boards: Marginalising Unions at Electrolytic Zinc, Tasmania, 1920–22", in Paul Griffiths and Rosemary Webb (eds.), *Work – Organi-zation – Struggle: Papers from the Seventh Labour History Conference, Held at the Australian National University, Canberra, April 19–21, 2001*, Australian Society for the Study of Labour History, Canberra Region Branch, Canberra, 2001, pp. 43–9; Barton, "The State, Labour Management and Union Marginalisation", pp. 57–8; Letter, Herbert Gepp to E.H. Shackell, 2 Jan. 1920. NS3753/1/19, E/872. Letter from C.R. Baker to Deputy General Manager, 29 Jan. 1926. NS569/1/147. EZCCTAH; *The Electrode*, Jan. 1921, pp. 19–20; University of Tasmania, *Employment Wages and the Basic Wage*, p. 14.

that the Works Committee was acting "improperly," ignoring this grievance procedure and directly hearing complaints that had not been heard by the relevant supervisor. Management issued a further memo calling for this practice to stop and for the Works Committee to send back these grievances to the department concerned.[38]

Table 8.1 EZ Works Committee – Issues 1936–38

Issues	1936	1937	1938
Committee governance %	3	2	16
Employment %	0	2	8
External political %	0	0	2
Hours %	3	2	6
Improvements to plant and machinery %	8	5	6
Industrial relations %	3	0	4
Labour discipline %	3	0	0
Train service %	8	12	6
Wages %	23	16	6
Welfare %	49	58	25
Workplace safety %	3	2	22
Issues per annum total	39	43	51
No. of meetings	4	4	4
Issues per meeting	10	11	13

Source: EZ Works Committee Minutes, 22 Jan. 1936 to 16 Nov. 1938. NS569/1/551. EZCCTAH. The percentages in the table have been rounded up

What did the EZ Works Committee do? A set of minutes survives for the period 1936–38 and Table 8.1 provides insights into issues dealt with by the Works Committee for this period. The meetings were held quarterly, which delayed the resolution of some key issues, and the minutes of the previous meeting were circulated around the plant before each meeting. While there are no data on the length of the meetings, 29 employee and management representatives attended on average. Welfare issues, such as the provision of

---

[38] EZ Memo, 18 Jan. 1924. NS569/1/95. EZ Staff Note, 29 May 1923. NS569/1/67. EZ Works Committee Minutes, 16 Feb. 1938. NS569/1/551. EZCCTAH.

crib rooms, where workers ate their meals, notice boards, superannuation and water fountains, dominated the matters dealt with by the Committee and formed the majority of issues in 1936 and 1937. Wage issues, such as classifications and the Christmas bonus, were an important but declining issue over the three years and management relied on the current wages board award to deflect criticism. There was an upsurge in governance and work safety issues. This paralleled the growing unionisation of the plant, criticism of the Works Committee procedures and even an allegation of victimisation of an employee representative. The increasing dust levels at the plant were a major health concern in 1938. The Works Committee received many complaints about the frequency of the service and the cleanliness of the carriages provided by the Tasmanian Government Railways. The Committee strayed into broader issues in February 1938 when it protested against the Tasmanian state government for lifting restrictions imposed on the population due to an infantile paralysis epidemic.[39]

There were some gains, such as the provision of soap to transport workers and the granting of a request by carpentry labourers to gain additional work on the plant's wharf. Management answered wharf labourers' complaints in December 1937 about their work transportation, placing a cover over the truck provided for the workers. However, by August 1938 the workers were complaining again that there were no covers on trucks and they were cold. There were tensions between worker representatives and management over delays in resolving grievances. Employee representatives criticised management in January 1937 for their failure to investigate poor conditions, such as inadequate ventilation, at the cadmium crib room despite a promise made at the Works Committee. When it was inspected, representatives "were not satisfied" as management refused to make any changes to the room. Employee representatives were still raising the issue in June. Management defended its prerogatives at the Works Committee meetings, claiming that it alone determined promotion to senior positions, whether by seniority or other factors, and selected applicants for apprenticeships.[40]

The EZ Cooperative Council, which later became the Community Council, predated the Works Committee and commenced operations in 1918. The Council initially consisted of 12, and later 13, annually elected employee representatives and four company representatives appointed by the General Manager, who was also the President of the Council. As with the Works Committee, the General Manager appointed the Chair of the Community Council who, unlike his counterpart on the Works Committee, was always

[39] Employees Section of the EZ Works Committee Meeting Minutes, 20 Jan. 1937. EZ Works Committee Minutes, 22 Jan. 1936 to 16 Nov. 1938. NS569/1/551. EZCCTAH.

[40] EZ Works Committee Minutes, 22 Jan. 1936 to 16 Nov. 1938. NS569/1/551. EZCCTAH.

an employee. While the Cooperative Council had executive authority over the Works Committee in principle, the creation of the Works Committee allowed more contentious issues relating to labour management to be dealt with elsewhere and allowed the Council to focus on managing the company's elaborate welfare programmes, which included employee housing, a company store, a doctor and a dental clinic. The Council also oversaw and funded various plant social and recreational clubs.[41] Management circulated the Council minutes and, according to Alexander, "on the whole the council functioned harmoniously."[42] Employees participated in the elections for the Council, with 90 per cent, 70 per cent and 85 per cent of ballots returned in 1927, 1929 and 1938 respectively.[43]

The elaborate participative practices at EZ did not prevent industrial action or the eventual formation of a union at the plant. During a dispute over the 44-hour working week in September 1922, members of the AEU, which covered skilled workers such as fitters and turners, walked out of the plant, which led to their dismissals and ultimately defeat in the worsening economic climate. An effort to form the EZ Employees' Industrial Union to cover unskilled workers in 1923 was unsuccessful following management's repeated refusal to allow an organiser in the plant. Workers did form the Zinc Workers' Union (ZWU) in 1936, but management preferred to keep the union from being involved in the purely "domestic matters" that were dealt with by the Works Committee. As noted previously, the rise of the ZWU paralleled growing criticism of the Works Committee and in 1937 there were not enough nominations to fill the employee representative positions. A ZWU ballot that year on whether the Works Committee should continue, however, saw 318 workers voting for its continuance and 278 against. An effort by worker representatives to have the ZWU Secretary attend all Works Committee meetings in February 1938 was rejected by management on the grounds that it would set a precedent and all the unions would request the same right. When the matter was raised again in June 1938 it was unresolved. The EZ Works Committee was active until 1948, when a successful ZWU ballot that prohibited union members from serving on it led to its demise.[44]

[41] Alexander, *A Heritage of Welfare and Caring*, p. 28; Letter to R.C. Belville, 23 May 1922. NS569/1/37. EZCCTAH; University of Tasmania, *Employment Wages and the Basic Wage*, pp. 14–16.

[42] Alexander, *A Heritage of Welfare and Caring*, p. 55.

[43] Alexander, *A Heritage of Welfare and Caring*, pp. 55, 70.

[44] Alexander, *A Heritage of Welfare and Caring*, p. 78; Barton, "The State, Labour Management and Union Marginalisation", pp. 47–65; EZ Works Committee Minutes, 16 Feb. 1938. NS569/1/551. EZCCTAH.

Conclusion

Though, as in the other countries examined in this book, an upsurge of interest in industrial democracy accompanied the political and economic crises at the end of the First World War, overall the forms of employee representation discussed in this book had the least impact in Australia. The small scale of Australian industry and the lack of a professional management ethos weakened management commitment to implementing these ideas. Policymakers viewed the Rockefeller Plan and its North American variants as inappropriate because of the strength of the labour movement in Australia and the presence of a compulsory arbitration system to determine wages and conditions. Even the preferred Whitley Scheme, which incorporated unions, had difficulties. The NSW Government Railways dropped the scheme in its Eveleigh workshops due to worker resistance. There was some support for union-management cooperation among union officials who participated in the 1927 industrial mission, but limited interest in German works councils.

One significant case in which employee representation did develop was EZ in Tasmania. The EZ plant was sophisticated by Australian standards as it relied on continuous production and had a relatively large workforce. It operated within a legal framework that did not give unions the full legal benefits of conciliation and arbitration enjoyed by their Australian counterparts, and the unions were particularly weak in the plant. Drawing upon overseas practices, including the Rockefeller Plan, EZ developed employee representation in combination with welfarism as a union-avoidance strategy. As elsewhere, supervisors at EZ were concerned with the loss of their status and authority and had to have their role in the grievance procedure reinforced by senior management. While the strategy was successful in the short term, workers grew dissatisfied with the Works Committee and had formed their own union by 1937.

9

Conclusion

Overall, this study generally supports the historical cycle approach to industrial democracy and notes a general wave of interest across all five countries from 1916 to 1922 and later a specific surge of interest in the US during the early 1930s. Labour unrest during and immediately after the First World War and concerns about the economic issues relating to post-war reconstruction fuelled interest. Some promoters of schemes believed that workplace employee representation could be part of an effective response to the threat of Bolshevism following the Russian Revolution. The period during and immediately after the First World War was very rich in experimentation with industrial democracy in the form of ERPs, union-management cooperation, Whitley works committees and German works councils, but all these ideas failed to sustain themselves significantly for the duration of the interwar period as wartime labour unrest subsided and the deterioration of several of the economies studied weakened labour. This was particularly notable in the UK, where government and employer interest in Whitley workplace committees diminished as the post-war boom broke in 1920 and the economy remained sluggish in the 1920s. There was a second wave of interest in ERPs in the US during the early 1930s as the New Deal encouraged labour organisation and employers looked at alternatives to trade unions.

Legislative intervention in the US, where ERPs were viewed as undermining legitimate trade unions, and in Germany, where the Nazis perceived works councils as an obstacle to their seizure of power, saw the banning of two of the ideas of workplace employee representation examined in this book during the 1930s. While the German works councils were re-established in West Germany in 1952, they were not seen as an improvement on the Weimar works councils, particularly from the perspective of the German trade union movement.[1]

---

[1] Weiss and Schmidt, *Labour Law and Industrial Relations in Germany*, pp. 222–3.

As Poole, Lansbury and Wailes note, though there may be macro conditions that favour industrial democracy, the adoption of employee participation at the level of the firm is subject to organisational choice by actors. It also reflects on the power of these actors and the organisational structures and processes at the level of the firm.[2] Certainly individuals, such as JDR Jr., Sir Alfred Mond, Daniel Willard and Henry Thornton, had the power and influence to ensure that these ideas were adopted and sustained in their organisations. These schemes tended to be found in larger and more complex organisations, such as major railways and ICI, where there was management concern to maintain contact with employees. Even where there was a mandated employee representation scheme, as in Germany, works councils were less likely to be found in smaller workplaces. The climate of labour relations was also important, particularly if management saw organised labour as a threat, as in the case of CF&I or EZ, or as a valuable ally in ensuring industrial peace or improving industrial efficiency, as in the case of B&O and CNR.

This comparative historical study has a number of implications for current debates concerning the revival of ERPs in the US. Industrial relations scholars, such as Kaufman, have focused on the North American experience with ERPs to provide lessons for today, but have overlooked the parallel experiences with Whitley works committees in the UK and German works councils in the interwar period. For scholars to resurrect the idea of ERPs is a problem for those industrial relations reformers who wish to give workers a voice in the workplace. While some employers may have seen ERPs as a way of improving communications with employees, increasing productivity and heightening worker commitment to the firm, CF&I and other firms saw the plans as a union substitute and the NLRA outlawed them on these grounds. While it is recognised that there may be circumstances in which workers prefer not to have union coverage, any NUER scheme built around the historical example of the ERP should be introduced on the basis of a clear choice by workers in a ballot and should also recognise freedom of association without employer interference.

Where ERPs operated successfully, they provided an opportunity for workers through their representatives to discuss workplace concerns and raise grievances. Workers were able to make improvements in working conditions through ERPs at places such as Pueblo, Colorado and Sydney, Nova Scotia. However, it should be recognised that schemes like those at Pueblo and Sydney were introduced following the defeat of unions in major industrial disputes and workers believed that there was no viable

[2] Poole, Lansbury and Wailes, "Participation and Industrial Democracy Revisited", pp. 25–6.

alternative and they had no choice but to participate in the ERPs. Workers also recognised that while some ERPs allowed for the external arbitration of disputes, management held the right of veto over decisions and set the boundaries as to what could be on the agenda, particularly if it affected managerial prerogatives.

While unions opposed ERPs, they recognised that they could be platforms for organising, that an ERP could be replaced by a local union branch. The evidence suggests that using ERPs as a vehicle for organising is very difficult, except in particular circumstances. The union requires both a well-resourced organising campaign and a favourable political and legal climate. Steelworkers in the US and Canada in the late 1930s successfully used the plans as a springboard for unionisation.

Unlike ERPs, the German works councils and the Whitley works committees were adjuncts to established systems of industrial relations and not able to deal with issues that were negotiated in collective bargaining. But this did not mean that these forms of workplace employee representation could not be effective where they existed. The German works council's role in protecting workers against unfair dismissal was extremely effective and encouraged German workers to support the retention of works councils. While the range of issues raised at the Orb Works Whitley works committee in the UK narrowed over time, it played an important role for workers in raising workplace health and safety issues.

The experiences of the Whitley works committees and the German works councils support the argument that is possible for unions to coexist and thrive alongside non-union forms of employee representation. While critics of these schemes, such as the AFL, argued that employers' funding of employee representation schemes compromised the latter's integrity and threatened union representation by creating a parallel organisation to trade unions, this was not necessarily the case with Whitley works committees or the German works councils. Where these schemes were voluntary, unions may have seen little need for them when there was a strongly established system of collective bargaining and management recognition of unions. When the schemes, however, were based on a legislative framework which recognised unions and provided non-union employee representation with a meaningful role, as was the case with the German works councils and their role in dismissals, unions generally appeared willing to live alongside these forms of employee representation.

There is also another important message for unions where non-union forms of employee representation existed. The fears that NUER could be captured by workers hostile to unions or manipulated by employers with an anti-union agenda could be realised if unions did not play an active role in ensuring that union candidates contest elections and win positions on these bodies.

The support of the British railway unions and German unions for their respective forms of NUER was built on them taking an active role in these bodies and ensuring through participation in the election of representatives that they did not undermine their interests. The ADGB in Germany went even further through the provision of education programmes to ensure that workers representatives were able to represent their constituents' interests to managers and the Supervisory Board.

Union-management cooperation, a form of union workplace employee representation, had its own limitations. This top-down approach, while attracting a large number of valuable employee suggestions for both the B&O and the CNR management, generally denied rank-and-file employees in workplaces the right to elect their representatives directly. This lack of trust among union officials of workers and their concerns about the possible creation of ERPs weakened this approach to employee voice. There was also the problem that union-management cooperation encouraged workers to promote the firms that participated in it. However, union promotion of organised firms that adopted union-management cooperation could weaken competitors that also had union shops but refused to adopt union-management cooperation. Further, unions' use of political pressure to win contracts for firms that adopted union-management cooperation could also undermine competitive tendering processes and bring the unions into disrepute.

There were also internal divisions within management ranks over these schemes, which could be perceived by supervisors as a threat to their authority and status. As in the case of EZ in Australia, management had to reassure supervisors that workers would bring grievances to them before they went to the Works Committee. At CF&I, JDR Jr. found it necessary to intervene on a number of occasions when management acted contrary to the principles of the Rockefeller Plan and even attempted to destroy it. As CF&I's Pueblo plant highlights, varying attitudes to employee representation among departmental managers can mean that employee representation varies in its impact across the same workplace. Even under union-management cooperation there were examples of supervisors victimising union representatives and refusing to bring agenda items to meetings.

A major problem for workers dealing with management was a lack of trust, particularly with regard to providing full information about the enterprise's economic performance. Burton argued that this was an important explanation for why ERPs failed to improve efficiency, output or employee morale.[3] There is evidence at CF&I that management even exaggerated the outcomes of the Rockefeller Plan in terms of suggestions approved, to provide a positive spin on its ERP. Even where there were legislative

---

[3] Burton, *Employee Representation*, p. 262.

requirements for management to disclose information to works councillors, as in Germany, some managers presented oral reports in the hope that works councillors would forget the details. Some German managers also constructed balance sheets that omitted important facts and adopted a pessimistic view of the company's financial fortunes to stop workers making claims for improvements. While the German works legislation implied a community of interest between management and labour in reorganising production and promoting efficiency, German management was generally reluctant to provide works councils the information necessary for this to occur.

The book has also explored the issue of the transferability of ideas concerning workplace employee representation. During the interwar period, there was a great deal of interest in these ideas in all five countries examined. While the US was a particular focus of overseas manager interest during the 1920s, and US firms received numerous delegations and visits from overseas managers interested in ideas such as personnel management, scientific management and mass production, the American ideas of employee representation had a limited impact on Australia, Germany and the UK, which all had stronger labour movements and more developed systems of industrial relations in terms of collective bargaining and industrial regulation. The scale of industry tended to be larger and more concentrated in the US, and Australia had the least developed industrial environment in terms of scale of industry and the development of a management ethos. The US experience had a greater impact on Canada due to the economic links between the two and the coverage of US-based international unions. There was an awareness of Whitleyism outside the UK, and the idea had some influence in US, particularly in terms of the development of union-management cooperation. Whitleyism also had some influence in Australia, where George Beeby, Minister for Labour and Industry in NSW, tried to provide a favourable legal environment for Whitleyism through amendments to state industrial arbitration legislation, and in Canada, as in seen in the findings of the Mathers Royal Commission. German works councils had their biggest impact in the UK, where the Liberal Party adopted this form of workplace employee representation as part of its employment policy.

What are the overall implications for the current debate concerning employee representation? Any proposal should recognise employee choice in terms of whether they wish to participate in these schemes and freedom of association. A legislative framework, built on the recognition of freedom of association, provides greater legitimacy for these schemes in the eyes of labour, particularly compared to schemes introduced by employers without consultation with employees or organised labour. Without a legislative framework, the survival of any employer-initiated programme will depend upon the firm's economic performance and the fate of its management backers. Workers and their unions have to be convinced that the scheme is going to be a permanent forum with meaningful powers, such as the oversight by the Weimar German works councils over dismissals, where issues can be discussed without victimisation. As the German interwar experience also highlights, meaningful forms of employee workplace representation built upon democratic practices can go beyond industrial relations and reinforce democratic practices in broader society. As noted previously, it is possible to reverse Robin Archer's argument that the basic ethical commitments that lead to political democracy should also promote economic democracy.[4] The ethical commitments that underlie economic democracy can promote and reinforce political democracy. The democratic principles that underlay the German works councils became a barrier for the totalitarian forces in Germany that were attempting destroy an independent trade union movement and liberal democracy in 1933. Similar arguments about encouraging direct forms of economic and industrial democracy outside traditional forms of representative democracy to frustrate authoritarianism can also be found in the literature on cooperatives.[5]

[4] Archer, "Freedom, Democracy and Capitalism", p. 590.
[5] Johnston Birchall, *Co-op: The People's Business*, Manchester University Press, Manchester, 1994, pp. 180–1.

Bibliography

Articles, Books and Reports

Ackers, Peter, "An Industrial Relations Perspective on Employee Participation", in Adrian Wilkinson, Paul Gollan, Mick Marchington and David Lewin (eds.), *The Oxford Handbook of Participation in Organisations*, Oxford University Press, Oxford, 2010, pp. 52–75.

Ackers, Peter, Marchington, Mick, Wilkinson, Adrian and Goodman, John, "The Use of Cycles? Explaining Employee Involvement in the 1990s", *Industrial Relations Journal*, vol. 23, no. 4, 1992, pp. 268–83.

Aitken, Hugh, *Taylorism at Watertown Arsenal: Scientific Management in Action 1908–1915*, Harvard University Press, Cambridge, MA, 1960.

Albert, Peter J. and Palladino, Grace (eds.), *The Samuel Gompers Papers, Volume 11: The Postwar Years, 1918–21*, University of Illinois Press, Urbana and Chicago, 2008.

Aldcroft, Derek, *The Inter-war Economy: Britain, 1919–1939*, Columbia University Press, New York, 1970.

——, *The British Economy between the Wars*, Philip Allan, Deddington, 1983.

Alexander, Alison, *A Heritage of Welfare and Caring: The EZ Community Council, 1918–1991*, Pasminco Metals, Risdon, Tasmania, 1991.

American Federation of Labor, *Report of the Proceedings of Annual Conventions*, Washington, 1919–40.

American Iron and Steel Institute, *Collective Bargaining in the Steel Industry*, New York, 1934.

Archer, Robin, *Why Is There No Labor Party in the United States?* Princeton University Press, Princeton, 2007.

——, "Freedom, Democracy and Capitalism: Ethics and Employee Participation", in Adrian Wilkinson, Paul Gollan, Mick Marchington and David Lewin (eds.), *The Oxford Handbook of Participation in Organizations*, Oxford University Press, Oxford, 2010, pp. 590–608.

Armitage, Susan, *The Politics of Decontrol of Industry: Britain and the United States*, London School of Politics, London, 1969.

Arnesen, Eric, "Charting an Independent Course: African-American Railroad Workers in the World War I Era", in Eric Arnesen, Julie Greene and Bruce Laurie Howard (eds.), *Labor Histories: Class, Politics, and the Working-Class Experience*, University of Illinois Press, Urbana and Chicago, 1998, pp. 284–309.

Aultz, C., "Union-Management Co-operation", MBA Honours Report, The University of Chicago, 1940.

Australian Federated Union of Locomotive Enginemen, *Report of Annual Conference*, 1928.

Ayçoberry, Pierre, *The Social History of the Third Reich, 1933–1945*, The New Press, New York, 1999.

Bagwell, Philip, *The Railwaymen: The History of the National Union of Railwaymen*, George Allen and Unwin, London, 1963.

Bailey, Stephen, "The Berlin Strike of January 1918", *Central European History*, vol. 13, no. 2, 1980, pp. 158–74.

Bain, George Sayers and Price, Robert, *Profiles of Union Growth: A Comparative Statistical Portrait of Eight Countries*, Basil Blackwell, Oxford, 1980.

Balderston, Theo, *Economics and Politics in the Weimar Republic*, Cambridge University Press, Cambridge, 2002.

Baritz, Moses, *The Danger of the Whitley Scheme*, Australian Socialist Party, Sydney, 1919.

Barton, Ruth, "Co-operation and Labour Management at Electrolytic Zinc and Cadbury-Fry-Pascal between 1918–1939", MA dissertation, University of Tasmania, 1989.

———, "Goose Clubs and Wages Boards: Marginalising Unions at Electrolytic Zinc, Tasmania, 1920–22", in Paul Griffiths and Rosemary Webb (eds.), *Work - Organization - Struggle - Papers from the Seventh Labour History Conference, Held at the Australian National University, Canberra, April 19–21, 2001*, Australian Society for the Study of Labour History, Canberra Region Branch, Canberra, 2001, pp. 43–9.

———, "The State, Labour Management and Union Marginalisation at Electrolytic Zinc, Tasmania, 1920–1948", *Labour History*, no. 101, 2011, pp. 53–70.

Beeby, George, "Industrial Conditions in Great Britain and the United States of America. Report of Investigations", *NSW Industrial Gazette*, Special Supplement, vol. 15, no. 2, 1919.

Beier, Gerhard, *Willi Richter. Ein Leben für die soziale Neuordnung*, Bund-Verlag, Köln, 1978.

Bernstein, Eduard, "The German Works Councils Act and its Significance", *International Labour Review*, vol. 1, no. 2, 1921, pp. 25–37.

Bernstein, Irving, *The New Deal Collective Bargaining Policy*, The University of California Press, Berkeley, 1950.

Berthelot, Marcel, *Works Councils in Germany*, International Labour Office, Studies and Reports Series B (Economic Conditions) No. 13, Geneva, 1924.

Bessel, Richard, *Germany after the First World War*, Clarendon Press, Oxford, 1993.

Beyer, Otto, "B&O Engine 1003", *Survey Graphic*, vol. 4, no. 4, 1924, pp. 311–17.

——, "Union-Management Cooperation in the Railroad Industry", *Proceedings of the Academy of Political Science*, vol. 13, no. 1, 1928, pp. 120–7.

Birchall, Johnston, *Co-op: The People's Business*, Manchester University Press, Manchester, 1994.

Bloomfield, Elizabeth, Bloomfield, Gerald, Holdsworth, Deryck W. and Macpherson, Murdo, "Economic Crisis", in Donald Kerr and Deryck W. Holdsworth (eds.), *Historical Atlas of Canada. Volume III: Addressing the Twentieth Century 1891–1961*, University of Toronto Press, Toronto, 1990, plate 40.

Boehm, Ernst, *20th Century Economic Development in Australia*, 3rd ed., Longman Cheshire, Melbourne, 1993.

Bothwell, Robert, Drummond, Ian and English, John, *Canada, 1900–1945*, University of Toronto Press, Toronto, 1987.

Boyce, Gordon and Ville, Simon, *The Development of Modern Business*, Palgrave, Houndsmills, 2002.

Bradley, Ian, *Enlightened Entrepreneurs: Business Ethics in Victorian Britain*, Lion Hudson, Oxford, 2007.

Bray, Mark and Rouillard, Jacques, "Union Structure and Strategy in Australia and Canada", *Labour/Le Travail*, no. 38/*Labour History*, no. 71, 1996, pp. 198–238.

Brinkley, Alan, *American History, A Survey. Volume II: Since 1865*, 11th ed., McGraw-Hill, New York, 2003.

Brody, David, *Labor in Crisis: The Steel Strike of 1919*, J.B. Lippincott, Philadelphia, 1965.

——, *Steelworkers in America: The Nonunion Era*. Harper & Row, New York, 1969.

——, *In Labor's Cause: Main Themes on the History of the American Worker*, Oxford University Press, New York, 1993.

——, "Why No Shop Committees in America: A Narrative History", *Industrial Relations*, vol. 40, no. 3, 2001, pp. 356–76.

——, *Labor Embattled History, Power, Rights*, University of Illinois Press, Urbana and Chicago, 2005.

Broken Hill Proprietary Co., *The BHP Review Jubilee Number*, Melbourne, 1935.

Broomhill, Ray, *Unemployed Workers: A Social History of the Great Depression in Adelaide*, University of Queensland, St. Lucia, 1978.

Brunner, Mond & Co., *The 50th Anniversary: 1873–1923*, no place of publication, 1923.

Buchheim, Christoph and Garside, Redvers, "Introduction", in Christoph

Buchheim and Redvers Garside (eds.), *After the Slump: Industry and Politics in 1930s Britain and Germany*, Peter Lang, Frankfurt am Main, 2000, pp. 1–8.

Burawoy, Michael, "Towards a Marxist Theory of the Labour Process: Braverman and Beyond", *Politics and Society*, vol. 8, nos. 3–4, 1978, pp. 247–312.

Bureau of Industrial Research, *The Industrial Council Plan in Great Britain*, Washington, DC, 1919.

Burton, Ernest, *Employee Representation*, Williams & Wilkins, Baltimore, 1926.

Cadbury Ltd., *A Works Council in Being: An Account of the Scheme in Operation at the Bournville Works*, Publication Department, Bournville, 1921.

Canada. Department of Labour, *National Industrial Conference, Ottawa, September 15–20, 1919. Official Report of Proceedings and Discussions*, Ottawa, 1919.

——, *Joint Councils in Industry*, Bulletin No. 1, Industrial Relations Series, Ottawa, 1921.

——, *Report of a Conference on Industrial Relations held at Ottawa. February 21st and 22nd, 1921*, Bulletin No. 2, Industrial Relations Series, Ottawa, 1921.

Canadian National Railways, *Annual Report of the Canadian National Railway System*, 1925–33.

Case, Harry, *Personnel Policy in a Public Agency: The TVA Experience*, Harper & Brothers, New York, 1955.

Catchings, Waddill, *Our Common Enterprise: A Way Out for Labor and Capital*, Pollack Foundation for Economic Research, Newton, 1922.

Chandler, Alfred, *Scale and Scope: The Dynamics of Industrial Capitalism*, Harvard University Press, Cambridge, MA, 1990.

——, *The Invisible Hand: The Managerial Revolution in American Business*, Harvard University Press, Cambridge, MA, 2002.

Chapman, Stanley, *Stanton and Staveley: A Business History*, Woodhead-Faulkner, Cambridge, 1981.

Charles, Rodger, *The Development of Industrial Relations in Britain 1911–1939*, Hutchinson, London, 1973.

Chase, Stuart, *A Generation of Industrial Peace: Thirty Years of Labor Relations at Standard Oil Company (N.J.)*, Standard Oil Company, 1947.

Chernow, Ron, *Titan: The Life of John D. Rockefeller, Sr.*, Vintage Books, New York, 1999.

Chickering, Roger, *Imperial Germany and the Great War, 1914–1918*, 2nd ed., Cambridge University Press, Cambridge, 2004.

Clegg, Hugh, *A New Approach to Industrial Democracy*, Blackwell, Oxford, 1961.

——, *The Changing System of Industrial Relations in Great Britain*, Basil Blackwell, London, 1979.

——, *A History of British Trade Unions since 1889. Volume II: 1911–1933*, Clarendon Press, London, 1985.

Clinton, Alan, *Post Office Workers: A Trade Union and Social History*, George Allen & Unwin, London, 1984.

Cobble, Dorothy Sue, "Pure and Simple Radicalism: Putting the Progressive Era AFL in its Time", *Labor*, vol. 10, no. 4, 2013, pp. 61–87.

Cochrane, Peter, "Company Time: Management, Ideology and the Labour Process, 1940–60", *Labour History*, no. 48, 1985, pp. 54–68.

Commonwealth of Australia, Advisory Council of Science and Industry, *Welfare Work*, Bulletin No. 15, Government Printer, Melbourne, 1919.

——, *Industrial Co-operation in Australia*, Bulletin No. 17, Government Printer, Melbourne, 1920.

——, *Report of Industrial Mission. Appointed by Commonwealth Government to Investigate the Method Employed in, and the Working Conditions Associated with the Manufacturing Industries of the United States and to Report Thereon*, Government Printer, Canberra, 1927.

Cook, Chris, *A Short History of the Liberal Party, 1900–1984*, 2nd ed., Macmillan, London, 1984.

Crawley, Ron, "What Kind of Unionism: Struggles among Sydney Steel Workers in the SWOC Years, 1936–1942", *Labor/Le Travail*, no. 39, 1996, pp. 99–123.

Darlington, Ralph, "Strike waves, union growth and the rank-and-file/bureaucracy interplay: Britain 1889–1890, 1910–1913 and 1919–1920", *Labor History*, vol. 55, no. 1, 2014, pp. 1–20.

Davis, Colin, *Power at Odds: The 1922 National Railroad Shopmen's Strike*, University of Illinois Press, Urbana, 1997.

Dellheim, Charles, "The Creation of a Company Culture: Cadburys, 1861–1931", *The American Historical Review*, vol. 92, no. 1, 1987, pp. 13–44.

Department of Manufacture, Chamber of Commerce of the United States, *Employee Representation or Work Councils*, Washington, DC, 1927.

Derber, Milton, *The American Idea of Industrial Democracy 1865–1965*, University of Illinois Press, Urbana, 1970.

Derkow, Willi, *The "Other Germany": Facts and Figures*, Trade Union Centre for German Workers in Great Britain, London, 1943.

Dersch, Hermann, "The Legal Nature and Economic Significance of the German Works Councils", *International Labour Review*, vol. 11, 1925, pp. 169–79.

Dietz, Graham, Wilkinson, Adrian and Redman, Tom, "Involvement and Participation", in Adrian Wilkinson, Nicolas Bacon, Tom Redman and Scott Snell (eds.), *The Sage Handbook of Human Resource Management*, Sage, Los Angeles, 2009, pp. 245–68.

Dodds, Joanne, *They All Come to Pueblo: A Social History*, Donning, Virginia Beach, 1994.

Dubofsky, Melvyn, *Hard Work: The Making of Labor History*, University of Illinois Press, Urbana, 2000.

Earle, Michael, "The Building of Steel Union Local 1064: Sydney, 1935–1937", in James E. Candow (ed.), *Industry and Society in Nova Scotia: An Illustrated History*, Fernwood Publishing, Halifax, 2001, pp. 39–56.

Eggert, Gerald, *Steelmasters and Labor Reform, 1886–1923*, University of Pittsburgh Press, Pittsburgh, 1981.

Eklund, Erik, "Intelligently Directed Welfare Work? Labour Management Strategies in Local Context: Port Pirie, 1915–1929", *Labour History*, no. 76, 1999, pp. 125–48.

Evans, Richard J., *The Third Reich in Power: How the Nazis Won over the Hearts and Minds of a Nation*, Penguin, London, 2006.

Fairris, David, "From Exit to Voice in Shopfloor Governance: The Case of Company Unions", *Business History Review*, vol. 69, no. 4, 1995, pp. 494–529.

——, *Shopfloor Matters: Labor-Management Relations in Twentieth-Century American Manufacturing*, Routledge, London, 1997.

Feldman, Gerald, *The Great Disorder: Politics, Economics, and Society in the German Inflation, 1914–1924*, Oxford University Press, Oxford, 1993.

Felgentree, K., "Praktische Arbeit der Betriebsräte im Wirtschafts-Gebiet Mannheim", *Gewerkschafts-Zeitung*, vol. 40, no. 18, 1930, pp. 276–8.

Ferland, Jacques and Wright, Christopher, "Rural and Urban Labour Processes: A Comparative Analysis of Australian and Canadian Development", *Labour /Le Travail*, no. 38/*Labour History*, no. 71, 1996, pp. 142–69.

Field, Gregory, "Designing the Capital-Labour Accord. Railway Labour, the State and the Beyer Plan for Union-Management Co-operation", *Journal of Management History*, vol. 1, no. 2, 1995, pp. 26–37.

Fitzgerald, Robert, *British Labour Management & Industrial Welfare 1846–1939*, Croom Helm, Beckenham, 1988.

——, *Rowntree and the Marketing Revolution*, Cambridge University Press, Cambridge, 1995.

Flatlow, Georg and Kahn-Freund, Otto, *Betriebsrätegesetz vom 4 Februar 1920*, 13th ed., J. Springer, Berlin, 1931.

Forbath, William, *Law and the Shaping of the American Labor Movement*, Harvard University Press, Cambridge, MA, 1991.

Foreman-Peck, James, *A History of the World Economy: International Economic Relations Since 1850*, 2nd ed., Prentice Hall, Harlow, 1995.

Forsey, Eugene, "The History of the Canadian Labour Movement", in Walter Cherwinski and Greg Kealey (eds.), *Lectures in Canadian and Working-Class History*, Committee on Canadian Labour History, St. John's, Newfoundland, 1985, pp. 9–22.

Fosdick, Raymond, *John D. Rockefeller, Jr: A Portrait*, Harper & Brothers, New York, 1956.

Fox, Allan, *History and Heritage: The Social Origins of the British Industrial Relations System*, Allen & Unwin, London, 1985.

Fox, Charlie, *Working Australia*, Allen & Unwin, North Sydney, 1991.

Frank, David, "The Cape Breton Coal Industry and the Rise and Fall of the British Empire Steel Corporation", *Acadiensis*, vol. 7, no. 1, 1977, pp. 3–34.

——, *J.B. McLachlan: A Biography*, James Lorimer & Co., Toronto, 1999.

French, Carrol, *The Shop Committee in the United States*, John Hopkins Press, Baltimore, 1923.

Geary, Dick, "Employers, Workers and the Collapse of the Weimar Republic", in Ian Kershaw (ed.), *Weimar: Why did Germany Democracy Fail?*, Weidenfeld and Nicolson, London, 1990, pp. 92–119.

——, "The Myth of the Radical Miner", in Stefan Berger, Andy Croll and Norman LaPorte (eds.), *Towards a Comparative History of Coalfield Studies*, Ashgate, Aldershot, 2005, pp. 43–64.

Gitelman, Howard, *Legacy of the Ludlow Massacre: A Chapter in American Industrial Relations*, University of Pennsylvania Press, Philadelphia, 1988.

Godard, John, "Union Formation", in Paul Blyton, Nicolas Bacon, Jack Fiorito and Edmund Heery (eds.), *The Sage Handbook of Industrial Relations*, Sage, London, 2008, pp. 377–405.

Goldenberg, H. Carl, "The Canada-United States Trade Agreement, 1935", *The Canadian Journal of Economics and Political Science/Revue canadienne d'Economique et de Science politique*, vol. 2, no. 2, 1936, pp. 209–12.

Gollan, Paul and Patmore, Glenn, "Transporting the European Social Partnership Model to Australia", *The Journal of Industrial Relations*, 2006, vol. 48, no. 2, pp. 217–57.

Gordon, David M., Edwards, Richard and Reich, Michael, *Segmented Work, Divided Workers: The Historical Transformation of Labor in the United States*, Cambridge University Press, Cambridge, 1982.

Gospel, Howard, "Employers and Managers: Organisation and Strategy, 1914–1939", in Chris Wrigley (ed.), *A History of British Industrial Relations Volume II: 1914–1939*, The Harvester Press, Brighton, 1987, pp. 159–84.

——, *Markets, Firms and the Management of Labour in Modern Britain*, Cambridge University Press, Cambridge, 1992.

Grant, Hugh Adam, *An Australian Looks at America: Are Wages Really Higher?* Cornstalk Publishing, Sydney, 1927.

Grant, H.M., "Solving the Labour problem at Imperial Oil: Welfare Capitalism in the Canadian Petroleum Industry, 1919–1929", *Labour/Le Travail*, no. 41, 1998, pp. 69–95.

Great Britain, *Report of the National Provisional Joint Committee on the Application of the Whitley Report to the Administrative Departments of the Civil Service*, HMSO, London, 1919.

——. Ministry of Reconstruction. Committee of Relations between Employers and Employed, *Supplementary Report on Works Committees*, HMSO, London, 1918.

——. Reconstruction Committee. Subcommittee of Relations between Employers and Employed, *Interim Report on Joint Standing Industrial Councils*, HMSO, London, 1917.

Grebing, Helga, *History of the German Labour Movement: A Survey*, rev. ed., Berg Publishers, Leamington Spa, 1985.

Gross, James, "National Labor Relations Board", in Melvyn Dubofsky (ed.), *The Oxford Encyclopedia of American Business, Labor & Economic History, Volume 2*, Oxford University Press, New York, 2013, pp. 9–10.

Grunberger, Richard, *A Social History of the Third Reich*, Phoenix Books, London, 2005.

Guillebaud, Claude, *The Works Council: A German Experiment in Industrial Democracy*, Cambridge University Press, Cambridge, 1928.

Hardach, Gerd, *The First World War 1914–1918*, University of California Press, Berkeley, 1977.

Haydu, Jeffrey, *Making American Industry Safe for Democracy: Comparative Perspectives on the State and Employee Representation in the Era of World War I*, University of Illinois Press, Urbana and Chicago, 1997.

Hendrickson, Mark, *American Labor and Economic Citizenship: New Capitalism from World War 1 to the Great Depression*, Cambridge University Press, Cambridge, 2013.

Heron, Craig, *Working in Steel: The Early Years in Canada, 1883–1935*, McClelland and Stewart, Toronto, 1988.

——, *The Canadian Labour Movement: A Short History*, James Lorimer & Co., Toronto, 1996.

Heron, Craig and Siemiatycki, Myer, "The Great War, the State and Working Class Canada", in Craig Heron (ed.), *The Workers Revolt in Canada 1917–1925*, University of Toronto Press, 1998, pp. 11–42.

Hicks, Clarence, *My Life in Industrial Relations: Fifty Years in the Growth of a Profession*, Harper & Brothers, New York, 1941.

Hogle, John, "The Rockefeller Plan: Workers, Managers and the Struggle over Unionism in Colorado Fuel and Iron, 1915–1942", PhD thesis, University of Colorado at Boulder, 1992.

Hogler, Raymond and Greiner, Guillermo, *Employee Participation and Labor Law in the American Workplace*, Quorum Books, New York, 1992.

Holme, J.B., *The British Scheme for Self-Government of Industry; and its Counterpart in New South Wales*, Government Printer, Sydney, 1918.

——, *The British Scheme for Self-Government of Industry; and its Counterpart in New South Wales No. 2*, Government Printer, Sydney, 1919.

Homburg, Heidrun, "Scientific Management and Personnel Policy in the Modern German Enterprise 1918–1939: The Case of Siemens", in Howard Gospel and Craig Littler (eds.), *Managerial Strategies and Industrial Relations*, Gower, Aldershot, 1983, pp. 137–56.

Howell, Chris, *Trade Unions and the State: The Construction of Industrial Relations Institutions in Britain, 1890–2000*, Princeton University Press, Princeton, 2005.

Hyman, Richard, "Foreword to the 1975 edition", in C.L. Goodrich, *The Frontier of Control*, Pluto Press, London, 1975, pp. viii–xli.

——, "Rank-and-File Movements and Workplace Organisation, 1914–1939", in Chris Wrigley (ed.), *A History of British Industrial Relations Volume II: 1914–1939*, The Harvester Press, Brighton, 1987, pp. 129–58.

International Harvester Company, *Harvester Industrial Council*, Chicago, 1919.

International Labour Organisation, *Works Councils in Germany*, Studies and Reports Series B No. 6, Geneva, 1921.

——, *Studies on Industrial Relations I*, Geneva, 1930.

Jacoby, Sanford, "Union-Management Cooperation in the United States: Lessons from the 1920s", *Industrial and Labor Relations Review*, vol. 37, no. 1, 1983, pp. 18–33.

——, *Employing Bureaucracy: Managers, Unions, and the Transformation of Work in American Industry, 1900–1945*, Columbia University Press, New York, 1985.

——, "Reckoning with Company Unions: The Case of Thompson Products, 1934–1964", *Industrial and Labor Relations Review*, vol. 43, no. 1, 1989, pp. 19–40.

——, *Modern Manors: Welfare Capitalism since the New Deal*, Princeton University Press, Princeton, 1997.

James, Harold, "Economic Reasons for the Collapse of the Weimar Republic", in Ian Kershaw (ed.), *Weimar: Why Did German Democracy Fail?* Weidenfeld and Nicolson, London, 1990, pp. 30–57.

——, *Europe Reborn: A History, 1914–2000*, Pearson Education, Harlow, 2003.

Jenkins, Jean and Blyton, Paul, "Works Councils", in Paul Blyton, Nicolas Bacon, Jack Fiorito and Edmund Heery (eds.), *The Sage Handbook of Industrial Relations*, Sage, London, 2008, pp. 346–73.

John, Richard, "Elaborations, Revisions, Dissents: Alfred D. Chandler, Jr.'s *The Visible Hand* after Twenty Years", *Business History Review*, vol. 71, no. 2, 1997, pp. 151–200.

John Lysaght Ltd., *The Lysaght Century 1857–1957*, Bristol, 1957.

Johnson, Paul, *Land Fit for Heroes: The Planning of British Reconstruction 1916–1919*, The University of Chicago Press, Chicago, 1968.

Johnston-Liik, Edith Mary, Liik, George and Ward, Robert, *A Measure of Greatness: The Origins of the Australian Iron and Steel Industry*, Melbourne University Press, Carlton South, 1998.

Kahn-Freund, Otto, *Labour Law and Politics in the Weimar Republic*, Basil Blackwell, Oxford, 1981.

Kaufman, Bruce, "Accomplishments and Shortcomings of Nonunion Employee Representation in the Pre-Wagner Act Years: A Reassessment", in Bruce Kaufman and Daphne Taras (eds.), *Non-Union Employee Representation: History, Contemporary Practice and Policy*, M.E. Sharpe, Armonk, 2000, pp. 21–60.

——, "The Case for the Company Union", *Labor History*, vol. 41, no. 3, 2000, pp. 321–51.

——, "Industrial Relations Counsellors, Inc.: Its History and Significance", in Bruce Kaufman, Richard Beaumont and Roy Helfgott (eds.), *Industrial*

Relations to Human Resources and Beyond: The Evolving Process of Employee Relations Management, M.E. Sharpe, Armonk, 2003, pp. 31–112.

——, *The Global Evolution of Industrial Relations: Events, Ideas and the IIRA*, ILO, Geneva, 2004.

Kaufman, Bruce and Taras, Daphne, "Introduction", in Bruce Kaufman and Daphne Taras (eds.), *Non-Union Employee Representation: History, Contemporary Practice and Policy*, M.E. Sharpe, Armonk, 2000, pp. 3–18.

Kealey, Gregory, *Workers and Canadian History*, McGill-Queens University Press, Montreal, 1995.

Kealey, Gregory and Patmore, Greg, "Comparative Labour History: Australia and Canada", *Labour/Le Travail*, no. 38/*Labour History*, no. 71, 1996, pp. 1–15.

Kelly, John, *Rethinking Industrial Relations: Mobilisation, Collectivism and Long Waves*, Routledge, London, 1998.

Kerr, Donald and Holdsworth, Deryck W. (eds.), *Historical Atlas of Canada. Volume III: Addressing the Twentieth Century 1891–1961*, University of Toronto Press, Toronto, 1990.

Kirk, Neville, *Labour and Society. Volume 2: Challenge and Accommodation, 1850–1939*, Scolar Press, Aldershot, 1994.

Krüger, W., "Employers Associations in Germany", *International Labour Review*, vol. 14, no. 3, 1926, pp. 313–44.

La Dame, Mary, *The Filene Store: A Study of Employees' Relation to Management in a Retail Store*, Russell Sage Foundation, New York, 1930.

Leuchtenberg, William, "The Tenth Amendment over Two Centuries: More than a Trueism", in Mark Killenbeck (ed.), *The Tenth Amendment and State Sovereignty: Constitutional History and Contemporary Issues*, Berkeley Public Policy Press, Berkeley, 2002, pp. 41–106.

Lewchuck, Wayne, "Fordism and British Car Employers, 1896–1932", in Howard Gospel and Craig Littler (eds.), *Managerial Strategies and Industrial Relations*, Gower, Aldershot, 1983, pp. 83–110.

Litchfield, Paul, *The Industrial Republic*, Goodyear, Akron, Ohio, 1919.

Littler, Craig, *The Development of the Labour Process in Capitalist Societies: A Comparative Study of the Transformation of Work Organisation in Britain, Japan and the USA*, Heinemann, London, 1982.

London Midland and Scottish Railway Company, *Scheme for Establishment of Local Departmental Committees, Sectional Railway Councils, and Railway Councils*, London, 1924.

Luff, Jennifer, "Labor and Anti-Communism", in Melvyn Dubofsky (ed.), *The Oxford Encyclopedia of American Business, Labor and Economic History, Volume 1*, Oxford University Press, Oxford, 2013, pp. 425–7.

MacDowell, Laurel Sefton, "Company Unionism in Canada, 1915–1948", in Bruce Kaufman and Daphne Taras (eds.), *Non-Union Employee Representation: History, Contemporary Practice and Policy*, M.E. Sharpe, Armonk, 2000, pp. 96–120.

MacEachern, George, *George MacEachern: An Autobiography*, University College of Cape Breton Press, Sydney, Nova Scotia, 1987.

MacEwan, Paul, *Miners and Steelworkers: Labor in Cape Breton*, A.M. Hakkert, Toronto, 1976.

Macgillivray, Don, "Military Aid to the Civil Power: The Cape Breton Experience in the 1920s", *Acadiensis*, vol. 3, no. 2, 1974, pp. 45–64.

Macintyre, Stuart, "Arbitration in Action", in Joe Isaac and Stuart Macintyre (eds.), *The New Province for Law and Order: 100 years of Australian Industrial Conciliation and Arbitration*, Cambridge University Press, Cambridge, 2004, pp. 55–97.

Markey, Ray, "The Australian Place in Comparative Labour History", *Labour History*, no. 100, 2011, pp. 167–87.

Markey, Ray and Patmore, Greg, "Employee Participation and Labour Representation: ICI Works Councils in Australia, 1942–75", *Labour History*, no. 97, 2009, pp. 53–73.

——, "Employee Participation in Health and Safety in the Australian Steel Industry, 1935–2006", *British Journal of Industrial Relations*, vol. 49, no. 1, 2011, pp. 144–67.

Marsh, D'arcy, *The Tragedy of Henry Thornton*, Macmillan, Toronto, 1935.

Mauldon, Frank, "Co-operation and Welfare in Industry", in D.B. Copland (ed.), *An Economic Survey of Australia*, *The Annals of the American Academy of Political and Social Science*, vol. 158, 1931, pp. 183–92.

——, *Mechanisation in Australian Industries*, University of Tasmania, Hobart, 1938.

McCallum, Margaret, "Corporate Welfarism in Canada, 1919–1939", *Canadian Historical Review*, vol. 71, no. 1, 1990, pp. 46–79.

McCartin, Joseph, *Labor's Great War: The Struggle for Industrial Democracy and the Origins of Modern American Labor Relations, 1912–1921*, The University of Carolina Press, Chapel Hill, 1997.

McCormick, Cyrus, "Employees' Representation. Co-operation and Industrial Progress", in *National Safety Council, Advance Copy of Papers to be Presented before the Employees' Representation Section of the National Safety Council Eighth Annual Safety Congress. Cleveland. October 1–4, 1919*, National Safety Council, 1919, pp. 3–12.

McDonald, G.W. and Gospel, Howard, "The Mond-Turner Talks, 1927–1933: A Study in Industrial Co-operation", *The Historical Journal*, vol. 16, no. 4, 1973, pp. 807–29.

McGovern, George and Guttridge, Leonard, *The Great Coalfield War*, University of Colorado Press, Boulder, 1996.

McIvor, Arthur and Wright, Christopher, "Managing Labour: UK and Australian Employers in Comparative Perspective, 1990–1950", *Labour History*, no. 88, 2005, pp. 45–62.

McLaughlin, Doris, "The Second Battle of Battle Creek: The Open Shop

Movement in the Early Twentieth Century", *Labor History*, vol. 14, no. 3, 1973, pp. 323–39.

McPherson, William, "Collaboration between Management and Employees in German Factories", PhD thesis, The University of Chicago, Chicago, 1935.

——, *Works Councils under the German Republic*, The University of Chicago, Chicago, 1939.

Merritt, Walter Gordon, *The Four C's of Industry*, League for Industrial Rights, New York, 1923.

Middlemas, Keith, *Politics in Industrial Society: The Experience of the British System since 1911*, André Deutsch, London, 1979.

Miller, Earl, "Workmen's Representation in Industrial Government", PhD thesis, University of Illinois, 1922.

Mizrahi, Shlomo, "Workers' Participation in Decision-Making Process and Firm Stability", *British Journal of Industrial Relations*, vol. 40, no. 4, 2002, pp. 689–708.

Mond, Alfred, *Industry and Politics*, Macmillan & Co., London, 1927.

Montgomery, David, *The Fall of the House of Labor*, Cambridge University Press, Cambridge, 1987.

Morton, Desmond, *A Short History of Canada*, 5th ed., McClelland & Stewart, Toronto, 2001.

Moses, John, *Trade Unionism in Germany from Bismarck to Hitler 1869–1933. Volume 2: 1919–1933*, George Prior Publishers, London, 1982.

National Guilds League, *Observations on the Interim Report of the Reconstruction Committee on Joint Standing Industrial Councils*, London, 1917.

——, *Notes for Trade Unionists. In Connection with the Adoption by the War Cabinet of the Interim Report of the Reconstruction Committee on Joint Standing Industrial Councils, Commonly Known as the Whitley Report*, London, 1918.

National Industrial Conference Board, *Collective Bargaining through Employee Representation*, New York, 1933.

National Liberal Federation, *Proceedings in Connection with the 45th Annual Meeting of the Council Held at Great Yarmouth on October 10th to 12th, 1928*, The Liberal Publication Department, London, 1928.

Naylor, James, *The New Democracy: Challenging the Social Order in Industrial Ontario*, University of Toronto Press, 1991.

Nehmer, Scott, *Ford, General Motors and the Nazis*, Author House, Bloomington, 2013.

Nelson, Daniel, *Managers and Workers: Origins of the New Factory System in the United States 1880–1920*, The University of Wisconsin Press, Madison, 1975.

——, "The Company Union Movement, 1900–1937: A Reexamination", *Business History Review*, vol. 56, no. 3, 1982, pp. 335–57.

——, "Employee Representation in Historical Perspective", in Bruce Kaufman and Morris Kleiner (eds.), *Employee Representation: Alternatives and Future*

Directions, Industrial Relations Research Association, Madison, 1993, pp. 371–90.

——, "The AFL and the Challenge of Company Unionism, 1915–1937", in Bruce Kaufman and Daphne Taras (eds.), *Non-Union Employee Representation: History, Contemporary Practice and Policy*, M.E. Sharpe, Armonk, 2000, pp. 61–75.

——, "Scientific Management", in Melvyn Dubofsky (ed.), *The Oxford Encyclopedia of American Business, Labor & Economic History, Volume 2*, Oxford University Press, New York, 2013, pp. 152–3.

Nolan, Mary, *Visions of Modernity: American Business and the Modernization of Germany*, Oxford University Press, New York, 1994.

Nörpel, Clemens, "Zehn Jahre Betriebsrätegesetz", *Gewerkschafts-Zeitung*, vol. 40, no. 8, 1930, pp. 120–22.

Norwood, Stephen, "Ford's Brass Knuckles: Harry Bennett, the Cult of Muscularity, and Anti-Labor Terror – 1920–1945", *Labor History*, vol. 37, no. 3, 1996, pp. 365–91.

Nyman, Richard, *Union-Management Cooperation in the "Stretch Out": Labour Extension at the Pequot Mills*, Yale University Press, New Haven, 1934.

Ozanne, Robert, *A Century of Labor-Management Relations at McCormick and International Harvester*, University of Wisconsin Press, Madison, 1967.

Palmer, Bryan D., "Class, Conception and Conflict: The Thrust for Efficiency, Managerial Views of Labour and Working Class Rebellion, 1903–22", *The Review of Radical Political Economics*, vol. 7, no. 2, 1975, pp. 31–49.

——, *Working Class Experience: Rethinking the History of Canadian Labour 1800–1991*, 2nd ed., McClelland & Stewart, Toronto, 1992.

Patmore, Greg, "A History of Industrial Relations in the NSW Government Railways, 1855–1929", PhD thesis, University of Sydney, 1985.

——, *Australian Labour History*, Longman Cheshire, Melbourne, 1991.

——, "Changes in the Nature of Work and Employment Relations: A Historical Perspective", in Ron Callus and Russell Lansbury (eds.), *Working Futures: The Changing Nature of Work and Employment Relations in Australia*, The Federation Press, Sydney, 2002, pp. 27–38.

——, "Industrial Conciliation and Arbitration in NSW before 1998", in Greg Patmore (ed.), *Laying the Foundations of Industrial Justice: The Presidents of the Industrial Relations Commission of NSW 1902–1998*, Federation Press, Sydney, 2003, pp. 5–66.

——, "A Voice for Whom? Employee Representation and Labour Legislation in Australia", *The University of New South Wales Law Journal*, vol. 29, no. 1, 2006, pp. 8–21.

——, "Employee Representation Plans in the United States, Canada, and Australia: An Employer Response to Workplace Democracy", *Labor*, vol. 3, no. 2, 2006, pp. 41–65.

——, "Iron and Steel Unionism in Canada and Australia, 1900–1914: The

Impact of the State, Ethnicity, Management and Locality", *Labour/Le Travail*, no. 58, 2006, pp. 71–105.

——, "Employee Representation Plans at the Minnequa Steelworks, Pueblo, Colorado, 1915–1942", *Business History*, vol. 49, no. 6, 2007, pp. 788–811.

——, "Federal Systems of Industrial Relations", *Journal of Industrial Relations*, vol. 51, no. 2, 2009, pp. 147–150.

——, "The Origins of Federal Industrial Relations Systems: Australia, Canada and the USA", *Journal of Industrial Relations*, vol. 51, no. 2, 2009, pp. 151–72.

——, "Industrial Democracy", in Melvyn Dubofsky (ed.), *The Oxford Encyclopedia of American Business, Labor & Economic History, Volume 1*, Oxford University Press, New York, 2013, pp. 363–68.

——, "Unionism and Non-Union Employee Representation: The Interwar Experience in Canada, Germany, the US and the UK", *Journal of Industrial Relations*, vol. 55, no. 4, 2013, pp. 527–45.

——, "A Tale of Two Employee Representation Plans in the Steel Industry: Pueblo, Colorado, and Sydney, Nova Scotia", in Fawn-Amber Montoya (ed.), *Making an American Workforce: The Rockefellers and the Legacy of Ludlow*, University of Colorado Press, Boulder, 2014, pp. 125–53.

Patmore, Greg and Rees, Jonathan, "Employee Publications and Employee Representation Plans: The Case of Colorado Fuel and Iron, 1915–1942", *Management & Organizational History*, vol. 3, no. 3–4, 2008, pp. 257–72.

Petridis, Ray, "Frank Richard Edward Mauldon (1891–1961)", in J.E. King (ed.), *A Biographical Dictionary of Australian and New Zealand Economists*, Edward Elgar, Cheltenham, 2007, pp. 183–5.

Phillips-Fein, Kim, *Invisible Hands: The Businessmen's Crusade against the New Deal*, W.W. Norton, New York, 2009.

Pinson, Koppel S., *Modern Germany: Its History and Civilization*, 2nd ed., Macmillan, New York, 1966.

Plomer, J., "Sir Henry: Some Notes on the Life of Sir Henry Thornton", *The Railway and Locomotive Historical Society Bulletin*, no. 103, 1960, pp. 5–20.

Poole, Michael, Lansbury, Russell and Wailes, Nick, "Participation and Industrial Democracy Revisited: A Theoretical Perspective", in Ray Markey, Paul Gollan, Ann Hodgkinson, Alaine Chouraqui and Ulke Veersma (eds.), *Models of Employee Participation in a Changing Global Environment: Diversity and interaction*, Ashgate, Aldershot, 2001, pp. 23–34.

Powell, Graeme, "The Role of the Commonwealth Government in Industrial Relations", MA dissertation, Australian National University, 1974.

Power, Terence, "Steel Unionism in Eastern Canada", BA dissertation, Saint Francis Xavier University, Canada, 1942.

Pugh, Arthur, *Men of Steel: By One of Them*, Iron and Steel Trades Confederation, London, 1951.

Ramsay, Harvie, "Cycles of Control: Worker Participation in Sociological and Historical Perspective", *Sociology*, vol. 11, no. 3, 1977, pp. 481–506.

——, "Evolution or Cycle? Worker Participation in the 1970s and 1980s", in Colin Crouch and Frank Heller (eds.), *International Yearbook of Organizational Democracy, Organizational Democracy and Political Processes*, Wiley, Chichester, 1983, pp. 203–26.

Reader, William, *Imperial Chemical Industries: A History. Vol. Two: The First Quarter Century 1926–1952*, Oxford University Press, London, 1975.

Rees, Jonathan, "'X', 'XX' and 'X-3': Labor Spy Reports from the Colorado Fuel and Iron Company Archives", *Colorado Heritage*, 2004, pp. 28–41.

——, *Managing the Mills: Labor Policy in the American Steel Industry during the Nonunion Era*, University Press of America, Lanham, 2004.

——, *Representation and Rebellion: The Rockefeller Plan at the Colorado Fuel and Iron Company, 1914–1942*, University of Colorado Press, Boulder, 2010.

Renold, Charles, *Joint Consultation over Thirty Years: A Case Study*, George Allen & Unwin, London, 1950.

Richardson, J. Henry, *Industrial Relations in Great Britain*, 2nd ed., Studies and Reports Series A (Industrial Relations) No. 36, ILO, Geneva, 1938.

Rockefeller, John D. Jr., *The Colorado Industrial Plan*, no publisher, 1916.

——, *Representation in Industry*, no publisher, New York?, 1918.

Rockoff, Hugh, "Until it's Over, Over There: The U.S. Economy in World War I", in Stephen Broadberry and Mark Harrison (eds.), *The Economics of World War I*, Cambridge University Press, Cambridge, 2005, pp. 310–43.

Roediger, David, "Industrial Workers of the World", in Melvyn Dubofsky (ed.), *The Oxford Encyclopedia of American Business, Labor and Economic History, Vol. 1*, Oxford University Press, Oxford, 2013, pp. 385–6.

Rose, James, *Duquesne and the Rise of Steel Unionism*, University of Illinois Press, Urbana and Chicago, 2001.

Rowntree, B. Seebohm, *The Human Factor in Business*, 3rd ed., Longmans, Green and Co., London, 1938.

Russell, Philip, "The Response of Management Policy to the Industrial Conditions of the later World War One and Reconstruction Era, 1917–1921", BEc (hons.) dissertation, Department of Industrial Relations, The University of Sydney, 1985.

Sangster, Joan, "The Softball Solution: Female Workers, Male Managers and the Operation of Paternalism at Westclox, 1923–1960", *Labour/Le Travail*, no. 32, 1993, pp. 167–99.

Scamehorn, Howard Lee, *Pioneer Steelmaker in the West: The Colorado Fuel and Iron Company 1872–1903*, Pruett Publishing, Boulder, Co., 1976.

——, *Mill & Mine: The CF&I in the Twentieth Century*, University of Nebraska Press, Lincoln, 1992.

Schumann, Dirk, *Political Violence in the Weimar Republic 1918–1933: The Fight for the Streets and Fear of Civil War*, Berghahn Books, New York, 2009.

Scott, Bruce, "A Place in the Sun: The Industrial Council at Massey-Harris, 1919–1929", *Labour/Le Travail*, no. 1, 1976, pp. 158–92.

Seager, Henry, "Company Unions vs. Trade Unions", *The American Economic Review*, vol. 13, no. 1, 1923, pp. 1–13.

Seavoy, Ronald, *An Economic History of the United States: From 1607 to the Present*, Routledge, New York, 2006.

Selekman, Ben, *Employees' Representation in Steel Works: A Study of the Industrial Representation Plan of the Minnequa Steel Works of the Colorado Fuel and Iron Company*, Russell Sage Foundation, New York, 1924.

Selekman, Ben and Selekman, Sylvia, *British Industry Today: A Study of English Trends in Industrial Relations*, Harper & Brothers, New York, 1929.

Selekman, Ben and Van Kleeck, Mary, *Employees' Representation in Coal Mines: A Study of the Industrial Representation Plan of the Colorado Fuel and Iron Company*, Russell Sage Foundation, New York, 1924.

Seymour, John, *The Whitley Council's Scheme*, P.S. King & Son, London, 1932.

Sharp, Ian, *Industrial Conciliation and Arbitration in Great Britain*, George Allen & Unwin, London, 1950.

Shearer, J. Ronald, "The *Reichskurotorium für Wirtschaftlichkeit*: Fordism and Organised Capitalism in Germany", *Business History Review*, vol. 71, no. 4, 1997, pp. 569–602.

Shepherd, John and Davis, Jonathan, "Britain's second Labour government, 1929–31: an Introduction", in John Shepherd, Jonathan Davis and Chris Wrigley (eds.), *Britain's Second Labour Government, 1929–1931: A Reappraisal*, Manchester University Press, Manchester, 2011, pp. 1–15.

Skopcol, Theda, *Protecting Soldiers and Mothers: The Political Origins of Social Policy in the US*, Harvard University Press, Cambridge, MA, 1995.

Slichter, Sumner, "The Current Labor Policies of American Industries", *The Quarterly Journal of Economics*, vol. 43, no. 3, 1929, pp. 393–435.

Sloman, Peter, *The Liberal Party and the Economy, 1929–1964*, Oxford University Press, Oxford, 2015.

Smith, Chris, Child, John and Rowlinson, Michael, *Reshaping Work: The Cadbury Experience*, Cambridge University Press, Cambridge, 1990.

Spates, Thomas, "Industrial Relations in the Zeiss Factory", *International Labour Review*, vol. 22, no. 2, 1930, pp. 177–98.

Stern, Boris, *Works Council Movement in Germany*, United States Department of Labor, Washington, DC, 1925.

Stitt, James, *Joint Industrial Councils in British History: Inception, Adoption, and Utilization, 1917–1939*, Praeger, Westport, 2006.

Storey, Robert, "Unionization versus Corporate Welfare: The Dofasco Way", *Labour/Le Travail*, no. 12, 1983, pp. 7–42.

Strauss, George, "Comparative International Industrial Relations", in Keith Whitfield and George Strauss (eds.), *Researching the World of Work: Strategies and Methods in Studying Industrial Relations*, Cornell University Press, Ithaca, 1998, pp. 175–92.

Taft, Philip, *The A.F. of L. in the Time of Gompers*, Harper & Brothers, New York, 1957.

Taksa, Lucy, "George Stephenson Beeby 1920–1926", in Greg Patmore (ed.), *Laying the Foundations of Industrial Justice: The Presidents of the Industrial Relations Commission of NSW 1902–1998*, Federation Press, Sydney, 2003, pp. 129–54.

Taras, Daphne, "Contemporary Experience with the Rockefeller Plan: Imperial Oil's Joint Industrial Council", in Bruce Kaufman and Daphne Taras (eds.), *Non-Union Employee Representation: History, Contemporary Practice and Policy*, M.E. Sharpe, Armonk, 2000, pp. 231–58.

——, "Portrait of Non-union Employee Representation in Canada: History, Law, and Contemporary Plans", in Bruce Kaufman and Daphne Taras (eds.), *Non-Union Employee Representation: History, Contemporary Practice and Policy*, M.E. Sharpe, Armonk, 2000, pp. 121–46.

Teagle, Walter, *Employee Representation and Collective Bargaining*, no publisher, 1933.

The Industrial Reconstruction Council, *Trade Parliaments. Why They Should Be Formed and How to Form One in your Trade. An Explanation of the Whitley Report*, London, n.d.

Thomas, A.J., "The Union Management Co-operative Plan on the Canadian National Railways", *Personnel*, vol. 5, no. 3, November 1928, pp. 219–25.

Thorpe, Andrew, "The 1929 General Election and the Second Labour Government", in John Shepherd, Jonathan Davis and Chris Wrigley (eds.), *Britain's second Labour government, 1929–31: A Reappraisal*, Manchester University Press, Manchester, 2011, pp. 16–36.

Tomlins, Christopher, *The State and the Unions: Labor Relations, Law and the Organised Labor Movement in America, 1880–1960*, Cambridge University Press, Cambridge, 1985.

Trades Union Congress, *Reports of Proceedings at Annual Trades Union Congresses*, London, 1917–18, 1928–29.

Trepp, Jean, "Union-Management Co-operation and the Southern Organising Campaign", *Journal of Political Economy*, vol. 41, no. 5, 1933, pp. 602–24.

Turner, Ian, *Industrial Labour and Politics: The Dynamics of the Labour Movement in Eastern Australia 1900–1921*, Australian National University Press, Canberra, 1965.

Uhl, Karsten, "Giving Scientific Management a 'Human Face': The Engine Factory Deutz and a 'German' Path to Efficiency, 1910–1945", *Labor History*, vol. 52, no. 4, 2011, pp. 511–33.

United Kingdom. House of Commons, *Works Councils (No. 2) A Bill*, HMSO, London, 1930.

——. Ministry of Labour, *Report on the Establishment and Progress of Joint Industrial Councils*, HMSO, London, 1923.

——. Ministry for Labour, *Report of the Delegation appointed to Study Industrial Conditions in Canada and the United States of America*, HMSO, London, 1927.

United States. Department of Labor, *Proceedings of the First Industrial Conference (Called by the President) October 6 to 23 1919*, Government Printing Office Washington, 1919.

University of Tasmania, *Employment Wages and the Basic Wage: Lectures and Papers Published in Connection with the Pitt Corbett Foundation*, Hobart, 1925.

von Bonin, Walter, *Die volkswirtschaftliche Bedeutung und die praktische Auswirkung des deutschen Betriebsrätegesetzes*, Verlag Ratsbuchhandlung L. Bamberg, Greifswald, 1927.

Vrooman, David, *Daniel Willard and Progressive Management on the Baltimore & Ohio Railroad*, Ohio State University Press, Columbus, 1991.

Wechsler, Robert, "Railway Labor Act", in Melvyn Dubofsky (ed.), *The Oxford Encyclopedia of American Business, Labor and Economic History, Vol. 2*, Oxford University Press, Oxford, 2013, pp. 115–16.

Weiss, Manfred and Schmidt Marlene, *Labour Law and Industrial Relations in Germany*, Wolters Kluwer, Alphen aan den Rijn, 2008.

Weitz, Eric D., *Weimar Germany: Promise and Tragedy*, Princeton University Press, Princeton, 2007.

White, Leonard, *Whitley Councils in the British Civil Service*, University of Chicago Press, Chicago, 1933.

Wilson, John F., *British Business History 1720–1894*, Manchester University Press, Manchester, 1995.

Withers, Glen, Endres, Anthony M. and Perry, Len, "Labour", in Wray Vamplew (ed.), *Australians: Historical Statistics*, Fairfax, Syme & Weldon and Associates, Sydney, 1987, pp. 145–65.

Wood, Louis, *Union-Management Co-operation on the Railroads*, Yale University Press, New Haven, 1931.

Wright, Christopher, "The Formative Years of Management Control at the Newcastle Steelworks, 1913–1924", *Labour History*, No. 55, 1988, pp. 55–70.

——, *The Management of Labour: A History of Australian Employers*, Oxford University Press, Melbourne, 1995.

Wrigley, Chris, "The First World War and State Intervention in Industrial Relations, 1914–1918", in Chris Wrigley (ed.), *A History of British Industrial Relations Volume II: 1914–1939*, The Harvester Press, Brighton, 1987, pp. 23–70.

——, *Cosy Co-operation under Strain: Industrial Relations in the Yorkshire Woollen Industry 1919–1930*, University of York Borthwick Paper No. 71, 1987.

——, *Lloyd George and the Challenge of Labour: The Post-War Coalition 1918–1922*, Harvester Wheatsheaf, Hemel Hempstead, 1990.

——, "Trade Unionists, Employers and the Cause of Industrial Unity and Peace", in Chris Wrigley and John Shepherd (eds.), *On the Move: Essays in*

Labour and Transport History Presented to Philip Bagwell, Hambledon Press, London, 1991, pp. 155–84.

——, "Labour Dealing with Labour: Aspects of Economic Policy", in John Shepherd, Jonathan Davis and Chris Wrigley (eds.), *Britain's Second Labour Government, 1929–31: A Reappraisal*, Manchester University Press, Manchester, 2011, pp. 37–54.

Zeiger, Robert, *American Workers, American Unions*, 2nd ed., Johns Hopkins University Press, Baltimore, 1994.

Zinke, George, *Minnequa Plant of Colorado Fuel and Iron Corporation and Two Locals of United Steelworkers of America*, National Planning Association, Washington, 1951.

Manuscript Collections

American Federation of Labor, Executive Minutes, George Meany Memorial Archives, Silver Spring, Maryland, US.

American Federation of Labor Congress of Industrial Organization Records, Railway Employees' Department, Kheel Archives, Cornell University, Ithaca, New York, US.

Australian Federated Union of Locomotive Enginemen Deposit, Noel Butlin Archives Centre, Australian National University, Australia.

BHP Billiton Archives, Melbourne, Australia.

Bundesarchiv, Berlin, Germany.

Canadian National Railways Collection, Library and Archives of Canada, Ottawa, Canada.

Colorado Fuel and Iron Collection, Bessemer Historical Society, Pueblo, Colorado, US.

Colorado Fuel and Iron Corporation Collection, Colorado Historical Society, Denver, Colorado, US.

Dominion Steel and Coal Corporation Collection, Beaton Institute, Cape Breton University, Canada.

Electrolytic Zinc Company Collection, Tasmanian Archive, Hobart, Australia.

Elton Mayo Papers, Baker Library, Harvard Business School, Cambridge, Massachusetts, US

Erich Lübbe Collection, Frederich-Ebert Stiftung Archive, Bonn, Germany.

Frank and Fred Hefferly Collection, University of Colorado at Boulder Archives, Colorado, US.

Great Britain Cabinet Office papers, Public Records Office, Kew, UK.

Great Britain Ministry of Labour papers, Public Records Office, Kew, UK.

Great Britain Ministry of Transport papers, Public Records Office, Kew, UK.

Harold T. Curtiss Papers, Pennsylvania State University Libraries Labor Archives, State College, Pennsylvania, US.

Historisches Arkiv Krupp, Essen, Germany.

International Labor Office Archives, Geneva, Switzerland.

Iron and Steel Trades Confederation Collection, Modern Records Centre, University of Warwick, UK.

Jesse Floyd Welborn Collection, Colorado Historical Society, Denver, Colorado, US.

John Fitch Collection, Manuscripts Library, State Historical Society of Wisconsin, Madison, Wisconsin, US.

Kurt Heinig Collection, The Labour Movement Archives and Library, Stockholm, Sweden.

Lamont M. Bowers Collection, Department of Special Collections, Glenn G. Bartle Library, State University of New York, Binghamton, NY, US.

London Midland and Scottish Railway Company Records, Public Records Office, Kew, UK.

Mary Van Kleeck Research Papers, Wayne State University. Archives of Labor and Urban Affairs and University Archives, Detroit, US.

National Archives of Australia, Canberra.

National Union of Rail Workers of Australia Deposit, Noel Butlin Archives Centre, Australian National University, Australia.

National Union of Railwaymen Collection, Modern Records Centre, University of Warwick, UK.

Otto S. Beyer Papers, Library of Congress, Washington, DC, US.

Rockefeller Family Archives, Rockefeller Archives Center, Sleepy Hollow, NY, US.

Rowntree & Co. collection, Borthwick Institute for Archives, University of York, UK.

Trade Unions Congress Collection, Modern Records Centre, University of Warwick, UK.

United Kingdom Admiralty Records, Public Records Office, Kew, UK.

United Kingdom Cabinet Office papers, Public Records Office, Kew, UK.

United Kingdom Ministry of Labour Records, Public Records Office, Kew, UK.

United Kingdom Treasury papers, Public Records Office, Kew, UK.

United States Courts of Appeal, Tenth Circuit Denver, Colorado Records, The US National Archives, Rocky Mountain Region, Denver, Colorado, US.

United States Department of Labor Library, Washington, DC, US.

United Steel Workers of America, Sydney Lodge collection, Provincial Archives of Nova Scotia, Halifax, Canada.

William Ashley Papers, British Library, London, UK.

William Leiserson collection, Manuscripts Library, State Historical Society of Wisconsin, Madison, Wisconsin, US.

William Lyon Mackenzie King diaries, National Archives and Library of Canada, Ottawa, Canada.

Newspapers and Periodicals

American Federationist (*AF*)
American Machinist
Baltimore and Ohio Magazine
Beilage zum Monatsbericht (Berlin)
BESCO Bulletin (Canada)
Bulletin of the Taylor Society
Canadian National Railways Magazine
Cape Breton's Magazine
Chicago Tribune
Colorado Fuel and Iron Industrial Bulletin
Correspondenzblatt Der GeneralKomission der Gewerkschaften Deutschlands
Factory and Industrial Management
Gewerkschafts-Zeitung
Labour Gazette (Canada)
Metalarbeiter-Zeitung
NSW Industrial Gazette (Australia)
New York Times
Pueblo Chieftan
South Wales Argus (UK)
Teamwork (Tennessee Valley Authority, Knoxville, Tennessee, US)
The Advertiser (Adelaide, Australia)
The Amalgamated Journal (US)
The Blast (CF&I)
The Canadian Railway Employees' Monthly
The Cocoa Works Magazine (Rowntree)
The Economist (UK)
The Electrode (Electrolytic Zinc Company, Australia)
The Iron Age (US)
The Mercury (Hobart, Australia)
The Ministry of Labour Gazette (UK)
The Nation (US)
The Railway Review (UK)
The Sydney Morning Herald (Australia)
The Sydney Record (Canada)
The Times (UK)
The Yeomans Guard (Yeomans Bros., Chicago, Illinois, US)
Way and Works (Union Construction Co., Oakland, California, US)

Index